2077646

APR 03 2013

The Problem of Slavery as History

THE DAVID BRION DAVIS SERIES

Since its founding in 1998, the Gilder Lehrman Center for the Study of Slavery, Resistance, and Abolition, which is part of the MacMillan Center for International and Area Studies, has sponsored an annual international conference on major aspects of slavery, its ultimate destruction, and its legacies in America and around the world. The Center's mission is to increase knowledge of this story across time and all boundaries, and to reach out to the broader public—in schools, museums, and historic sites, and through filmmakers and general readers—where there is a growing desire to understand race, slavery, abolition, and the extended meanings of this history over time.

In the name of David Brion Davis, the founder of the Center, Sterling Professor Emeritus at Yale, and the world's leading scholar of slavery in international perspective, we have established an occasional lecture series. A single distinguished scholar, or a group of noted writers on a subject, is invited to speak on a theme out of which we then produce an original book such as this one.

Because the research, discoveries, and narratives presented at our conferences do so much to enrich our knowledge of one of humanity's most dehumanizing institutions and its place in the founding of the modern world, as well as of the first historical movements for human rights, we are immensely grateful to Yale University Press for engaging in this joint publication venture. The Gilder Lehrman Center is supported by Richard Gilder and Lewis Lehrman, generous Yale alumni and devoted patrons of American history. The Center aspires, with Yale University Press, to offer to the broadest possible audience the best modern scholarship on a story of global and lasting significance.

David W. Blight, Class of 1954 Professor of History at Yale University, and Director, Gilder Lehrman Center for the Study of Slavery, Resistance, and Abolition

JOSEPH C. MILLER

The Problem of
Slavery as History

A GLOBAL APPROACH

Yale UNIVERSITY PRESS
New Haven &
London

Published with assistance from the foundation established in memory of Calvin Chapin of the Class of 1788, Yale College.

Yale University Press books may be purchased in quantity for educational, business, or promotional use. For information, please e-mail sales.press@yale.edu (U.S. office) or sales@yaleup.co.uk (U.K. office).

Set in Sabon type by IDS Infotech, Ltd.
Printed in the United States of America.

ISBN: 978-0-300-11315-0 (pbk.)

Library of Congress Control Number: 2011943036

A catalogue record for this book is available from the British Library.

This paper meets the requirements of ANSI/NISO Z39.48–1992 (Permanence of Paper).

10 9 8 7 6 5 4 3 2 1

To Jan Vansina,

for teaching me about history and about Africa

And in memory of

Phil Curtin (1922–2009),

for teaching me about the world and slaving, and

insisting that I try to write cogently about it all

Contents

Preface

The chapters in this book express some of the historical insight that a recovering Africanist has gained over several decades spent learning to appreciate the epistemological core of a humanistic discipline, itself in a century-long recovery from its urgent pretensions to discern truths of a scientific, replicable order. They are therefore not an integrated global narrative of the history of slavery told in conventional terms of the "institution" that it is all-but-ubiquitously characterized as having been. Readers will find mentioned here only aspects of slaving relevant to understanding these practices as historical strategies rooted in times, places, cultural heritages, and momentary opportunism. With regard to slaving, the argument focuses on the recurring pattern of the principal slavers' positions as marginal to the contexts in which they lived and competed. It thus adds the historical political dimension of slaving to the relatively familiar psychological, cultural, and economic aspects of the outcomes of these struggles. It stresses processes of creating slavery rather than examining features of an "institution" taken for granted. It emphasizes the experiences of the enslaved as isolated, betrayed, and vulnerable rather than the masters' claims of absolute domination.

But the following chapters also represent, perhaps primarily, a reflection on history as process and on the experience and challenges of initiating change through time. I examine change of a particular historical sort, rooted in human experiences and motivations rather than in abstractions as common-place as the "slavery" and "freedom" that prevail in the literature. Nor do I here attempt to cover the vast historiography of this field as such, though I will attempt to problematize some of its emblematic works in relation to the precise epistemology of history that I will develop. So these chapters, as their titles indicate, problematize slavery not as a moral issue of social exclusion or as an economic anomaly but as an illustration of the problematic limitations of the significant structuralism in the recent practice of history. I am trying to historicize the conventional narrative.

I will also spend some time distinguishing an exact practice of slaving and the experience of enslavement from the strong rhetorical overtones of injustice, inhumanity, social and political exclusion, personal abuse, and inequality that the notion of slavery carries in modern culture. Thus I need to contrast slaving, as a historical strategy, from other means of mobilizing human effort for the benefit of others, sometimes compiled into a negative category of unfree labor to contrast with modern wage labor practices now taken as normative. "Slavery as an institution" has also been compared extensively with race, class, and gender, all abstracted modern forms of exclusion. These debates about abstract definitions explicitly do not enter a discussion aimed to historicize slaving and enslavement as particular contextualized strategies. Nonetheless, I will comment on what I regard as the logic of these structural alternatives, by way of contrasting my historical approach to slaving, as many readers will approach this book from intellectual and cultural backgrounds that do not draw the distinctions I hope to underline.

An even greater challenge for some readers may lie in my presuming a general familiarity with the world's history. The small format of this volume severely limits my ability to provide narrative framing. So I cite widely ranging examples, though neglecting Asia and most of the Islamic world, in favor of concentrating on Africa, my own area of expertise, and the Americas, presumably the field in which most readers will have some background. The modern Americas, or rather, the antebellum United States, are the single source of the politicized epistemology of studies of slavery as an institution. I do not stop to gloss the historical contexts, and even less any sort of narrative, of the laws of slavery (or, as I argue, manumission) characterized as Roman. I sketch elements of the conventional histories of Africa and Brazil, but those do not reflect the historicized framework I want to develop here. The background necessary for readers new to these narratives would overwhelm this book's central arguments about history itself and understanding slaving as a historical strategy as a significant alternative to thinking of slavery only as an institution. I hope that the epistemological argument will provide the coherence that will be lacking as narrative history. Every chapter begins with an explication of the issues of conceptualization raised by the challenge of historicizing slaving in differing contexts chosen to highlight the patterns of slaving recurring through them all.

The final challenge lies in the invitation I am offering here to rethink a subject—slavery, as an institution—that looms so large in the immediate background of all of us in the modern world, though of course for some far more than others, or at least more than some of the others usually allow themselves to realize. Slavery is a politically loaded, emotional subject, and for important reasons in a modern world that is in so many ways a product of its recent practice, and in which practices arguably constituting slaving (even by my historical definition) still continue, and may be increasing. My hope is that historicizing slaving, as these chapters are intended to do, will suggest relevant strategies of moderating the circumstances that render some people vulnerable to enslavement and induce others to slave at their expense.

"The problem of slavery" that I have strung through the titles of the lectures in this book, of course, I take from the justly famed and seminal masterpiece of Professor David Brion Davis of Yale University and the founding director of the Gilder Lehrman Center for the Study of Slavery, Resistance, and Abolition at Yale University, where earlier versions of these chapters were given as the inaugural annual lectures named for him. I choose the title of this book not only to begin with suitable honors the series in which lecturers for years to come will surely continue to draw inspiration from the rich insight of Davis's many works. It is not uncommon to commemorate a foundational thinker by providing a forum like this one for thinking further about the subjects to which that scholar's life was dedicated, but it is rare to sense that thoughts of the honoree will remain the starting point for a vast range of ongoing research and reflection yet to come.

In Charlottesville, Virginia, where I have spent my professional career, we draw in this way on another foundational thinker, to whom we do not compare others lightly. However, I am struck by the similarities in commanding erudition and inspiring dedication to human welfare, and the nobility of the human spirit, between the founder of the University of Virginia—at his best—and our honoree. David Blight, thank you for making all of this possible. My sincere gratitude goes as well to Richard Gilder and Lewis Lehrman for recognizing the uniqueness of this man and making possible the ongoing commitment of the Gilder Lehrman Center at Yale University to bringing an utterly central element of the American experience out from the shadows of embarrassed denial, and—I will argue in this book—also a no-less-central aspect of human history on the broadest imaginable scales. Davis's accomplished scholarship and dedicated social commitment present qualities all the more inspirational when one recalls all the other tones—apologetic, economic—in which it is possible to approach the somber complex of slavery and abolition to which he has devoted his professional life.

I

The Problem of Slavery as History

Slavery was and is a tragedy. It provokes outrage among the modern heirs to its divisive damages, as it should. All of us, whether white or black or merely observers to its racialized polarities, are in that same agonized company. These modern legacies of the Atlantic slave trade in the Americas and in Europe remain an emotional field of battle in the culture wars of modern nations. For racially identified descendants of the enslaved in the present, slavery in the past provokes animated claims for justice, apologies, and financial reparations. The complementing heritage on the part of those who seem potential beneficiaries of the slaving past has long provoked equally intense denials, from descendants of planter families to citizens of former slaving ports like Nantes, Liverpool, and Warwick, Rhode Island, to insurance companies, banks, and universities, and to many communities in modern Africa. Only recently have families and institutions begun to acknowledge the intricate embrace of slavers and enslaved in the New World. Everyone in the slaveholding colonies and countries of the Americas, and in the slaving centers in Europe, in one way or another was implicated. It is also now becoming clearer how many people in Africa bear parallel legacies from their own slaving pasts.

Important as these neo-abolitionist politics may be today, their portrayals of "slavery as an institution" transcending time and space have frozen the dynamics of slaving in most parts of the world as a historical process. The prevailing concept of institutionalized slavery in fact primarily represents abolitionist depictions of the U.S. antebellum South, with the enslaved as one-dimensional victims of similarly one-dimensional brutal masters. The whip is the dominating symbol. In American English, Simon Legree is a trope for an abuser. Emblematic fictionalized mothers sacrifice infants to save them from these horrors.

Without diminishing the domineering excesses that the vulnerability of the enslaved encouraged—or the rapes, psychological abuses, maiming, and deaths—these stereotypes have also inhibited academic understandings of slaving as a subject of intellectual inquiry. It is the intellectual challenge of thinking about slavery outside the box of contemporary politicization that I want to introduce in this chapter. Then I will present three efforts to apply an alternative understanding of *slaving*, as a historical strategy, and *enslavement* as a human experience prior to the personal brutalities, to selected, illustrative aspects of the history of the world. The last of these applies this global approach to slaving to the familiar, seemingly paradigmatic slavery of the modern Americas, concluding with reasons why this unique North American warping of a practice of introducing outsiders into local fields of political competition led, for the first time, to its institutionalization, and thereby finally to its abolition.

To problematize slaving as a historical strategy asks readers to suspend the images of slavery conventional in modern popular culture—in the United States, essentially African-American men working in the cotton fields of the antebellum South; in England or France, African men toiling in canebrakes under a scorching Caribbean sun; and for others, perhaps girls and women secluded and seduced in exotic harems somewhere in a sexualized Muslim palace. The considerable company of scholars who think about the subject professionally will find similar challenges to their essentially sociological assumptions about "slavery as an institution," "slave societies" or "societies with slaves," "slave modes of production," forms of "unfree labor," "slave/creole cultures," and "the idea (or ideology) of slavery."[1] I am thus inviting my readers—scholars and others—to reconsider not only what we think about slavery but also the deep-seated assumptions that underlie *how* we can think most comprehendingly, and hence most productively, beyond existing understandings of slaving. In the parlance of the professional literature on slavery, I want to problematize the utility—even question the elemental accuracy—of the familiar, all-but-ubiquitous phrasing of slavery that historians study as an institution. Hence the play on the word "problem" in the title of this book, and in those of each of its chapters. I hope to problematize slavery as an institution by exploring slaving as a historical strategy.

"Problem" also references the occasion that prompted the present elaborated form of these essays. I presented them as the inaugural David Brion Davis Lectures at the Gilder Lehrman Center for the Study of Slavery, Resistance, and Abolition at Yale University, to honor David Brion Davis, its founding director. Davis is perhaps the defining thinker in the modern field, a writer for the public as well as for the most sophisticated of the professionals. His famous and foundational book, *The Problem of Slavery in Western Culture* (1966), set the standard for problematizing historical clichés.[2] *The Problem of Slavery* is a sweeping survey of the idea of slavery in Western culture over two millennia, from Greek antiquity to its abolition in the nineteenth century. To the amazement of most modern historians at the time, Davis revealed the continuity of slaving throughout the Christian European Middle Ages and Renaissance, as well as the resigned toleration of dehumanizing other human beings as things, from Aristotle to Aquinas to the sixteenth-century Spanish theologian Las Casas to political economists in seventeenth-century England and France. For him, the problem of slavery was why none of the great humanistic thinkers of Western civilization had developed their consistent unease about the institution toward the abolitionist impulses that finally burst forth in the North Atlantic in the eighteenth century, primarily in England and then in the United States. The capacious discourse of humane justice in which he framed the problem reflects popular discomfort with the very idea of slavery, and it is the framework within which scholars still discuss slavery productively.

In this opening chapter I hope to frame these important moral issues of enslavement in ways that are more capacious still, ways that I conceptualize as historical. The second chapter in this book applies the historical epistemology outlined in the first chapter to explain the contexts—political and ideological—that led discerning commentators (from Aristotle to Aquinas) to lament the personal failings of abusive masters but not to invoke public sanctions of the sort claimed by modern abolitionists. In effect, I add the political and intellectual contexts of slaving to the primarily economic analyses that have otherwise tended to prevail.

By training and experience I am a historian of Africa and a student of the overwhelming prominence of slaving in that continent's recent history. My primary research focuses on Angola, one of the African regions most profoundly engaged in those tragic historical processes. But my studies of Africa—like those of many of my Africanist colleagues working on other parts of the continent—leave me with an acute awareness of the utter irrelevance there of the defining qualities of slavery "as an institution" that we read about, mostly in the Americas. The third of these chapters therefore presents slaving as a historical process within the particular historical contexts of Africa, which include virtually none of what turn out to be quite a few unrecognized and no less particular assumptions underlying the thoroughly modern conception of slavery as an institution. Historians must escape the premises of their own times and places if they are to sense the motivations of people in the other places and times that they study, and so I offer a historical approach that I believe illuminates aspects of slaving in Africa not evident, or seemingly anomalous, to modern understandings.

If one grasps the possibility of seeing slaving in terms radically different from what we modern heirs to the Enlightenment have taken all too comfortably for granted, then one is prepared to look again at slavery in the Americas. Chapter 4 places some of the conventional issues of the large field of comparing New World slaveries—for example, in the United States and Brazil—in this historicized perspective, in a historical framework centered not on comparing geographical regions (or culture areas, or colonies or countries or other abstract entities) as relatively timeless contrasts. Instead, it suggests a historically coherent sequence of incremental developments from fifteenth-century circumstances in the Mediterranean region, and also slightly later in northwestern Europe, that were very different from the challenges that Europeans faced later in the Atlantic. Following this sequence—from sixteenth-century strategies in the Hispanic Americas to seventeenth-century extensions in Brazil and then to the Caribbean, through the distinctive circumstances in eighteenth- and nineteenth-century North America—historicizes slaving as a process resulting from changing strategies of people in consistent positions of marginality to the quite distinctive times and places in which they resorted to slaving to intrude on older, more established interests.

Perils of Presentism

First, I will need to elaborate what I mean by historicize. As I use the term, it means a good deal more than merely looking at the past or even narrating events then in terms of changes. Here I use the term to emphasize the human meanings that have motivated people's actions (in the past) in contexts that are not only particular to their times and places but also include ephemerality—prominent, pervasive, dynamic, fleeting change itself. Beyond problematizing slaving as strategy, in contrast to slavery as an outcome, the book also problematizes thinking historically, in this specific way. The title of the book as a whole, *The Problem of Slavery as History*, is meant to emphasize as much. Introducing the problematic of thinking historically is the burden of this introductory chapter in particular. I want here to consider explicitly what the best historians do instinctively to bring earlier times and other places alive for readers and viewers and listeners—all of us, including the historians—very much anchored in the here and now. Generally, we professionals tend to lumber on in the academic modes of abstraction and generalization that we favor, because they highlight orderly aspects of the disorder of human life and—not incidentally—make us look good for making some sense of the chaos. This tendency to favor selective sense in our understanding of slavery over existential ambiguities, I propose to problematize as sociological.

This inclination to find coherence, even if only the brutality of domination, in the essential uncontrollability of a life imagined as entirely subject to the whims of another, adds an emotional edge to the customary contemplation of slavery. The subject, in its academic formulations as well as in its politicized cultural ones, may derive some of its elemental intensity as a kind of distillation of the helplessness and isolation underlying the radical individualism of modern life, not least among scholars. We thus tend to draw curtains of the abstract concepts in common currency today around the exquisite particularities of the past. I will refer later, for examples beyond slavery, to the historical irrelevance of familiar, seemingly unproblematic contemporary notions like kingdoms or states or empires to understanding Africa, or—for that matter, as the second chapter will suggest—anywhere in the world's past. Historians of the ancient Mediterranean have recently become productively critical of their predecessors' tendencies to find straightforward origins of modern forms of democracy in Greece in the fifth century before the current era, an age claimed as classical; Athens in that era was in fact a place very different from both Philadelphia in the 1780s and nineteenth-century republican France.

Historians use the technical term "teleological" to refer to viewing the past significantly, and thereby distortingly, in terms of their own present—that is, painting the purposes of people in the past as though they had meant to invent prototypical versions of whatever we might today claim for ourselves. For readers for whom such technicalities might as well be Greek, this in-group jargon refers to historians' Cardinal Sin, a logical offense that negates the fundamental focus of the discipline on the past on its own terms rather than on ours. The word, which derives from Greek *telos* for "purpose," means writing about the past as if it could hardly have led anywhere but to the present, however selectively we may understand ourselves here and now. Such arguments eliminate the contingency, indeterminacy, and sheer uncertainty of how everyone everywhere, caught in the flux of time, inevitably blunders along.

One teleological habit, all too common even among historians who claim to know better, is a quest for origins of later outcomes, often those of the historian's own times. In this book I seek to avoid contemplating the problem of slavery in terms of what Robin Blackburn calls this "idol of origins": that is, looking for elements in the past, presumed known to actors then but in fact usually only imagined by the historian, then isolating those elements from their contexts to equate them with similarly selected parts of equally complex more recent practices.[3] It is one of the celebrated sins of the historical profession, at least in theory, because all celebrated sins are condemned so urgently precisely because they are so tempting, and so common. Such self-centeredness is not difficult to achieve, since our limited evidence from those times usually reveals so little about the fullness of lives back then. It is thus easy for the historian to notice, to select as analytically significant, only aspects of the past readily recognizable today; these seeming continuities are, by the standard of familiarity, the ones that seem to have led toward later times, and particularly our own. This myopic misrepresentation of others in the past is also called presentistic. To explain what happened historically, one instead relies on context analytically, rather than merely making passing mention of it, mostly for local color, in a logic subtly (and arrogantly enough) predicated on knowing how it has all turned out now.

Teleology is so tempting to historians, further, because history is inherently perspectival, in two senses. The historian therefore attempts to discern the multiple perspectives motivating the actors in every viably historicized context. But historians live in historical contexts of their own, and so they always add the perspective of the historian trying to make sense of them. Historians' own positionality requires them to write with reference to their own times, at least implicitly, if they hope to be intelligible. Although historians must therefore keep in touch with themselves and with their readers or audiences, they must do so without also imputing these necessary and appropriate presentistic referents onto people in the pasts that they study. Instead historians' reliance on contextualization of their subjects obligates them to distinguish the terms of those, back then, whose motivations alone can explain what they did. Being in the present does not preclude constructive engagement with the past; rather, the historian must merely avoid conflating the two. The historian's engagement with the past is constructive both in the sense that it is productive of understanding the past as well as acknowledging the mental world of the historian-observer. The two senses of "construction" are complementary rather than contradictory; in fact, they are mutually interdependent.

Years ago Moses Finley, the late, great historian of slavery in the ancient Mediterranean, famously showed how the emotionality of slavery as a political issue at the end of the nineteenth century, in the nationalistic aftermath of abolitionism in Europe and of the triumphalism of European imperialism at the time, rendered slavery in the ancient Mediterranean past anything but dead for social and political theorists there. Rather, they resurrected antiquity by imagining classical Greece and Rome as fields of battle over slavery, primarily by analogy with then-recent, often Christian abolitionist formulations of the problem.[4] For some of them, ancient Christians had triumphed over the earlier slaving of Roman pagans and assorted barbarians. For others, the enslaved had rebelled against their miseries. The story attributed to ancient slaving at the end of the nineteenth century paralleled the simultaneous strategies that politicians in late nineteenth-century Europe, bent on justifying imperial conquests of "backward" regions around the globe as a civilizing mission, epitomized by eliminating the slaving of Muslims and "native" people there. This displacement of the present politics of slaving into the remote past paralleled the highly political abolition campaigns of late eighteenth-century England, when reformers had projected the social costs and amorality of growing capitalism onto slavery in politically safely remote West Indian colonies.[5] But reasoning by analogy is hopeless as history, since projecting even viable patterns from one time and place into any other violates the fundamental emphasis of history's epistemology on setting the action in past times and other places in its own distinguishing circumstances. Instead, analogous reasoning, like the originary fallacy, selects easily recognizable aspects out of their historical contexts for their (alleged, usually only nominal or abstract or formal) similarities to political or ethical concerns of the present.

The temptations of teleology, at a slightly higher level of abstraction, and therefore also at a more basic level of the thinking processes of our modern era, explain why—and how—we tend to view the institution of slavery, as well as the rest of the world, so unproblematically through the modeling of the modern, progressive social sciences. These historically problematic concepts include notions as seemingly obvious as society itself, or even economics as a domain of monetized supply, demand, and exchange. In an instance of direct relevance to slaving, we think of ourselves as living amid abstract structures, as in "social structure," or in the past with slavery as an institution. Even human rights, race, and the primacy of the individual—concepts that to us seem utterly obvious and beyond discussion—are ideological products of modern times, and the historian ought to be able to recognize them as such. All of these seemingly self-evident abstractions presume historical contexts of commercialization, individuation, and civic (national) governments that did not exist throughout most of the history of the world. In fact, in spite of our pretensions to universality, it is obvious that none of them work today around the globe as fully as their more zealous proponents tend to presume. However valid these ideals may be in principle, every day we read in the media, or personally experience, behavior that by these standards appears anomalous, deficient, or outrageous.

For the historian, all of these structures—political, economic, or mental—are ideologies, or abstractions, strategic, normative, homogenizing statements of how things *should*—or, in the case of slavery as an institution, how they *should not*—work. They are not descriptions of the actual variability of human behaviors, as motivated strategies, that are the proper business of historians. In fact, they calculatedly deny or demonize most of the multiplicity. But historians focus on what people actually did, insofar as we have evidence to know about it. Historians do not contemplate what people in the past might or should have done, and so the stories we tell are not always pretty. Nor should historians attempt to animate these abstractions, to make religions or nations or slavery itself, into quasi-anthropomorphic actors. How many ahistorical sentences have historians written that place societies and kingdoms in the driver's seat of accounting for change, as if these states of mind could influence or spread or otherwise act on their own? For a historian, a single such sociological violation of the humanist way in which one must think historically would be one instance too many. All of these structural abstractions are outcomes, and not always or even often intended ones, of the strategies of interested historical parties to the struggles of their own times. For historians, they explain nothing in themselves; they are rather what historians must explain.[6]

The deceptively simple core of the humanistic definition of history that I will develop is how and why *people* actually behaved, however long ago or far away. Motivated human action, carefully contextualized, is thus the starting point for my understanding of *slaving*. I propose strategies of introducing outsiders for private local purposes that recurred in infinitely variable particulars throughout the history of the world. The precise sense in which I am historicizing *slaving*, then, is to explain human actions (though, of course, only the particular ones indicated in the body of random evidence from the past that we can now detect) as intentional and motivated by meanings that people derived from the contexts (of times, places, cultural heritages) in which they imagined themselves as being. The concluding phrase about "imagining themselves" is crucial, since they lived in times no less ideologically ordered than our own. But their ideologies were not ours; we cannot apply *our* modern, sociologically tending abstractions to attribute intent to whatever they did, often in much more personalized terms. Further, they didn't know all that historians can now reconstruct about their contemporary circumstances, any more than we now know all that much about the blur of experiences and impressions through which we blunder every day. Historians have to take imaginative leaps beyond their own cultures, including our social-science modeling of the world. We must put ourselves in others' places, whether or not we like them or what they did.

Slavery as a Problem in Contemporary Culture

Our strong moral aversion to slavery as an institution makes particularly difficult the challenge of avoiding the sociological tenor of modern structuring of the problem. The subject is deeply politicized, and hence inherently ideological—in a neo-abolitionist mode, to be precise—virtually by the genesis of the subject in the nineteenth-century aftermath—or, internationally, ongoing imperialist context—of abolition. The subject of slavery thrives on as a fascination of both scholarship and popular culture because we are still engaged significantly, if not primarily, in condemning its injustices. In a world in which human rights, as we rightly insist, ought to prevail, they do not. Just as mid-twentieth-century liberalism has gained ground in its battles against the racial consequences of modern slavery, new forms of slaving appear to be surging all around us in the contemporary world. The horrors that we attribute to slavery, ancient, nineteenth-century, or modern, seem to modulate contemporary concerns about other injustices closer to home, insofar as they confirm for us that the world could be worse than it is. Contemplating slavery as an abomination, and its abolition as having made the world a better place, gives liberals cause for hope now no less than in the nineteenth century.

But unless we make the effort to step far enough outside of our own lives to at least comprehend what all those slavers, and those whom they enslaved, were all about, we end up lamely lamenting the fates of the enslaved, or condemning the slavers as congenitally evil. We not only leave the enslaved as relatively passive victims but also condemn the slavers as motivated only by greed and sadistic needs to dominate. That retrospective judgment and—worse yet—leaving any human being helplessly inert or hopelessly driven contradicts the essence of thinking *historically*, that is, by understanding humans as meaningfully and coherently motivated. To invoke another Greek-derived philosophical term, judgmental approaches to the past violate the essence of history's *epistemology*. Epistemology is not what you think about a subject, for example slavery, but how you think about it; it is a thinker's logical "operating system" rather than the "application" that one launches to achieve a particular task. In a sentence: Thinking about slavery in an epistemologically historical way means tracking observable outcomes of human strategies of slaving, particularly as motivated and enabled in unsettling contexts of rapid change, and intended (by the slavers) to effect further changes in their historical contexts. Slavers were motivated to dominate outsiders by their own sense of being dominated within historical contexts in which they found themselves marginalized. Details, nuances, and applications of this compressed declaration of method follow throughout these pages.

The continuing emotionality of the subject of slavery is so immediate a problem in contemporary American culture, and around the modern world, that we seldom pause to make this intuitive and historically necessary leap of imagination into the minds of other people in other times or, for that matter, in other places in the world. We do not perceive even the possibility of understanding how ordinary people like ourselves might have indulged in the exploitation that masters supervised or how the enslaved might have found meaningful lives even amidst what we perceive as severe deprivations. It is the essential genius of the historian, part of the craft about which the great French historian, Marc Bloch, wrote, to attempt to imagine our ways into the times and places of others very unlike ourselves.[7] Contrary to the hopes of many of the positivist founders of the modern discipline, history is not a science. It is essentially humanistic in its necessary reliance on the imaginative, even intuitive leap of the historian, to sense the motivations behind the observable outcomes of human actions.

But the prominent presence of historians themselves in what they think and convey about the past makes it all the more important to turn off the automatic pilots by which we fly through the mists of our own lives. Through awareness of ourselves, we can then discount what we draw from our presents to understand what *others* did, back then and out there. For slaving, the subject at hand, my objective is to present a historicized way of understanding how and why the slavers did what they did, in terms that comprehend, though not thereby condoning, their motivations. That I can understand does not mean that I endorse, or that I am making excuses for anyone or anything. Comprehension allows me, as a historian, to present the dilemmas of the past in ways that the moral philosophers might proceed to judge on bases informed by their training and experience. But to apply their training and experience, they need to draw on the historian's understandings, informed by knowledge of contexts and human intuition as to their meanings. The same historicized sort of understanding allows us also to respect the enslaved for what they managed to do, even under severe hardships of enslavement. Some of them suffered flesh flayed by the lash, but we need to see them more fully than as victims, or as mechanically resisting the lack of Freedom that the modern historian imagines as the primary privation that they endured.

Structures of Slavery Unproblematized

At this epistemological level, I cannot turn to the very rich literature on slavery for much insight. The scholars who have studied it have only begun to consider how slaving in Roman times, or in Africa, or even in seventeenth-century Virginia, might have differed from the way in which we have come to think about it now. Here at the outset, then, I want to guide readers through the thicket of challenges posed in attempting to escape present concerns about slavery to intuit the minds and meanings of others in the past. This challenge is difficult enough for modern Americans trying to think outside the popular image of Africans at Jamestown, for example, and it is all the more demanding when one tries to do so across the apparently yawning gulfs that separate the many cultures around the world.[8] That obstacle is one reason why my third chapter here focuses on slaving in Africa, since the continent from which so many of our ancestors came to the Americas, and elsewhere around the world, often labors under the metaphorical millstone of being made to stand for everything that "we" are not, or hope not to be.[9] However, we all learn most about ourselves when we can suspend the pressures of our day-to-day lives to sense how others think, including the ways in which we appear to them. Thus, thinking *how we think about slavery* forms the core of these lectures. In the end, understanding slavery *historically*, that is in others' terms, as I propose, may open a window through which we can view ourselves in otherwise unexpected ways.[10] Historicizing, as I propose to pursue it through these essays, is humbling: it puts us, ourselves, in historical perspective.

David Brion Davis's classic *Problem of Slavery in Western Culture* provided just such a surprising view on the persistence of slavery within the Western cultural tradition over a stunningly *longue durée* of more than two millennia. Why, he wondered in broadly historical terms paralleling the ones I propose here, had humanists, Christians and others, from the classical Greeks down to the eighteenth century, not been repelled by practices rife in antiquity, far from unknown in the Renaissance Mediterranean, and pervasive in the Spanish and Portuguese Americas? Why did eighteenth-century English abolitionists finally recognize its obvious inhumanity and only then launch the political campaigns that led to government-decreed bans of "slavery" in the monarchical domains of western Europe, then to ending Atlantic trading in slaves, and finally, in the nineteenth century, to emancipations of millions of Africans and their African-American children enslaved throughout the Americas?

This fundamental paradox that Davis phrased in such dramatically historical terms of change has framed nearly all subsequent work on modern slavery, including inspiring many Africanists. It is not a criticism to note that his wide-ranging survey of slaving in the cultures of the West did not seriously engage slaving elsewhere, in what were then called non-Western cultures—negatively enough in relation to his chosen topic and in the discipline as a whole at that time, and a characterization of most of the world in negative terms that were analytically less than robust. The conceptual vacuity of understandings of slaving in the rest of the world as "not us" had not yet fully struck even most historians of those other parts.

Though since 1966 historians and anthropologists have revealed a great many details about slaving in Africa, among Native Americans, in southeastern Asia, even in India, they have tended to retain the modern Western premise of *The Problem of Slavery*, that slavery—in all times and all places—has been a single institution subject to straightforward comparisons. They have reasoned more by analogy than from considered contexts. They have not gone on to consider how practices in the parts of the world they know best might have differed fundamentally from the familiar modern practices, implicitly taken as defining, as the norm. They recognize that plantation regimes based on slave labor were not common outside the modern Americas, but they have seemed almost relieved when they have found them, as in nineteenth-century Zanzibar or in what is now northern Nigeria.[11] Though they recognize that race as an all-but-defining dichotomous correlate of slavery was distinctive to the United States in the nineteenth century, they approach slavery earlier in the Western Hemisphere and everywhere else in the world as though it must have worked through some sort of cognate category of differentiation, preferably heritable. Even more fundamentally, they implicitly define slavery as the opposite of, or absence of, a particular kind of political freedom implicitly derived from the civic polities unique to the Americas and, increasingly, western Europe, and also only by the nineteenth century.

My own experiments in trying to think about Africa historically have left me also considering slaving around the globe in ways more substantive and more dynamic than these static negative contrasts with the Western concept of slavery as an institution. These are the bases of my respectful and appreciative audacity in appropriating these essays to focus on the logical problematics of the copious and continuing approach of which Davis's work is paradigmatic. I hope that problematizing slaving as a strategy will end up explaining how slavery became institutionalized in unprecedented ways in the late eighteenth-century Americas and to suggest that it was these novelties that attracted the attention of the moralists, and then politicians, whom Davis has discussed in elegantly insightful detail. Thus, as I suggested in an earlier paragraph in more general terms, by looking at slavery as a recurring historical strategy dating from earliest humanity, through which its perpetrators created historical processes of change, I hope in turn to problematize its changing characters over the long course of Western culture before the modern Americas. Delineating these changes is the purpose of the second chapter in this book.

First, then, a brief appreciation of *The Problem of Slavery in Western Culture*. This was the single book that inaugurated modern studies of "the peculiar institution,"[12] and it is still—probably more than twenty thousand scholarly publications later[13]—an utterly foundational text. Its eminence makes it a solid and familiar base from which to attempt to move on to the further thoughts on the subject that I want to present here. In that master work, Davis subtly traced the ambivalent acceptance throughout Western philosophy, theology, and political theory of the slavery evident—indeed embedded—in ancient Greece and Rome and then Christian medieval Europe. Slavery's all-but-continuous persistence in a Western civilization dedicated to Christian fellowship and human salvation was far from fully appreciated at the time, even in academic circles. Scholars in Europe had ignored the slavery in their own past out of neo-abolitionist embarrassment over the shame it brought, which at the end of the nineteenth century was still a living memory for the founding generation of professional study of the past.[14] But Davis, in emphasizing its long and tolerated presence, took the first step toward detached contemplation of the problem,[15] in order to frame the fundamental question in the history of the institution. Why, he asked, had the abolition movements of the eighteenth century seized on the very same, celebrated intellectual traditions inherited from these millennia of apologists for the "legal and philosophic concept . . . the *idea* of slavery"[16] to reject the institution definitively during the modern Age of Revolution (the subtitle of a second volume, published in 1975).[17] The seeming paradox of sudden and radical change that he presented as arising out of preceding profound continuities was, and remains, the stuff of high and vital historical drama.

In a third volume, *Slavery and Human Progress* (1984), Davis deepened the paradox by highlighting the coincidence of European slavery's greatest prominence at celebrated moments of progress itself.[18] Over more than two millennia of Western history, he stressed, slavery had flourished at the very moments most celebrated in the Western tradition of freedom. These paradoxical combinations of slavery and freedom included classical Athens, otherwise known for democracy; the Roman Empire's civilizing of barbarian northwestern Europe; fifteenth-century Florence at the height of Renaissance humanism; and eventually in the Americas at the very birth of modern civic freedoms. How could these champions of the story of Western progress toward modern human rights not have recognized obvious need to eliminate the inhumanity of human bondage?[19] Davis's penetrating paradox provided a deeply ironic counterpoint to the dominant celebratory tone of progressive mainstream history at the time, which treated state-mandated general emancipation as a direct extension of humanism dating from antiquity. However, emphasizing continuities in this way (focusing on outcomes for the freed ex-slaves) blurred key distinctions between earlier ethical stress on the personal responsibility of a master for his—or her—dependents of many sorts, including slaves, and the abstract institutional authority that abolitionists begged formative modern nation-states to assert by liberating people whom their citizens had claimed as *their* own—or claimed *to* own in the sense of fungible private property.

Davis reconciled continuity in his central focus on slavery as an institution, or, to cite his exact wording, the "legal and philosophic concept . . . the *idea* of slavery," with profound changes in other, arguably equally central, aspects of Western history by acknowledging that practices of slavery in the New World after the sixteenth century, to which abolitionists finally reacted, might have become harsher than those of their predecessors. But the novelty of slavery in the New World did not inhere in the institution itself but rather was found in an added degree of social exclusion based on race that somehow came to define only Africans as enslaveable, and all others not. Racism, at least in the antebellum United States, extended to all-but-absolute prohibitions against manumission of slaves (all of whom were attributed descent from Africans), the practice that earlier and elsewhere had released at least some of the enslaved from the burdens of enslavement. In the end, Davis not only maintained his emphasis on the "institutional continuity" of "chattel servitude"[20] but also located the "fundamental problem" of this constant feature of European history to be "the simple [i.e., axiomatic, enduring] fact that the slave is a man."[21] Practices of the principle were thus explicitly backgrounded.

Davis's resort to explaining the difference between slaveries, ancient and modern, through the prominent racial aspect that slaving acquired in some parts of the modern Americas[22] followed a conceptual slippage that pervaded academic studies at the time, as well as popular culture. Both conflated bondage and race as quintessential evil twins of civic exclusion. To the first post–World War II generation of liberal critics of both racism and slavery, the two seemed so closely related that they formulated the modern study of slavery out of their concern to explain, and thus begin to reduce the denial, on grounds of race, of constitutional civil rights guaranteed to all in the United States to American citizens of African descent. So congruently politicized seemed race and slavery in the 1950s and 1960s that academics generated quite a lot of academic heat—though less historical light—out of the chicken-and-egg conundrum of whether the institutionalized racism seemingly inherent in Western—particularly English—culture might have predisposed northern Europeans to enslave Africans when they encountered them in course of Atlantic "discoveries" in the sixteenth century. The alternative pairing of this terrible twosome reversed the order: it had been the degradation of enslavement, undertaken for economic or other historical reasons, that left Africans and African-Americans exposed subsequently to racialized scorn.[23]

This ahistorical conflation of race and slavery as the abstract dual demons of prejudice derived from even earlier evocations of it in the domain of public policy and culture in the United States. In the interwar years, scholars concerned with the nation's acute racial divisions had looked back to slavery's destructive effects on families—seen then, as now, as core institutions in raising productive future citizens for the republic—to explain subsequent sociological differences white middle-class ideals seen as normative and African American communities interpreted as deficient.[24] This explanation of contemporary racism as an extra-legal legacy of slavery's exclusion of African American families from civil marriages led to a seminal essay phrased in quasi-historical terms by a historian of Latin America, Frank Tannenbaum. Tannenbaum turned to two countries' differing chronologies of slavery to contrast the racially polarized United States with Brazil, an exotic place in the tropics viewed—however dubiously, in retrospect—as a national paragon of many races coexisting without discrimination according to color. The Portuguese ancestors of Brazilian colonizers had lived with dark-skinned Moors in Iberia since the twelfth century, much longer than English settlers who had encountered Africans first in North America in the 1600s. Long familiarity with Africans in Iberia evidently had bred not contempt but rather greater interracial acceptance as well as a large population of people of mixed racial backgrounds in hot and steamy Brazil.[25] By some mysterious mechanical chronological calculus, the argument concluded, the harsh racism of the United States might fade similarly with time, perhaps in another four centuries or so. It is a tragic comment on that post–World War II era of still barely challenged biological racism, that a wait of four hundred years seemed promising. Still, the prospect that culture, not genetics, might tell the tale and that timing mattered seemed reassuring, no matter how long Americans might have to wait for their national dilemma to fade.

Tannenbaum and others drew their impressions of a multihued but nonracial Brazil from a no less revealing conflation of slavery and racism in the writings of the brilliant Brazilian sociologist Gilberto Freyre.[26] In the 1930s, Freyre had addressed the future of his native country, seemingly condemned by the large proportion of "mulattos" in its population to mediocrity among modern nations, by substituting culture and cultural diversity for biology and racial miscegenation in determining its prospects.[27] For Freyre, slavery in Brazil had brought Africans to contribute positively to a rich amalgam of cultures—including those of Native Americans, Jews, nineteenth-century European immigrants, and Japanese, as well as the Portuguese population seen nonetheless as the core of the culture. Slaving—if not slavery itself—had been an unfortunate means to a praiseworthy end.[28] Reverting to the physical racism then on everyone's minds, Freyre added a bio-corollary to his theme of cultural mixing, pointing out that slavery had facilitated interbreeding between the wealthy Portuguese sugar barons of Brazil's early centuries and the African women enslaved in their "great houses" (*casas grandes*). The overwhelming force of racism (and sexism) in the postwar world may be sensed from his admiring, and widely accepted as praiseworthy, assessment of patriarchal power, which we now would condemn as rape, as racially constructive.

The highly politicized backgrounds of both modern scholarship and popular understandings of slavery acquired a further ideological overlay from their development during the aftermath of a world war fought in defense of national freedoms. "Freedom" referred rhetorically both to personal autonomy underwritten by government-guaranteed civil rights and to the analytical dedication of neo-liberal economists to the efficiencies attributed to free markets, free trade, and—most of all—free waged labor, all coinciding with the civic freedoms of democratic constitutional government.[29] The ensuing Cold War era, in which the academic field of studies of slavery flowered, embedded the virtues of free labor as anchors of Free World economic prosperity, in contrast to the economic failings and personal oppressions of government-controlled socialist economies.

Thus economic historians tended to explain the economics of slavery, particularly in its antebellum U.S. context, by contrasting the presumed inefficiencies of its reliance on forced labor with the undoubted efficiencies of free wage labor: as a system of labor slavery was unfree. Economists found ample precedent for equating abstract efficiency and wages in debates among the eighteenth-century political economists, founding fathers of their discipline, who were trying to understand how this nonwaged labor system fit into an emerging global commercial economy based on cash wages.[30] Wages were incentives supposed to motivate independent workers, theoretically free to flock to the most efficient employer, who would then be able to attract the most productive employees by paying them more than less-competent competitors could manage. Economic historians accordingly condemned the constraints of compulsion on the initiative of enslaved workers. By the progressive Darwinian market laws of survival of only the most efficient, inefficiency doomed slavery as an institution to extinction. Inversely to the case for capitalist global progress, seen as keyed on free wage labor, slavery not only condemned the enslaved workers to impoverished living conditions to pay its high and unnecessary costs of control but also translated into unprofitability for masters and for their nation.[31] The economists' identification of slavery as an institutional developmental drag paralleled the unfortunate structural hangover that sociologists found in families destroyed by slavery and the biological burden attributed to it by racialists.

Economic historians, and often also segments of the public committed to some version of the American way of capitalism, have thus positioned slavery among a vaguely defined set of unacceptable, outdated, and inefficient abstracted forms of labor termed "bonded" or—grouped negatively enough— "unfree."[32] Both concepts are essentially inversions of the ideal of free wage labor, taken as normative. As negations, they are not analytically productive in understanding the particular historical dynamics of any of these quite distinct arrangements, including slaving, in fact normative in the history of the world before the late eighteenth century, in the northern Atlantic. They therefore must be vacuous in order to accommodate what is in fact an enormous variety of quite distinct terms of engagement, through time and around the world. On a global scale, these alternative ways of organizing productive effort extend well beyond the usual list of suspect arrangements grouped as unfree, all of them in fact state sanctioned. The composite category of unfree labor—serfdom, debt bondage, peonage, and so on, in addition to slavery, as well as state corvée, conscription, prisons, and coercion of other public sorts—in fact includes only a subset of the world's historical strategies of organizing production: ones found on the margins of the more thoroughly commercialized minority of all the world's economies.[33] However comfortably cognate with the tendency to link slavery with racism primarily as inhibitions of personal freedoms these generic regimes of bonded labor may seem, they are analytically obscuring.

Broadly, then, the rather stereotyped notion of slavery in both the academic literature and in modern popular culture derives from a nineteenth-century abolitionist negative contrast—in fact a politicized caricature—designed to stir the emotions of an emergently modern world against all limitations of the personal liberties that it seemed to promise. The potential of modernity to yield civic freedoms and material progress then seemed unlimited, and so no human institutions should be allowed to limit these possibilities. In view of the subsequent histories of civic exclusion by gender, race, and other discriminatory social categories, slavery as an institution has remained a convenient target, and not least because—for well-intended progressives—it was nearly always presentable as someone else's problem, and, as institutionalized, it could be, and was, abolished.

Slavery continues to bear this array of negative associations, often more rhetorical than analytical. We hear emblematic usages of the word every day in media that invoke its horrors to attract public attention to alleged injustices of every sort, in fact not infrequently expressing personal frustrations at not getting one's own arbitrary way. Activists deploy the word to condemn one or another of the inevitable partisan ambitions that constitute politics, as well as in many other evocative but intellectually imprecise ways. Exclusionary, racial, unfree slavery, invoked by analogy to protest other dimensions of difference and diversity in modern cultures ideologically dedicated to equality, blurs into class and gender, as well as race. Oppression, evoked as slavery, can potentially be anything, anywhere.

My intent here is to move beyond this presentistic rhetoric of popular culture and its echoes in the analytical vacuity lurking in academic study of slavery by presenting a more systematically historical approach to slaving as both a product and a strategy of change itself, of time and timing. My method is to contextualize slavers, as they have thrived in specific times and places in enormously varied ways, and also to contextualize the enslaved to sense their meaningful experiences as human beings and to identify their resultant responses. Since the existing literature on slavery as an institution is so profoundly sociological—as perhaps befits a subject of such social intensity—I will first establish the parameters that I believe frame a rigorously *historical* way of viewing the human experience. I will then sketch a few of the novel, sometimes surprising, insights that emerge from historicizing the perennial problem of slavery. The following chapter sketches specific examples of slaving evident through the *longue durée* of human history by distinguishing them as historicized human strategies from the loaded connotations of "slavery (abstracted) as an institution."

Defining Slaving as a Historical Strategy

It's now more than forty years since Davis confronted the inevitable limits of opening a virtually new intellectual field: pioneer thinkers always raise more questions than they answer, as they recognize as unknown what others had not imagined as knowable. But in 2010 we have those twenty thousand or so products of the scholarly quest that he inspired to understand slavery worldwide, most of them pursued with all the imagination and intensity generated by the continuing ethical and political difficulties of living with the lamented legacy of the modern institution. To use this wealth of recent work *historically*, I begin by replacing the sociological, structural language employed in nearly all of them with other concepts that derive from the distinctive epistemology of the discipline of history.

Historicizing slaving in this way, globally, provides an analytically sub-stantive—not a negatively conceived—range of contrasts with the publicly acknowledged, modern American practice of human domination that we now condemn as peculiar.[34] Within that global context, we see how pro-foundly anomalous slaving had become in the eighteenth-century Americas, in its enormous scale, in its concentrations of male workers on productive sites—plantations and mines, and in the emergent uniquely civic political context of the northern Atlantic. Though Davis's humane emphasis on the ongoing problem of slavery in Western culture rightly emphasized its continu-ous, even constant, moral contradiction,[35] I want to treat slaving not only as the transcending contradiction of dehumanization that it created against the background of modernity but also as a strategy that people in historical positions of marginality have pursued, since time immemorial, with signifi-cant consequences for themselves and for others around them, beyond the sufferings that the practice imposed on the people they enslaved.

Effecting this transition from a sociological to a historical mode requires several logical steps, perhaps demanding ones, in view of the intensity of neo-abolitionist structuralism that surrounds the subject. First, one must suspend the usual virtual exclusivity of focus on the intense and tense relationship between paradigmatically dominating masters and paradigmatically domi-nated slaves, the all-but-defining dyad of slavery as an institution.[36] Instead I want also to acknowledge, robustly, the historical contexts in which both parties, masters and slaves, were trying to influence not only one another but also others around them. The sympathetic reader must then follow the implication that contextualizing this master–slave dyad forces us to abandon the very notion of slavery as an institution; that is, we must think beyond the static abstraction, independent of time or place that we imagine by observing it as such. Rather, one must think experientially by imagining oneself in the positions of the historical creators, sensing the range of meanings of their actions to them, recognizing intentions of theirs beyond their fraught relationship with one another. The moral resonance of "slavery" in our own culture makes this step a particularly difficult one; our interests in the subject lie essentially in condemning the relationship, comprehensively, and hence abstractly. But we might also wonder what led slavers to create and endure so problematic a situation; they had other purposes relevant to the changing contexts in which they lived.

Thinking historically also requires one to abandon the recent intensely structural inclinations of the historical discipline generally. The notion of slavery as an institution has created few waves among historians, whose discipline was defined at the end of the nineteenth century primarily through an unproblematized focus on the origins of nation-states that we now understand to be imagined—that is, not natural entities but rather ideological strategies.[37] A historical approach to the past, through the motivations of the slavers and the experiences of the enslaved, and the changes they wrought together, affirms—indeed exploits—the humanistic aspects of what people have done. By focusing on motivated and contextualized strategies of the slavers and the enslaved, one arrives at the logical axis of historical narrative, the kind of story that one may tell: processes (of incremental, inadvertent changes) that slavers initiate and the enslaved manipulate. Slavery is our retrospective (streamlined) observation of the outcomes of the myriad actions on which historians properly concentrate. To repeat: "slavery" explains nothing; it is what historians ought to try to explain.

Because studying slavery as an institution rests on such deep commitment to these structural, abstract conventions, I begin by querying aspects of the existing literature that illustrate the contrasts between what I term its sociological (in a nontechnical sense) tone and the historical dynamic I hope to elaborate, one by one, en route to suspending them in favor of a historicized alterative.

Orlando Patterson's definitive synthesis of the logic of the field, in his avowedly sociological *Slavery and Social Death* epitomizes the decontextualization of what I call the master-slave dyad.[38] For a quarter of a century this masterwork has justly been accorded pride of place, and it will not soon be superseded as a vivid evocation of the lived Hegelian problem of personal domination. Slavery, as he abstracts it, singular among human relationships in its extremity of claimed domination, is utterly ubiquitous in recorded human societies. Patterson's book takes on slaving on a sweepingly global scale, though not historically. In his hands slavery has dynamic elements, to be sure, though not of a historical sort that would embed particular masters and their slaves in specific times and specific places. His data come from a comprehensive range of very specific ethnographic sources, but his essentially statistical analysis of them extracts generalized masters and their slaves from these specific situations in which they lived. His resonant metaphor of "social death" isolates the pair axiomatically, indeed by definition. Masters monopolize the lives of their slaves, to the absolute exclusion of all others around them, thus condemning the enslaved to the living historical hell of decontextualization.[39] *Slavery and Social Death* then essentially goes on to elaborate the psychology of such obsession within the isolated intimacy of his sequestered master–slave dyad more than it provides a sociology in the sense of positioning masters or their slaves in the larger social or temporal matrices in which they lived. It thus excludes historical context by definition.

Patterson's treatment of masters and slaves as individuals, rather than as relational beings embedded in social—or, as I would phrase the point, historical—contexts is also thoroughly modern in its implicit assumption of society itself. The autonomous, calculatingly self-centered individual stands at the core of all the modern behavioral social sciences. He, or she, then acts in ways that may be combined with the similarly individuated actions of others into aggregates susceptible to description in terms of their statistical tendencies. The implicit dehumanization, or at least anonymity, of sentient historical beings through application of statistical techniques to slavery and, most prominently, to the demographics of the Atlantic slave trade, have excited emotional objections from both scholars and members of the public intent on understanding identities and experiences of the enslaved obscured by the abstractions of the modern social sciences.[40] The intensity of these reactions, of course, reflects the political sensitivity of the subject itself, a metonymic essence of the metaphysical modern isolated individual.

In contrast, since historians are epistemologically humanists, a historical approach starts by focusing on the contexts that Patterson backgrounds to sense the strategic considerations that motivated the people who managed to acquire slaves at all. Patterson merely presents the historian with the enslaved already on hand and in hand, unproblematically subject to a master's compulsion to dominate.[41] Most other works on slavery have, in varying but considerable degrees, treated this assumption of abstracted dyadic domination as the dominating aspect of slavery. One reason Patterson's book immediately attained the seminal status that it has earned is that in it he brilliantly distills to an explicit essence the axiom that hovers implicitly in nearly all other works in the field.

Axiomatic denial of social existence to both the slavers and the individuals enslaved predicts the remainder of Patterson's argument. Implicitly lonely masters end up depending on their slaves so intensely that they have to acknowledge them personally as the vibrantly alive individuals who they in fact always were. Indeed their very recruitment and retention for their masters' service must have called upon them to be exactly that. The dynamic counterpart of "social death" is intense personal vitality. So intense a relationship is necessarily filled with dialectical contradictions that make relations between slaves and masters anything but stable. Thus, for Patterson, slavery itself is process, a growing engagement from the perspectives of both the enslavers and the enslaved. Beyond the rich intended irony of rescuing the seemingly dominated slave and placing the nominal master in the position of a parasitical dependent of the enslaved, this Hegelian dynamic of twisted psychological interdependency also reflects existential anxieties inherent in the book's axiomatic reliance on the individualism of modernity (and its discontents).

Patterson's slavery is also processual in a sense of acknowledging the growing social contextualization of the enslaved, other than in the modern Americas. Elsewhere the enslaved move from the "social deaths" of their moments of violent capture, through arrivals at remote and unfamiliar locations, to subordination to their masters' wills, to contesting the domination (all but tautologically) inherent in such engagements (but primarily, even only, on individual terms), and eventually, for some, at least, on through manumission to the social resurrection of conditional, negotiated, but recognized public standing.[42] A contradiction may lurk in Patterson's due attention to social rituals of exclusion by naming, dress, and other social markers apparently necessary to isolate the enslaved; the enslaved person is thus not socially inert but only liminal and thus anxiously evident to all. A title parallel to Patterson's appropriate to accent the master–slave dyad contextualized historically might be "slavery and social dread," or "slavery and social denial."

Patterson's accent on assimilation generates several of the many appealing insights of his sociology, as they show the peculiarity of the permanent, inherited civic exclusions of slavery as institutionalized in the United States. Slaves, as vital human beings working to gain the recognition in the wider societies initially denied them, challenge their masters' claimed monopolization of their attentions, mostly by burrowing from within their enslavement. They use strategies of resistance of the oblique and opportune sorts long featured in the general literature on slavery as a relationship of domination.[43] However, the totality of the domination that lies at the base of Patterson's definition of "slavery"; the analytical isolation of the master–slave dyad by definition converts any sign of life from the enslaved into resistance. Conceptually, they have no other option. But these are generic passages of abstracted slaves, anywhere, anytime. The principal exception to this generic sociological process was denial of this final step toward freedom (as Davis had noted, obliquely attributing the blockage to racialization) in certain colonies in the New World, and preeminently in the United States. Patterson's process thus operates ubiquitously through the myriad specific realizations that he documents, but in analytical significance it recedes to incidental background, mere cultural variants on the prioritized regularity, indeed ubiquity, of "social death."[44] The principal particularity—truncation of an otherwise uniform process (one hesitates to think also "progress") toward manumission in parts of the Americas—is not a positively explained event with a historicized, that is contextualized, logic of its own, but remains a dichotomous absence left an unexplained exception to the general model.[45]

The primary ahistorical analytical alternative to Patterson's sociological synthesis of the historically varying local results of slaving has been to compare the outcomes as cases of a generic phenomenon, with their differing features analyzed as variables around a constant no-less-abstract essence. In the early decades of modern studies of slavery, the apparent mildness of the practice in Brazil (in racial terms, of dubious direct relationship to slaving as such) offered a tempting contrast to the presumed (also racialized) harshness of slavery in the United States.[46] This and other quasi-social-scientific historical comparisons explicitly assume, in the spirit of true experimental science and parallel to Patterson's implicit backgrounding of context, that other things are equal. But things involving human perceptions—on which history properly concentrates—never are the same or even comparable, and things in the past cannot be ascertained to have been so in a rigorously scientific sense. Moreover, the things that scientific method attempts to hold constant are limited, even unique, in their numbers, whereas the aspects of historical context relevant to motivating human actions are infinite and ephemeral, by definition. As a result, historians attempting to compare slavery in different places have acknowledged contexts but left them as decorative background, analytically inert, effectively dismissed as insignificant.

In the comparative method, time itself is among these analytical residuals. Comparisons are inherently static, and so comparison entirely misses slaving's inherently dynamic qualities. These comparisons assume away the historical processes that the slavers appropriated to engage in slaving in addition to the further changes they may be assumed to have intended to effect by slaving, not to mention the radical disruptions experienced by the enslaved. As historical strategists, slavers operate effectively primarily in contexts of rapid change, as I will go on to illustrate, and the enslaved survive only by drawing on their deepest reserves of adaptability, agility, and opportunism.

Slaving, as motivated human action, was itself fundamentally historical also because it was a particularly efficacious strategy of making a difference in people's lives, thus generating historical processes. Slavers introduced resources from outside and protected them from local rivals. Their slaving strategies motivated competitors to react, on scales ranging from interpersonal relations, between individual masters and the people whom they acquired; to local and regional competition, between slavers seeking power through slaving and opponents less committed, if not actively opposed, to their strategy; and to domestic relations, between the legitimate wives of patrimonial householders and the slave girls brought in for domestic services but available to attend to their masters also in more intimate ways. Slavers from early times to the eighteenth-century Atlantic arguably achieved significant changes on the grand scales of humanity: that is, as world history, by slaving, as the following chapter sketches. This historicized approach to slaving—or, in the formal language of the discipline, viewing human initiatives through the lens of a rigorously historical epistemology—explains the association of "slavery" with "human progress" that Davis acutely noted, but not merely as a paradoxical, or unexplained irony, but rather as an eminently intelligible, intended historical process. Slavers succeeded in moments of momentous change and also used their unrestrained control of their slaves to apply their energies to further, radically novel ends. Slaving is inherently historical. Sociological structures and institutional comparisons cannot capture this fundamental dynamic.

Problematizing History

But why is doing something that in the present day sounds as obvious as historicizing the concept of slavery the problem to which the title of these essays alludes? No one has ever denied that things change, slaving included, and Davis certainly considered changes on encompassing scales, beyond his operative focus on the profound change in the hearts of the eighteenth-century pietists and humanists who recognized slavery as a moral problem of proportions so enormous that eradicating it required mobilization of all the overwhelming civic, and eventually military, force of emerging modern governments.[47] Nonetheless, for the ethical and political reasons I have sketched, nearly all academic literature on the subject, implicitly or explicitly, anywhere in the world, has continued to treat slavery as an implicitly static institution: that is, sociologically.

In an epistemological sense history involves a good deal more than just mining the past for human behavior to describe, or even to analyze with an ad hoc assortment of sociological models. Historical sociology also does this, often revealingly enough with regard to illustrating regularities in human behavior. Sociological approaches may even acknowledge change, but they do not rest analytically on its dynamics. In contrast to historical thinking, which contextualizes in order to suggest the meanings and intentions behind human actions, sociology decontextualizes by selecting specifics to illustrate the generalizations and theories in focus, creating the models on which it properly—and productively—concentrates.

Putting the point less abstractly and thus more historically, changing contexts, not the seemingly universal constant of inhumane domination,[48] explain how *people in positions definably marginal* to the societies in which they lived *recurrently resorted* to slaving to convert their marginality toward centrality. Historians thus would not say that slaving abstractly persisted, even though people in this position of marginality, a logically necessary component of any coherent—and thus conceptually centered—historical community, have therefore, also logically, necessarily turned up ubiquitously since the very beginnings of human time. Historians instead focus on the specific circumstances in which peripheral parties,[49] again and again, in different places and different times found slaving an accessibly advantageous strategy and so reinvented it out of their own moments, and therefore always in novel ways and to particular strategic ends. These historical contexts of change, which both motivated and enabled these specifiable interests to use slaving to appropriate the changes already under way around them for purposes of their own, also always differed, depending on where in their particular historical contexts the slavers stood.[50] That is, the historian would not start from the intellectual, or philosophical, or ideological problem of an institution, frozen in timeless analytical space, but rather with the historical, that is dialectical/processual, specifics of what Davis noted—but reluctantly backgrounded—as "economic functions and interpersonal relationships . . . for which we lack satisfactory data."[51] Historians then account for such recurring patterns by reasoning from the particulars of human experiences rather than contemplating the abstract logic of the patterns that the particulars may form.[52]

By explicitly problematizing slaving as a *historical* strategy, in processual historical contexts, rather than implicitly as a sociological institution, I accent change of a very particular historical sort. Situating the slavers and the enslaved in the specific contexts in which the innumerable master–slave dyads in the world's history in fact lived requires precise definition of context. I intend this concept in the most comprehensive sense possible, including momentary (and individual) adaptations of received cultural heritages; societal frameworks as dynamic and manipulable outcomes of historical actions rather than as constraining structures; imagined political, military, or economic opportunities; and the sheer ephemerality of the series of presents in which we all always live.

This phrasing of the dynamic aspects of slaving is thus intended to draw on what strike me as the three distinguishing components of history's epistemology. Our purpose in thinking historically is to explain, in ways historians and their audiences find plausible.[53] We seek truth less than we seek to communicate meaning; whatever truth we achieve is consensual at best, probably fleeting, and significantly rhetorical. It may thus be said that historians distinctively *explain* by focusing on

1. *humans* (people rather than abstractions, institutions, or structures of any kind—mental or social or economic or otherwise)

    Thus for historians, abstractions do not act. Christianity, or civilization, or modernity do not spread; rather, people may adopt and adapt elements of these logical constructions for their own immediate purposes.

Civilizations do not endure, but rather people may preserve them, and necessarily change them in the course of making the efforts necessary to maintain elements in them against the erosive flow of time. Ideas cannot influence, but people may manipulate them ideologically to attempt to influence others.

In the present context, slavery as an institution is an abstraction and thus not a premise viable for historians, though historians may trace how certain interests in the very particular context of British North America eventually institutionalized the unintended consequences of intense slaving in the Atlantic.[54]

2. humans *acting* (in whatever baffled ways they can manage) out of incomplete, impressionistic, and significantly inaccurate awareness of momentary and particular circumstances from which they derive meanings, and hence motivations for whatever they do.

Historians reconstruct contexts as richly as they can, to discern as many as possible of the always multiple, not always (or perhaps seldom) coherent, aspects of actors' contexts to which they may plausibly have reacted in ways that historians can identify.

"Cause" is thus an entirely false problematic for historians. It is necessarily attributed to structural sociological abstractions, in a futile search for coherence in the eye of the analyst/beholder. Causation may be possible to discern in defined scientific reactions, or mechanical processes, but among historians the word almost always attributes agency to an abstraction, in response to some phrasing parallel to "what [abstraction] caused the Second World War, or the Great Depression." In a historical mode, it cannot be said that "race caused slavery" in the Americas, or vice versa. This sort of statement is mechanistic, regular, and deterministic; human actions are subtle and complex, unique, and contingent. It should be no wonder that historians never agree on the answers to questions posed as these historical red herrings.

Even if masters abused enslaved persons to the point of provoking flight or retaliation, the historian cannot assume a causal link between provocation and rebellion, both abstractions. Rather a historical assessment of such incidents would consider as much of the context of the fugitive's circumstances, at the moment of flight, as can be evaluated. Historians thus assess contexts as fully as possible to identify all the aspects of them significant in motivating what people may be observed to have done. To repeat: historians do not prove anything but rather explain, in the sense of rendering others' actions plausible, even convincing, to readers or audiences also positioned in swirling flows of time. The place of abstract causation in a historical epistemology, as distinct from ascertainable or plausibly inferable motivations, is rhetorical.

3. humans act more with the intention of forestalling changes than of effecting them, that is, dealing with the consequences stemming from the motivated initiatives of others. Such externalities as climate are often prominent elements of contexts, but they are historically significant only as filtered (still) through human reactions to noticeable aspects of them, as the meanings people may attribute to them.[55]

The further implication of change, construed historically in terms of the multiple actions producing it, is that it is an ongoing dialectical process. People are inherently social beings, or—in the context of this discussion of the epistemology of history—by definition they act in historical contexts. Every human action may be said to produce unanticipated and asymmetrical human reactions. How otherwise would Patterson depict the forlornness of the enslaved so effectively through his isolating metaphor of "social death"? Consummate powerlessness is the inability to provoke anyone; "social death," as I emphasized in a preceding context here, is historically inert. Historically, slaves are actors, and every historical action is itself also a reaction to and part of infinite sequences of reactions.

These processual sequences are the aspects of contexts that the historian strings together in plausible narratives. Since each action arises from a preceding one, in an established context of multiple meanings, the processes that historians track are incremental, even minimally so. The historian sees change as an extension of the philosophical rule of Ockham's razor. This law of logic, in effect, urges elegance in explanation: what explains most elegantly requires the fewest assumptions. In mathematics, it is a "least-moves" sequence. In terms of historical action, it means that the most accessible move is the one that alters contexts (including existing positionality) least, adapting to changed contexts by attempting to modify only a selected few aspects, or even obsessively singular aspect, of contexts that are infinitely complex. Historical actions are therefore minimalist, at least in principle.

Explanations of least moves succeed most often also because change is not cheap. Historians therefore must also account for actors' access to means available and adequate to effect change. Stating the point in yet another way, humans relish changes of dramatic, transformational proportions; clear-cut contrasts make great stories. But such stories are not historical. They are magical, essentially illusions achieved by the sleight of hand of focusing attention on orderly contrasts abstracted from the messy realities of experience. Realistically, that is historically, actors maneuver opportunistically within the realm of the apparently possible. People also inherently seek security, and the security of the known motivates them to seek change in forms that preserve as much as possible of the past; alternatively, they misinterpret unavoidable novelty as familiar. People are conservative; they create change in spite of their best intentions.

The historian's definition of "change," beginning with contextualized human initiative, is therefore incremental, and it generates infinitely complex, subtle, even contradictory chains of human relations and reactions that the historian uses to explain outcomes by arraying them as processes plausible in the present.

A former colleague presents these three components of history's epistemology alliteratively (and hence masterfully and memorably) in terms of the particularities of "people, places, and processes."[56] To his alliterative play on "p" I would add an accent on taking analytical account of, or *problematizing*, the *partiality* of the vast array of individuals' *perspectives* on their surroundings. We all create simplified illusions of our historical contexts to reduce the anxieties that anyone must feel who wallows along in ongoing uncertainties of time itself. I mean "partiality" in both senses of the word: incomplete, as well as involving feeling or commitment. To continue the play on "p," history is therefore also fundamentally *perspectival*. Historical narrative may involve *participants* in the *past*, as well as subsequent historians in the *present* contemplating them. History, finally, then, is inherently *plural*: multiple "mystories" and "ourstories."

The historian thus thinks in registers that include human emotions, while avoiding abstractions presumed to be calculated, logical, and hence operative only at selected levels of rationality. Since history takes account of what, to the actors, was unaccountable (the limited aspects of the contexts in which people found themselves that they actually experienced) its epistemology is richly ironic, filled with unpredicted outcomes, consequences of actions not intended by the initiators of the changes to which they ended up having contributed, indirectly, through the reactions of others that they provoked. The alternative to historians' reliance on ambivalence and ambiguity, the sociological abstractions of the literature on slavery leaves people as merely passive, at best participating as accepting without reasons of their own, or accepting for reasons attributed to them by some analytical observer in the present, hopefully not including historians. These attributed characteriological ways of explaining may employ ethnic or racial discourses, may be presented as matters of faith, or humanized (and secularized) as psychological, but none of these entirely valid ways of rendering people subject to abstract logics approximates history's existential epistemology.

Slavery presented as an institution is a fait accompli, accomplished, a done deal, general, and static. Conceived in this conventional abstracted form it axiomatically becomes the intractable problem that scholars have accepted it as being, however they lament the dilemma that they have themselves thus created by structuring it as such. Without thinking about slaving historically, as contextually motivated strategies, we have logically accepted the moral abomination that we condemn; we have left slavery as an evil lurking eternally in the hearts of men (and women).[57] It is in this politicized sense that "slavery is good to think with." But the historian instead follows ordinarily ambitious and unsettling "slaving strategies," in all their dynamic particularities—though decidedly not in their peculiarity as a human experience.

Evil, however, is precisely what I will argue slaving, and the slaveries eventually built on it, became—but only in a historical sense that specifies the modern context of civic nationhood that imbued it with the strong and negative meanings that Davis problematized. Since history is elementally perspectival, a historian cannot attempt a comprehensive judgment—which would be omniscient, godlike—as would a moral philosopher, or a politician (at least for rhetorical purposes). Rather, "evil" refers to human perspectives on actions and on the processual changes following from others' reactions to them. It demonizes to displace responsibility from the initiators of the process by blaming the reactors; in a playground brawl, the kid who hits back is always the one who ends up being noticed and sent to the principal. In the case of slaving, "evil" refers to a quite specific destructive intent—not primarily to destroy the enslaved, who are needed, but rather of the status quo, the contexts that motivate the slavers to slave. Their slaving, in turn, is threatening from the perspective of the rivals at whose expense the slavers advance themselves by slaving. Slaves were the slavers' means of gaining, from the margins, on more established rivals otherwise capable of inhibiting moves of the sort that slaving enabled.

Marginality as a Historical Problem

Historically, it is possible to identify quite consistent circumstances in which the greed present in us all breaks through the constraints of culture and becomes historically significant as slaving.[58] The definable and distinguishing position of slavers is their marginality to the historical context in which they live and compete. It is a very precise situation in terms of the historical contexts that both motivated and enabled slavers to slave. The contexts, defined historically, include whomever the slavers intend to overtake by slaving and also whatever resources they find accessible to do so. These relevant motivating contexts are fluid, inchoate, and even incoherent from the perspectives of the people who inhabit them and act in terms of them, but they include all that the historian may now surmise as having framed their motivations. Discerning that historically coherent, or relevant, domain of action is the responsibility of the historian, since it includes not only considerations that the actors then could arguably take into account but also other considerations evident only now to the historical observer.[59]

For slavers, marginality means quite literally "on a margin" of a network of people who were in control of whatever the key resources might have been in the relevant contexts. Marxists would state this control in materialist terms of physical means of production, but recent cultural theorists from Gramsci through Foucault have highlighted the intellectual, ideological, or cultural, or elementally linguistic aspects of exercising such power. Merchants in fifteenth-century Europe, for example, may be said to have been in positions of marginality relative to the military, aristocratic, and ecclesiastical interests then in control of the peasant farmers, the productive contributors central to an agricultural economy.[60] These commercial interests were not excluded: rather, they were vital to the dominant figures who controlled military power, land, and people, the secular and ecclesiastical aristocracies who supported themselves (but only with merchant support) at levels of material splendor and cultural idolization that still stand, in a romanticized sort of way, as paradigms of power in modern culture. Merchants on the margin of the wealth and honor and power of kings and bishops were thus close enough to that establishment to imagine themselves as potentially sharing its privileges but rigidly barred from entering the ranks of the exalted. Marginality thus accounted for merchant ambition, for their motivation, to belong.

The same marginality also accounted for how merchants turned to slaving as a novel, indirect avenue to the quite conventional, integrative objectives they sought. Merchants of a stature sufficient to harbor these ambitions not only had financial means but also operated, almost by definition, beyond the territorial domains claimed by military rulers and human souls claimed by the Church. In the world outside these internal spheres of contested eminence, merchants were positioned to operate effectively beyond the control of their aristocratic sponsors. There also they could acquire people, by purchase, whom they transported back home. They lodged them as personal retainers—beholden to no competitors in the internal establishment they wished to join—or even deployed them to unseat the settled. Contextualizing the slavers as marginal in this specific sense of motivations, means, and independent access to outside resources, then, positions the historian to track the incremental steps that led to *strategic slaving*, and then to consider the reactions that innovations of such substance always provoked on the parts of those they threatened.

The historical problem of slaving, as I develop it in the following essays, is thus political: who, under what circumstances, by what means, with what ends in mind, and with what failures as well as what successes, managed to get their hands on individuals so culturally and socially isolated that they could induce, if not directly compel, the outsiders they added to internal politics to support the slavers in advancing themselves at the expense of more established interests. The historical issue between the enslavers and the enslaved was appropriating outsiders' energies in support of insiders' strategies.

To recall the lingering historiographical issue of slavery and progress, slaving as a strategy is inherently innovatory: it is a means of turning changing contexts to specific advantages for hangers-on. The literature of the field, in a theorized moment inspired by the determinism of both progressive and Marxist historiologies, once debated whether the institution of slavery in the modern Americas represented an atavistic retreat to earlier, less efficient means of production, or was part of the progressive move toward modern capitalism then under way. The logic of this debate considered slavery in terms of the logics of alternative structures, arrayed along an essentially evolutionary continuum, or rather series of separated, contrasted abstract types. But as a historical strategy, slaving enables slavers to promote change relative to any of an infinite set of existing contexts. Not forward or backward, nor for better or for worse in any comprehensive sense, but in a historical process in which some, with access to outside resources, challenge others in control of the significant resources within the sphere in which they compete—a conceptual space that I term a historically coherent entity. Slaving illuminates the historical processes behind Davis's powerfully ironic association of slavery with progress.

This historical definition of *slaving* further implies a contextualized definition of the experience of *enslavement* as isolated helplessness, or helpless isolation. This accent on the slave's positionality contrasts with Patterson's famous sociological definition of slavery as "*the permanent, violent* [personal] *domination of natally alienated and generally* [that is, socially] *dishonored persons*"[61] in nearly every one of its five or six decontextualizing components. It emphasizes the contexts in which both masters and slaves acted rather than centering on the paradoxical relationship between masters and slaves. In Patterson's definition the intense, even obsessive, relationship between master and slave all but tautologically states the obverse of the condition of "social death." In contrast, this historical approach draws attention to the slavers' relations with the social, or economic, or political, or military rivals of their particular, changing moments. Competition, not domination, motivates and enables masters' strategies of improving their (relative) positions by slaving.

This definition is therefore from the point of view of the enslaved rather than one of the masters' conceit of total control. Patterson's definition of slaves as dominated rests not on the experiences of the enslaved but rather on a reductive—because decontextualized—vision of the masters' intention to dominate. It, in effect, elevates to definitional status what is demonstrated to be no more than a masters' conceit. Defining enslavement historically (that is, experientially and including the perspectives of the enslaved), starts with the backgrounds of the enslaved, assesses individual personalities, considers the experience of capture and removal, seeks motivations, and assesses their means to act in the social/cultural/historical contexts in which they find themselves. This approach goes beyond the passivity of suffering and domination. An example at an elemental level: enslaved women and children had experiences, opportunities, and objectives significantly different from those of men enslaved.[62] Taking account of enslaved people's historical contexts—from before their captures and removals and through their calculated manipulations of their masters' authority—positions them as autonomously motivated historical actors. Giving them contextualized hopes for comfort or personal satisfactions and fulfillments other than the abstract freedom (through manumission) that constitutes the primary significant escape for Patterson's slaves, makes them historical people with realistic choices—or agents as some of the current discourses abstract the people hidden behind the mask of slavery in much of the literature.

Arguably, isolation is a—if not the—prominent motivating aspect of enslavement as experienced. For the enslaved, isolation is the existential obverse of the component of Patterson's abstracted "natally alienated," as it is also their experience of what Patterson phrases—again abstractly and negatively—as "social death." In fact, Patterson's definition—"*the permanent, violent domination of natally alienated and generally dishonored persons*"—does not describe the thesis of the book, which emphasizes not "permanent . . . domination" but rather the slave's process through arrival, engagement with masters, and—usually—eventual manumission, not to say ironic ultimate psychological mastery of the master. Phrased more accurately, the definition would read "*the violent domination of* permanently *natally alienated and* socially *dishonored persons*," and it would suggest the corollary that violence is necessary only because in every realistic historical context the enslaved have, and take advantage of, options, whether they find them on plantations or in mines, harems, villages in Africa, or complex households of the sort that Patterson refers to as "palaces."

The isolation of the enslaved upon arrival is also their principal weakness, the circumstance, or aspect of their historicized contexts, that leaves them vulnerable to abuse or exploitation. But isolation is ephemeral. All human beings are social; they depend fundamentally on one another. The enslaved arrive alone, with no one to whom they can turn for protection or affection. They lack cultural knowledge or even the language to communicate. This vulnerability is psychological as well as physical, more demoralizing and more emotionally debilitating than the stereotyped occasional lashings of the whip or the drudgery of (collective) labors in a cotton field. The principal historical strategy of the enslaved, living in processual time, is therefore to overcome their initial isolation, to make human contacts with whomever they find accessible, to build committed relationships of whatever sorts, and to defend whatever connections they manage to make with whatever means may be available, including imaginative ones. Permanently "natally alienated," historical persons isolated by enslavement primarily seek new ways to belong in their new situations.[63] There is no turning back, and so they move on, as Patterson's emphasis on assimilation implies. Their personal strategies may center on obsessive and manipulative relationships with the masters, including playing on the psychodynamics of Patterson's master–slave dyad, but over time the enslaved extend these connections in other opportune directions, flying well under the radar of abstract social/civic acknowledgement that Patterson emphasizes. Human fulfillment thrives on multiple relationships, appropriate to the unpredictably varying moments in everyone's lives. The slaves' informal networks, invisible in structural terms, are the contributions of the enslaved to Patterson's abstract social process of assimilation. By contextualizing, the historian of slaving and being enslaved contemplates the opportune strategies of the enslaved as well as the opportunism of the slavers.

However Patterson's slaves may preserve some sense of personal dignity, and however they may play off the contradictions within the (presumed, axiomatic, accepted, given) relationship of domination to find places of their own in society, they are unpromising agents of historical change. Historical actions affect their contexts, from which Patterson's slaves are definitionally isolated. Within this logic, slaves are positioned to make a historical difference only in rebellion, that is, no longer as dominated slaves but rather by asserting themselves outside of the intentions of their would-be masters. In fact, by devotedly and brilliantly celebrating the agency of the enslaved, Patterson's book as a whole disproves his own defining quality of domination; this definition is thus the perspective of the masters, not of the enslaved, and more an ideological assertion than historical behavior.

The Prospect of Problematizing Slaving

The prospect of understanding slaving historically immediately confronts historians with the "problem" of construing the situation of vulnerable outsiders in positions of abject dependency as anything other than an institution. To date, the field has increased its geographical and temporal range either by analogy with the highly peculiar—even unique—image of the American South or in dichotomous contrasts, noting the absence of features taken to characterize it. The conventional definition derived from the antebellum southern United States, or abolitionists' caricatures of it, defines "slavery" as a legal institution that positions people in a proprietorial regime otherwise reserved for things and domestic livestock—that is, as productive animals of commercial value.[64] Such modern slavery also involved coercive and highly disciplined exploitation of the efforts of the persons thus reduced to serving the monetary aims of their owners. However, the proprietorial accent that became prominent in Atlantic slavery, or at least in parts of the region (and even there only during certain moments), was just that: an emergent, localized accent not inherent in the long-run political efficacy of the historical strategy of slaving. Property was thus a metaphorical—in fact, technically legal—aspect of slaving in the commercialized circumstances that arose from the distinctively capitalistic contexts of these recent times. In effect, studies of slavery in the antebellum American South, as well as elsewhere in the world, have appropriated the past as prologue to our subsequent present politics.

This ahistorical selectivity, a problem for historians because it violates their epistemological premise of comprehensive contextualizing, became all the more exaggerated as studies of slavery expanded to global scales. The dynamics of building a new field, that is, defining a logic to guide specific research along paths not previously taken, or even imagined, is as random as looking for a needle in a haystack. New fields are inherently cantilevered precariously out over yawning chasms of "lack [of] satisfactory data."[65] In the case of slavery studies, historians accordingly projected a base of empirical research resting largely on highly politicized abolitionist accounts of the antebellum U.S. South out into world areas then unknown. They advanced tentatively outward first from an initial, almost obsessive fascination with their own North Atlantic late-nineteenth-century selves to others in the ancient world whom, as Finley noted, Europeans had grown to fancy, hardly less narcissistically, as exemplarily ancestral to themselves. In the twentieth century, the interwar celebration of Pan-Americanism brought attention next to the tropical Americas. Then, but more faintly, European socialists interested in the Marxian postulate of a transition from (ancient) slavery to (medieval) serfdom added medieval Europe into the picture, with faint Soviet parallel interests in ancient China. Only in the post-Sputnik era of the 1960s did the search for slaveries extend into the rest of the world, with the growth of regional "non-Western"[66] histories.

This introductory chapter on history's proper epistemology argues that the recovery of information on slavery elsewhere in the world, collected over the past half century, positions historians now to break free of their then-necessary, but now increasingly transitional, inherently modern reliance on the social sciences. That is, historians are now equipped with a vast array of specifics to historicize their understanding of the inherently historical process of slaving. The following chapters explore the potential yield of problematizing slaving there as history, and then historicizing the cliché of slavery as an institution.

2

History as a Problem of Slaving

The demonstrated—but relatively timeless, and lamented more than explained—ubiquity of slaving throughout the world's history, historicized, becomes a strategy readily explicable in terms of the marginality of the slavers suggested in the opening chapter in this book. This chapter extends the discussion of the epistemology of history to problematize the conventional, still significantly Eurocentric and structural approach to the history of the world. Here I sketch a historical vision of slaving over some thirty to fifty thousand years, centering on strategies of slaving as both means and consequences of major innovations in the human narrative. The historical processes sketched here in terms of slaving form the basis for the following, more elaborated—though still hardly nuanced—chapters on Africa and the Americas. Readers knowledgeable in the often highly specialized regions and epochs in which professionals normally cluster, and into which here I intrude, however recklessly (but always respectfully), will surely—at least initially—have acute impressions of what I have omitted, or of hotly debated nuances of their fields that I have ignored. However, I hope that these first impressions will be modulated by awareness of the potential insight to be gained from contextualizing their expert knowledge in the broader patterns revealed by a global synthesis centered on strategies of slaving. Inspired by the words of the Malian sage, Tierno Bokar of Bandiagara, I hope for indulgence on a first reading:

If you wish to know who I am,
If you wish me to teach you what I know,
Cease for the while to be what you are
And forget what you know

Toward a Comprehensive Global Approach

Slavery around the world pulled off one of the more artful disappearing acts of the early twentieth century. Not that slavers ceased to slave, though the widespread slaving violence of the late nineteenth century did decline with imposition of a rough *pax coloniana;* instead slaving was marginalized in public discourse and not yet embraced as a subject suitably remote for contemplation as history.

In the imperialist campaigns of the generation before World War I, European governments had sent armies through Africa and Asia under high-flying banners of eradicating there the abominably inhumane slaving practices of which they had only recently purged themselves, closer to home. Then in the following generation of interwar colonial politics a deep silence fell over the subject. Professional ethnographic descriptions of the largely unknown residents of European colonies in Africa, South Asia, the Indonesian archipelago, and the Sino-East-Asian region concentrated on rendering rational, and hence intelligible, the strange ways of the "people without history"[1] for whom European governments had taken responsibility for nudging into their own visions of the twentieth century. Similar wishful attentions to order and social harmony pervaded understandings of the Native Americas. Slavery, retrograde in the extreme according to the progressive "civilizing" standards of the time, was not part of those pictures, and the reforming European heirs to the anti-slavery components of imperial conquests shifted their attention toward the forced labor policies to which new, struggling, underfinanced colonial regimes not infrequently resorted.[2]

The colonial regimes themselves had other secrets to keep with regard to slaving. Their minimal resources and personnel, and their innocence of the unprecedented scale of the responsibility they had theoretically assumed for hundreds of millions of people around the world, in practice left them significantly dependent on the collaboration of local authorities in their colonies. Extreme weakness on the ground was the reality of colonial occupation that the British, in particular, dignified as policy, the doctrine they celebrated as "indirect rule."[3] The problem of slavery inherent in this quiet concession to political reality was that the local authorities on whom colonial officials relied had gained the positions that gave them value to colonizers largely because they had profited, as slaveholders, from the violence of the late nineteenth century that the colonizers had allegedly colonized to terminate. The less said in public about this quiet compromise, the better, and so the classical generation of ethnographers in the 1930s and 1940s found other rural exotica in the colonies to engage the interests of their government sponsors in political control and of social theorists in the harmoniously integrated societies they believed they had discovered.

Historical interest in slavery increased in the 1950s and 1960s as a generation of scholars who had not known the subject as politics turned their attentions to a subject sufficiently remote to contemplate. This interest in slavery coincided with growth of academic attention to the remote parts of the world, then emerging from the shadows of colonial propaganda into the light of national independence. But, for reasons having as much to do with the interested scholars' perspectives from the Americas and Europe, historians found slavery all but invisible there. Whatever echoes of slavery they found bore so little resemblance to stereotypical cotton plantations in the Mississippi Delta of the 1850s that the practice seemed infrequent at best (or worst). They found it mild in contrast to the hard labor that defined the harshness of slavery in the Cotton South and on the sugar plantations of the eighteenth-century Caribbean. The mitigating absences they attributed to it nearly always included the racial aspect entangled with the American institution as they thought they knew it. Slavery in Africa seemed to admit of assimilation of the enslaved rather than exhibiting the inherited permanent exclusions of institutionalized slavery in the Americas. Legal formulations of the institution were absent or, in the case of Islam, less comprehensive than seemed appropriate. It was particularly difficult to identify economic exploitation reminiscent of American plantations.

These efforts to seek slavery around the world only in the familiar terms of abolitionist characterizations of American plantations highlight the selective logic employed in this self-fulfilling quest: one can always find (at least some bits of) whatever one is looking for, particularly when one looks intently enough. But always at the cost of finding only that. In the case of seeking slavery construed as a legal institution applied for economic purposes of commodity production, *not* finding what one thought one was looking for came to the evident relief of neo-abolitionist historians, embarrassed by their own racialized heritage and eager to redeem the "people without history" throughout the world from any taint of practices—like slavery—that progressive historiography had consigned to the dustbin of the past. Bringing the "natives" into the historical world—where they belonged—meant endowing them with progress too, and progress did not involve slavery.

For Africa, as the following chapter elaborates, historians faced the added challenge of rescuing the ancestors of the people wrongly enslaved in the Americas from the stigma of having been involved in the institution from which they had suffered so much. A prominent part of their neo-abolitionist heritage from the earlier politics of abolition had been eighteenth-century European slavers' ardent defense of their business practices as relieving their captives of their sufferings in Africa as slaves who would be sacrificed by savage kings far more brutal than the charitably Christian planters in the West Indies. A historian raising the prospect of slavery in Africa risked appearing to shift responsibility for the tragedy, or crime against humanity, away from the European participants in the process. Mid-twentieth-century politics of race associated people in Africa with people of African descent in the Americas. And, at the inauguration of research into the regional histories of the world, the empirical limits—the lack of research that Davis had noted, in another context—provided little basis for even the most cautious and respectable members of the historians' guild to recognize when they were projecting their own pasts, and the politics of the present, or inversions of both, into the voids of real knowledge that they were entering.

The historian should consider the historicized alternative in defining slaving strategies in terms of objectives other than producing commodities and should approach enslavement in terms of the experiences of the enslaved—of wondering how people might have experienced the hardships and disabilities of betrayal, isolation, vulnerability, and humiliation—and then assess how enslaved people might have responded constructively in terms of those understandings. A half century later, innocence no longer imprisons Western scholars in their own perspectives, and scholars from these once-remote parts of the world are beginning to broach a subject of a continuing sensitivity no less intense for them than for modern Europeans and Americans.[4]

However, the enabling studies of slavery extended into other parts of the world over the last four decades built on evidence grounded in the structural anthropological concepts—lineages, states—available at the time. This sociologically framed scholarship has remained only incipiently historical, in the rigorous sense defined in the first essay in this book. Alternative inspiration, or inspired alterity, has been slowest to contribute to understanding slavery in the New World, including North America. Here (from where I am writing, in Virginia), in spite of recent masterworks,[5] historians' personal positioning in the midst of slavery's modern legacies have made many of them confident that they understood what they were looking for, even in earlier times, well before the classic antebellum formulation of slavery as an institution. Alternative perspectives have also been slow to permeate work on slavery in the ancient Mediterranean, because so many historians identified with it so strongly that they thought they knew what to make of the very limited sources at their disposal.[6]

Elsewhere, Africanists and specialists in the Muslim world (often led by historians working on Islamic Africa) started with a clearer sense of how little they knew, although they compensated for the initially fragmentary evidence at hand by attempting to fit whatever they had into the sociological framework of an institution rather than seeing the array of particular historical strategies or practices.[7] Asia, particularly maritime southeastern Asia, came into focus next, though again only partially on terms of its own, with occasional extensions to China and Korea, where world historians had long, and comfortably, interpreted empires and civilizations by their resemblances to the modern West's congratulatory image of itself, and thereby marginalizing slaving yet again.[8] Ethnohistorians of Native North America followed the lead of the Africanists into positioning slavery in small communities structured in metaphors of kinship.[9] Non-Muslim India lingered even longer in the obscurity of exoticizing colonial conceptions of caste and of labor bonded by means other than slaving, though South Asia is now becoming a fascinating example both of the unsuspected strategies of slaving employed there and of the ideological processes of colonial rule that obscured them from ethnographers and historians.[10] There is, of course, a salutary lesson here for historians: they should be careful about presuming what they are looking for, because they are likely to find it.

A new and growing scholarly cottage industry is now finding copious evidence of slaving in all the prosperous regions of the Renaissance Mediterranean: Italian cities, parts of the Iberian Peninsula, the Balearic and other islands. Among these discoveries are the complementing seizures of hostages, most of them enslaved, by the Christian and Muslim adversaries confronting one another through the religious tempests then roiling that conflict-torn sea.[11] Everywhere, including Europe, rereadings of anthropological accounts, reexamination of archives and other seemingly familiar sources, and new research have now established an empirical base sufficient to support a serviceably contextualized, hence humanly motivated rather than model-driven, *history* of *slaving* on a globally inclusive, and perhaps even analytically comprehending, scale.[12]

In the Beginning

Having suggested how treating slavery as an institution, peculiar or not, has obscured the global historical processes in which marginal interests thrived by slaving, having offered the epistemological parameters of a rigorously historical approach to the problem, and having alluded to the range of the recent research that makes it possible here to attempt such an integration on a global scale, I turn to some highly selected, but I hope also highly suggestive, aspects of a world history of slaving.[13] On these global scales, slaving arguably contributed to the very beginnings of human history, tens of thousands of years before times recorded in any conventional document-based sense. An approximate date for when history in this inclusive sense may be said to have begun is roughly forty thousand to twenty thousand years ago. I propose that date partly for purposes of debate, but also with a degree of consideration that leaves me confident that the remote era I suggest is at least a professionally responsible estimate. It was the threshold of both humanity and history, marked by abilities to strategize collectively, in contexts of shared meaning. The marker of such strategically effective collectivity is functionally syntactical language: that is, language sufficiently grammatical that speakers can wield it flexibly enough to succeed in confronting novel, unexpected historical contexts. Someone, somewhere, perhaps many competing bands, gradually elaborated syntactical, hence creative, language from cranial capacities that had earlier enabled efficacious, but rote, signaling. In complex ways language enabled the collective creativity and intentionality that distinguish fully human beings from even the most alert of other animals. That remote epoch is also an analytically considered starting point for slaving.

With language, early humans learned to strategize together, giving them the unprecedented advantage of being able to rely on knowledge accumulated and then shared and on actions coordinated, and to pass along the successful strategies that they worked out as learned cultures. Slaving was arguably one successful strategy that these earliest peoples hit upon as a means of creating and maintaining the commitment to mutual loyalties that gave such humans the edge in confronting other contemporary, but less inventive, hominids, as well as the changing environmental and other contextual challenges that have brought us to where we are today. That is, humanity, history, and slaving were inherently linked; they were fundamentally mutually constituted. Slaving has also proved exquisitely adaptively efficacious, including subsequent resort to slaving by key initiators in new ways in new contexts during the last twenty thousand years. This deep imbrication ought to be obvious, given the ubiquity of the practice, even today, though our progressivist conviction in our own slavery-freed perfectibility has tended to obscure its elementally human temptation.

Historical linguistics provides the primary evidence for my dating of the beginning of efficaciously historical strategizing.[14] Research in this field dates the broad origins of the modern language families of the world—that is, the languages that generations of heirs to talkative ancestors found useful enough to maintain them—to approximately the time depth I propose. The last generations of clever hominids, including media favorites like the bulky but slow and mumbling Neanderthals in western Europe, had been adept imitators, but their limited imaginations also narrowed the range of innovations they could copy to random, unintended accidents. Noticing accidents to copy them was a further very low-percentage process and produced cumulative change only through slow processes of evolution. History, defined as humans acting purposefully in collective, or social, contexts out of shared systems of meaning, in contrast follows the subsequent accelerating sequence of collaborative strategies that strategizing humans developed to try to preserve what their ancestors had achieved.

Focusing more specifically on change as the incremental, inadvertent outcomes that constitute the processes characteristic of history in an epistemological sense, this essentially conservative historical motivation,[15] of course, reverses the future-oriented vector of intention that underlies the vision of history as progressive held by people like us who seem, or claim to be, anything but sentimental about their pasts. The progressive ethos of this conventional modern western idea of history confuses the hope that springs from the key human ability to imagine with the lumbering, still basically imitative realities of how humans in fact think and act. In the aggregate, people are risk-averse, wary of the unknown, skeptical about novelty. They generally respond to dilemmas arising from circumstances that they could not influence directly (that is, historical contexts) by changing other aspects of their lives that they sense as of secondary value in the moment in order to conserve other values, regarded as core, that circumstances seem to threaten.

An epistemologically historical vision, based on actors' experiences rather than sociological modeling, therefore perceives change as unintended in its most significant aspects. Long-term changes follow inadvertently from reactions to what initiators are trying to preserve. They are outcomes of intensifications or extensions secondary to initial short-term responses—means to immediate ends, often sacrifices made in pursuit of another losing cause. Even calculated innovations made to escape intolerable circumstances often failed, because all strategies are contextualized in the competitive circumstances of scarcity in which all human endeavors wallow. Adaptations therefore created their own contradictions; anyone's gain someone else always perceived as their loss, and the losers reacted. This dialectical, ironic, accidental, and historical sort of change tolerates, even welcomes, the lessons in humility that it teaches, even while acknowledging the nobility, virtue, and good intentions of individual actors in the past, by the standards of their times.[16] In history, all are responsible, but no one is in charge.

With this ironic quality of historical change in mind, we return to understanding those very early humans, and their strategies, in their times, without anticipating what we may now think about what others did later. My emphasis falls on suggesting how slaving may plausibly have contributed, within the generically human ability to communicate and strategize, to fashioning the intensely communal ethos of collective (historical) action that they created. What I am calling a communal ethos was—and is—an enveloping moral commitment to the collectivity, a commitment sufficiently intense, naturalized, that it produced the consistent, dependable degrees of collaboration that enabled small groups to sustain themselves, against enormous odds. Elders and parents instilled such loyalties in their children, passing along what then became the sociability and culture that define humans and also history: they think and act routinely in terms of collectivity. This prioritization of the group, in an enduring sense, over the transient individuals in it at any given moment, succeeded widely, though not universally, in early human history, so that its beneficiaries around the world preserved it, and it was observed ethnographically in the first half of the twentieth century. For historians working outside the domain of the modern West's heavily ideological celebration of modern individualism, it is commonplace, and normatively human. Community is the heart of the historicized problematization of slaving that this essay develops.

But community was a historical creation, not a given. Back at the beginning I am positing, someone invented a communal ethos intense enough, and thus sufficiently efficacious, that its heirs literally used it to populate the world. My historical candidates for the credit can be no one but those earliest humans whose historicized context placed them in positions of recovering from late hominids' lingering, instinctual solitude. They somehow had to forge communal loyalties of sufficient emotional intensity to motivate reliably collective action spontaneously, even—or particularly—under the kind of duress that might otherwise have provoked panicked reversions to "each hominid for himself . . . or herself." Knowing, as we do now, how difficult it is to change what we think of as basic "personality traits," we can imagine the mental trauma—or shock therapy—necessary to effect so fundamental a transition as the inauguration of history itself. In emergencies, abominations concentrate the mind.

Drawing on these arguably universal qualities of the human mind,[17] the historian can imagine a kind of twelve-step program of humanization. Someone had to induce—more than impose, since coercion could not have been viable as a continuing strategy to control individuals then only just learning to rely consciously on one another—collaboration as an efficacious premise for historical action. To create such conditioned trust in others it was necessary to move relatively amoral creatures operating primarily with only hominid predation—and with associations with one another beyond family groups limited to instinctual, self-interested, incidental, and instrumental moments (as all other animals have continued to behave)—toward not only functional but also sentimental, future-oriented mutual dependency. The basic premise is the historical one: community itself was not obvious to people who had never experienced it, or easy for them to invent. A considered historical logic like this contrasts with the mechanistic teleology of characterizing very ancient moves of this sort as inevitable, as abstractly somehow necessary, as some sort of advance, or as inherently obvious progress. Human collaboration is usually acknowledged as an abstract contrast with preceding hominid independence, described as a transition or transformation from one abstract state to another. But for historians, this contrastive logic merely defines the difference; it does not explain how it happened, that is, shifting from abstractions to human historical actors, who did it, why, and how.[18]

The doubtlessly numerous incidents that opportunistic leaders seized on to induce enduring, functional groups included the strategy of amplifying contrasts between people within momentary assemblages of people, counted as insiders, with others whom they scorned as outsiders. Since these elemental contrasts would not then have been presumed, it is plausible to imagine that they appropriated moments of threat, experienced incidentally (or calculatingly interpreted) as shared. By dramatizing, memorializing fear, they instilled what they could of emotional,[19] routinized, hence stabilized commitments to one another among individuals in what had been incipient, unstable, open, and still-ephemeral aggregates. And they could have done so, at least in part, by alienating individual enemy combatants seized in violent encounters with others as inherently dangerous to all within. Since ritual is a powerful collectivizing tactic, they then assembled everyone available as direct participants in, or as witnesses to, collective torture of the captive. The more gruesome the immolation, the more effective the process of forging internalized collective identities, extending even to no less intensely ritualized consumption of the physical remains.[20] Such bloody, intimate violence concentrated the [collective] mind. Ritualized immolation of others would have constituted the first appropriation of alienated outsiders for internal purposes, or for purposes of internalizing the essential mutuality of human history. In this sense, slaving contributed to the beginnings of history itself.

The most direct evidence of strategies of appropriating outsiders for *collective*, or *collectivizing*, purposes comes from scattered recent ethnographic reports of small foraging modern communities living in low population densities approximating conditions of long ago—the Brazilian Amazon and the Maori in New Zealand, and in the background of what we know about other Native American practices, not least in pre-Columbian Mesoamerica, where Mayan and Aztec warlords seem to have elaborated ancestral techniques to consolidate an agonistic sort of personal authority over large concentrated populations, otherwise strangers.[21] The conventional sense of slavery as an institution hardly accommodates sanguinary ritualized destruction of captured enemies, since they are not held as property and produce nothing of commercial value, but such appropriations of human resources external to given historical contexts, in this case the formative community, for internal purposes readily fits my historical definition of slaving as strategy. The historical effects, the changes it facilitates, are political. The historian also notes that the dialectical qualities of history's epistemology also flow from the intensity of human relatedness; every human action generates an equal, and likely opposing, reaction. Only an ethos of community holds these in bounds.

From the beginning, then, one may define "slaving" as a strategy and practice of agents defined other than as masters, thus acting within specifiable contexts, of claiming absolute power over outsiders to pursue specific purposes internally. At that earliest stage of fully human collaboration, of course, these strategies were as emotional as they were rational, since they were more collective than individual; individuals may think, cognitively, but crowds, as such, react without reflecting. At that initial stage—or subsequently in moments intensely felt to be critically threatening—slaving was imminent and cathartic rather than coolly deliberated in terms of the longer-term consequences evident now to the historian. Historical motivations—but not causation—need always to be considered in terms of varying combinations of these and other, multiple levels of impetus to act. The real-time chaos of actual human lives, the multiplicity and contingency of historical contexts, our lack of direct information about them (because the actors were themselves not articulately aware), make these nonrational impulses central for historians because they are powerfully generative of meanings, motivators of action, and hence change. Speaking historically, rationality slips easily into rationalization, which generates ideologies, and those primarily retrospectively, and so calculatedly obscuring significant aspects of the moments of their creation. A rational focus on cognitively accessible, and thereby only short-range, objectives necessarily makes the eventual significant consequences unintended by the initiators of historical action. The apparent rationality of history lies primarily in the cognitive coherence that historians attempt to impose on the past, more than in the past human behavior that they chart.

Coherence is much easier to model sociologically than motivations are to infer historically.

Contradictions of Collectivity and Slaving

On the supramillennial timescale of these beginnings, the epistemological point is that a hypothesis of this sort offers a historical dynamic for how slaving originated with humanity itself, or how humanity employed slaving to develop its distinguishing ethos of sociability. The strategy of using outsiders contributed to effecting the major cumulative change[22] of the remote era at the dawn of history. These collective strategies of immolatory slaving would have prevailed for at least ten thousand years, as successful communities defined themselves to reliable degrees of coherence and continuity by building other strategies of maintaining collaboration in less anguished moments, primarily as ranked interlocking obligations, or debt. Successful strategies of creation are not the strategies of continuation. In the instance at hand, distinguishing languages and cultural displays defined communities' ongoing terms of engagements with others as conceptual contrasts, largely complementing one another. Groups defined themselves around the shared environmental niches in which they lived and exchanged specialized products from their distinctive resources with neighbors. Within these environmentally anchored communities, reproducing lineages exchanged daughters or nieces as wives. Beyond this intensifying range of familiarity, more remote others gradually became human reservoirs of enslaveable outsiders.

But, historically speaking, success always breeds its own discontents. The next significant appropriation of these outsiders for the purposes of insiders emerged dialectically and thus again historically enough as a response to the very successes of consolidating the ethos of community. Its ideology of selfless sharing subordinated the individual self to the interests of the group. By the collective standards of the communal ethos, success lay in larger numbers, achieved both by bearing and claiming heirs through time and also by attracting and assimilating others into groups large and coherent enough to pass their distinguishing cultural heritages down through the generations.[23]

The creators of the early ethical (and eventually also ethnic) communities thereby extended truly ancient sentiments of parental and family attachment to political groupings manipulable historically, that is, in response to changing circumstances. They converted a primordial universal constant of human sentiment into a contingent historical strategy of forming political collectivities. Historical change, as slaving strategies repeatedly confirm, often results from incremental extensions of existing habitual behavior. Humans are inherently conservative, seeking to preserve what in the recent past has seemed valuable or efficacious or even comfortable. But attempting to extend existing circumstances against an ebbing tide of time requires effort—in this case population pressures resulting from the efficacy of sustained collaboration. Intensification is necessary because the circumstances that once favored routine are already eroding. Intensification of focus on immediate needs forces concessions in other, less critical aspects of life, producing radically unintended consequences in the longer term of history, where change is a long-term process composed of the outcomes of short-term struggles to preserve positions against the encroachments of others with access to outside resources, prominently including slaves.

Eventually, something like ten thousand years or so ago, consolidation of effective, thoroughly socialized (and hence humanized) communities confronted the winners of the first round of human history with the next macrohistorical challenge: coordinating the contributions of the larger numbers of people thus assembled. These larger collectivities, increasingly organized by a manageably few elders or represented to others by chiefs, had to devise ways to call for the personal sacrifices of the many, at least nominally on behalf of the whole.[24] Not everyone in larger, more structured groups—by definition—experienced the fullness of the personal attachments and commitments that characterize these small face-to-face communities or possessed the patience or the vision to take much satisfaction in persisting in giving without getting much, or very immediately, in return. Ideology of reciprocity aside, that is to say, the earlier hominid isolation that I've implicitly characterized as the challenge that the first humans had to overcome thrived on in the new historical context of strong group loyalties as individualism. Africans, among others, understand this additive, or accumulative, quality of history and celebrate it; ongoing presents are strained extensions of the past. In contrast, modern linear notions of time force us to pretend that we can build the edifice of the future without a solid foundation in what we have been.

Since, in a historical epistemology, it is lived contexts that generate meanings, the ideological (or cultural) emphasis on the community had changed individuation from the hominid norm to a human anomaly, if not an abomination. Slaves in the communal ethos, for example, are defined by their exclusion from recognized standing in communities defined by relationality, whether as family or extended kin or clan or any of an infinite variety of other associational collectivities that people around the world created ad hoc, from many historical exigencies of many moments. The extreme vulnerability of the enslaved ensues upon abandonment or betrayal by, or capture from, their own communities of birth, where they otherwise belong ineradicably. Comparable individuation sensed within the community on the parts of their own members was condemned as witchcraft and extirpated in ritual performances of unified rejection reminiscent of the physical immolation to which captured enemies had been subjected long before.

In the communal ethos individualism was correspondingly muted or converted to making personally distinguishing contributions to the group. Individuals exercising degrees of personal authority within such groups merely channeled specific, often ad hoc aspects of an abstract, collective domain of potential power, whether imagined as ancestors, nature spirits, or deceased predecessors, all ultimately accessed through the authority of the group. The personal presence of influential individuals was closer to modern notions of earned respect than to our vested, single-vectored notion of power. Chiefs, in a historically precise sense, did not exercise an exclusive personal power within the group but represented it as a whole to outsiders; their authority was oriented externally on behalf of the collective, not exercised individually and internally. Within this collective context individuals who claimed personal power overtly—and few managed to do so until relatively recently[25]—did so in significant part through fears of them as witches, since the only way they could have stood apart in the ways they seemed to do must have been through secret access to powers external to the group and invisible to and inaccessible by others within it. Operating surreptitiously, they were dangerously uncontrollable.

Nonetheless, within larger, complex groups hierarchy and personal rivalries inevitably emerged. Struggles for centrality to groups created to promote human reproduction often revolved around competition for women as means of reproducing children as heirs—that is, to propagate the future of the collectivity by creating potential successors outnumbering the descendants of rivals and prepared to enshrine their fathers and grandfathers[26] in the ancestral sphere of spiritualized collective authority. Particularly after the development of agricultural strategies capable of sustaining large settled communities (and continuing into the recent past in times and places where growing populations had not put demographic pressure on available land), internal ideologies of legitimacy accorded respect to those who acquired enough experience and who had waited for genealogical seniority to envelop them in descendants and other human relationships of obligation within the group.

Consolidation of control by seniority and siring of children by these elderly few disadvantaged no less ambitious and much more impatient junior males, or at least delayed their progress toward marrying the women who would become mothers of children recognized as members of the group, propelling them along the internal road to eventual prominence. Since greater population densities had made land scarce and valuable, marginalization developed along the dimension of residence and rights to using it; precedence generally went to first occupants, and later arrivals were tolerated only in formally subordinated ways. Younger men, guests present only on contingent terms, and other marginal residents were thus dependent for access to the primary valued local resources and had nowhere to look for the dependents who spelled success (respect, honor) other than outside the group. Outsiders, people from other communities or from the communities of others conceptually vulnerable to capture and reincorporation as slaves became reservoirs of personnel, mostly female, where marginal men could obtain dependents and bring them into the community, under their personal control, by means other than the reproductive ones validated culturally, guarded collectively, and hence beyond their reach.

That is to say, once large communities or other more categorically differentiated local groupings intensified internal competition for personnel, the acquiring of isolated, vulnerable outsiders became the strategy by which the internally marginalized in communities nominally structured by local descent pursued ambitions as individuals against the restrictions of the community. Slaving of this individuated sort, which challenged the communal ethos rather than maintaining it, would have prevailed in more populous areas of the world from the consolidation of (female) labor-intensive hoe cultivation—and all the social complexity entailed in managing its dependencies—into the twentieth century. Elements of its practice survive in more than a few communities even today. As a result, rich ethnographic evidence illuminates the dynamics of slaving in contexts of hoe cultivation throughout the world.[27] In them, male outsiders are appropriated opportunistically, usually as captives taken in wars, and appreciated at least as much for their sheer subordinated presence, often in humiliating assignments to women's work, as for any material thing they might produce. Or they may be employed in utterly excessive and superfluous displays to manifest or perform the prestige of patrons who can afford to indulge in such competition and whose prominence depends on such displays. The value even of male slaves rests not only on the personal obeisance they display, on their conspicuous availability for the most whimsical of demands rather than routine services necessary to the group, but also on the reserves of distinctive knowledge and skills from elsewhere that they might add to a local community's ability to tap its resident talent to deal with unpredictable historical contingencies.[28]

However, everywhere in the world before the sixteenth-century in the Americas, women and children were the great majorities of those enslaved.[29] They joined in performing the literally vital responsibilities of reproducing and maintaining the community assigned to females, most of them accorded internal status as wives, or, in the relational context of the communal ethos, eventually as mothers of the children they bore for it. The respectable wives controlled by the older men were protected by accessible and attentive kin of their own in neighboring communities, through guarantees affirmed in formal marriages that were more treaties between the groups of kin of the married pair than the isolating coupling of individuals established by marriages in the modern West. But isolated females acquired by slaving lacked the protections of these ongoing local relationships. They were accordingly vulnerable to arbitrary disposition or to abuse by the men who had claimed them. Their captors might marry them and claim for themselves the children they might bear, or they might distribute enslaved females as wives to others within the community, thereby making clients of the favored husbands or currying the favor of influential senior men.[30] Both of these strategies allowed younger or marginalized individuals to simulate descendants and dependencies otherwise reserved to insiders and elders. The spuriousness of using dependent outsiders to simulate legitimate methods of attaining rank limited the attractions of this strategy mostly to men of lesser standing—that is, the marginality of slavers generally as they turned up in historical contexts of reproducing communities.

Yet such individuated ambition, as with all initiatives considered in historical contexts, provoked dialectical responses. Slaving to advance individually by assembling outsiders undermined communal solidarity and so challenged elders, the guardians of the communal ethos.[31] Hence communities tended to regain control of outsiders acquired by slaving by absorbing them into their own collectively recognized universes of multiple dependencies, including juniority, clientage, and marriage.[32] The recognized internal status of wife (but not the protection of kin recognized by legitimate marriages) accorded women acquired by slaving left them less directly and personally manipulable than their captors or purchasers might have intended. Communities, in effect, translated the female outsiders introduced as an external resource dangerously empowering to marginal individuals within the group into a collective asset by according them the internal status of wife. Women acquired through slaving gained additional standing, in the form of more and different relationships, when they achieved motherhood. The anthropological literature and most quasi-historical treatments based on it characterize this strategy from the sociological perspective of the abstract structure of the group, into which the female newcomer appears to be assimilated. The familiar ethnographic examples are the natives of North America, who made captive women wives[33] or adopted men they captured as sons,[34] but the parallel with African strategies has been obscured by structural analyses focused instead on assimilation to the group.[35] The historical strategy of integrating women acquired through slaving is a political process of domesticating human resources from outside the group to defuse challenges to its internal rankings, to defeat marginal members' attempts to advance personally in terms of the very ethos they had used slaving to evade.

Without elaborating further specifics, I make the epistemological point here to suggest how history explains slaving not by mechanistic association of isolated variables (as behavioral social-science comparisons of cases would attempt to correlate them) but rather in positioning particular slavers as motivated and enabled in changing specific, complex, multifaceted, and contradictory contexts—in this case, small reproducing communities defined by nominal kinship. The slavers tend to be motivated by and to strategize from positions of marginality; young warriors sent out to roam among strangers are removed from the disabilities of juniority in the presence of elders but gain access to the opportunity to kidnap young women from far enough away to bring them back to their home communities in positions of personal dependence and social isolation.

Putting the historical dynamic of slaving in these strategic terms, it is almost a truism to observe that the vulnerabilities of the enslaved, and therefore their utility to their captors, derived from the structural quality that Patterson, Moses Finley,[36] and many other students of slavery have stressed as definitional: the slaves' *origins* outside the social contexts into which they ended up being introduced, confined, claimed, and deployed against their claimants' rivals, often also their sometime sponsors. As the products of the politics of slaving contextualized in the complex ethos of community, rather than simply subjected to the theoretical domination of a master, outsiders were new resources adding to the strength of challengers otherwise too weak to compete locally for the resources available within the relevant historical context—in the contexts elaborated here, that of communities structured by descent. Slavers, by seizing or buying outsiders and incorporating them as slaves, evaded the zero-sum, self-defeating calculus of attempting to mount challenges from within.[37]

The Problematic Politics of Slaving in the Era of Agrarian Empires

If one gulps down millennia at a time, the historical dynamics of slaving become more apparent.[38] Particular, usually marginal, interests slaved to effect changes in the historical communities in which they lived, sometimes momentously, since the outsiders were new resources. I am phrasing these dialectical processes carefully to avoid any implication of attributing causation to slaving, much less to the abstraction of slavery. Causation is alien to history's distinctive epistemology.[39] The recurrent efficacy of slaving for particular, usually marginal interests implies no deterministic contribution to the much broader processes leading to greater social complexity, involving many strategies and resources, all with their own corollary complications and contradictions, many of them—technological, ideological—internal to communities and consequently not introducing human resources from outside, as slaving critically did.

Slaving focused on introducing specifically human resources, directly and privately controlled, to the exclusion of collective interests, however the controlling collectivity was formulated—from face-to-face communities of the sort that it had helped to create at the dawn of history to the integration of such communities under military warlords across temperate Asia five thousand years ago, and on to the public interests of modern civic nations. In this way slaving, again, contributed to creating the ancient age of military empires two thousand years or so before the current era among large agrarian populations along the Asian latitude running from the Yangtze River in China west to the Mediterranean and northeastern Africa. There, alluvial floodplains improved with irrigation channels, ox-plough agriculture, and wheeled transportation to move the vast quantities of grain produced with these technologies also became the focus of investments of local labor. The resulting agricultural production was sufficient to support the significant militarization that defined the empires of the era, specially trained professional troops and heavy weaponry that replaced ad hoc militias fighting only occasionally, on the strength of personal valor, and for the communities in which they lived. Militarization, as a strategy, mobilized communities on a permanent basis to fight for others' interests. Elaborate hierarchies of priests performed the rituals of state cults to deify and legitimate the power of rulers who were, in origin at least, warlords. Approached from the point of view of the underlying agrarian communities, these seemingly familiar ancient empires were externalities, superimposed on the underlying productive population and engaged dialectically with them over control of the local resources and the products of their own efforts.[40]

Like the integration of community itself through slaving tens of thousands of years earlier, at least in (crucial?) part, someone had to build these ancient military and, eventually, literate civilizations out of contexts of earlier, smaller, but resilient local communities. Warlords had to impose military control over, rather than induce loyalty within, these existing communities of agrarian peasants, living in peasant-adapted versions of the intensely collective ethos at the base of all human history. Local communities recognized no ongoing need for external, and especially not extremely expensive, military overrule, any more than early humans had anticipated the eventual potential and personal constraints of what had become the communal ethos. Families, villages, and districts commanded everyone's primary day-to-day attention; authority in these communities was multiple, in the sense that people recognized different scales of responsibility in the differing scales of their lives as they participated experientially in these collectivities. The relatively autonomous power of remote, singular military authorities (notionally figures we might term rulers, but only by not quibbling over historical technicalities of *how* they managed to rule) to exploit ruthlessly rested on their ability to set themselves outside— and ranked as above—the reciprocities of local communities. The resulting tendency of the successors to the conquering generals who had created such warrior regimes to deify themselves, thus transforming their political weakness into an ideological strength, achieved a kind of institutionalized extension of individuation, or precisely what the communal ethos condemned as preda-tory greed itself.

That is to say, from the perspective of the communal ethos, rulers of this imperial (not to say imperious) sort were the epitomes of outsider, though in positions of irresponsible strength rather than the vulnerability of the enslaved, the other outsiders on the scene. Successors to the military conquerors who characteristically established dynasties, but were in practice rarely able to live up to the exalted standards set by or attributed to the founders, exaggerated all the more in memorializing them, went on to celebrate themselves through monumental construction or military plundering abroad. They limited their demands on local peasants to levels that they could provide, on an occasional basis, without destroying the local residents' ongoing devotion to agriculture that sustained their regimes. They therefore accumulated material wealth on the grandiose scales that we, modern individualists and materialists that we are, now admire as civilization. These military rulers had few local allies on whom they could depend or on whose ethic of loyalty they could count. They also slaved, to surround themselves personally with other outsiders, similarly unencumbered by competing obligations to any in the local communities that they thus sought to transcend. Such militarized political power rested inherently on slaving.[41]

The strategy of political integration by military plundering and slaving that characterizes imperial rule is very expensive and ultimately self-defeating. The elaborated infrastructure, ideological and monumental as well as military, built by slaving strains the ability of local populations to support them, and increasingly so over time. Otherwise, military rulers would not have to use the force at their command locally to extract taxes and other revenues. Mili-tary successes intensified the zero-sum competition for local resources. Until nineteenth-century fossil fuel technologies enabled economic growth through radically increased local productivity,[42] the human resources drawn off to fight on remote battlefields or assault distant cities drained agricultural economic sectors at home. Militarized regimes therefore tended to cover their growing local deficits by plundering, though also at very high costs, more and more remote regions for the wealth they need, including captives to supplement strained local supplies of labor.[43]

In ancient Mesopotamia in particular, local military elites came to tap distant populations susceptible to capture, removal, and reintegration as dominated newcomers, and rulers accordingly filled their palaces with attendants acquired through slaving. Slaves also supported the priests of the ideological cults that deified rulers. Enslaved retainers became critically differentiating supports for temples and large royal and aristocratic households filled with domestics, eunuchs, soldiers, concubines, children, and highly trained, widely experienced, powerful personal agents, emissaries, and enforcers. In the long-term historical process of imperial conquests and consolidation, military rulers slaved on imperial scales to support themselves independently of the ethos of communal reciprocities in which individuals had previously (or elsewhere) recruited women through slaving to support personal challenges to the ethos. They had no need to conceal enslaved women as wives or to adopt children but rather flaunted them to display the dominance they asserted, dominance not only of the enslaved but also of the local communities whom they claimed to protect as subjects. Slaving became a significant strategy by which military elites consolidated the infrastructural and then the ideological strength they claimed.[44] Early Egypt, whose roots were deeper in time than those of Mesopotamia, peripheral to the commercialized crossroads of southwestern Asia, and less militarized in its basic political economy before the rather late definition of the pharaoh,[45] may have relied on slaves correspondingly less.

To the extent these rulers turned to slaving to maintain institutionalized military power and to implement a cover of divine legitimacy, they correspondingly structured the populations of outsiders they enslaved ideologically as eligible for, or rather innately suited to, such predation. In the communal ethos, demonization of enemies, both strangers and internal deviants, had taken forms reported in ethnographic descriptions of them as witchcraft. But as larger military consolidation and commercial networks became dependent on slaving in the Aegean Peninsula, the Greeks wrapped a pan-peninsular identity around their congeries of highly diverse, local polities and ethnologically reduced those they excluded to "enslaveable barbarians," although they continued to acknowledge, if only ironically, the ethnically random quality of earlier opportunistic slaving there. This historical dynamic suggests that the dehumanizing qualities attributed to the enslaved intensify with the systematic dependence of the slavers on capturing them; racialization, the modern formulation of this recurrent tendency, is not a peculiarity of Western culture but rather the most recent in a long sequence of other discourses of difference, each reflecting its own times.[46]

Slaving accordingly staffed large aristocratic households in the cities of the Old World, and later also in more of the New World than acknowledged by the econocentric plantation paradigm of American slavery. The sensitive aspect of this domestic slaving was not labor in some abstract sense, although many of the enslaved were surely worked hard to maintain the households in which they found themselves. Neither were they held exclusively for products they might contribute, though some were trained in artisan skills that could be deployed to engage the domestic household with the commercial sectors of the economy. Significantly, their values also lay in the incremental political advantages that their sheer presence brought to householders engaged in otherwise delicately balanced composites of competing and interlocking personal and family networks.[47] A marginal advantage that one such household, enlarged with slaves, gained in the highly competitive politics of singular imperial rule, without incurring reciprocal obligations to others through marriages or other legal arrangements, could compound to a significant superiority. Slaving in such composite, personalistic polities—as nearly all such entities were throughout the world before the consolidation of monarchies and their modern derivatives, nation-states—was significantly political.

The political dynamics of the military regimes of ancient Eurasia, usually known as empires, hinged on systematic slaving to assemble captives from outside the historical spheres of internal, zero-sum competition and to employ them in whatever capacities within that enabled the slavers to gain on more established local rivals. Before the modern era, when direct control of human effort counted for more than military or other technology or money, successful slavers could move from their original positions of marginality to pose direct challenges and even achieve dominance within. Absent modern technologies, for five millennia of the world's history these political dynamics were exquisitely sensitive to slaving, tending in the long run to favor merchant interests, who at first prospered from supplying armies in the field and handling the logistics of disposing of the captives they took. Depending on how many slaves the marginal merchants managed to acquire—and these numbers were fundamentally contingent on the historical outcomes of competition in particular times and places and in theory entirely indeterminate—their resort to slaving could fail, leaving the old guard safely embedded, if they, in effect, bought out the slavers by acquiring the captives as dependents for their own households or as workers for estates and temples or as soldiers for their armies. On the other hand, if circumstances brought more captives into the hands of the merchant slavers than their established rivals could relieve them of, the captured outsiders accumulated in the hands of the upstarts, empowering them. In the former case, the human resources of the society or polity or economy increased by means of slaving but resulted in no cumulative historical change. In the latter, it was the merchant-slavers who ended up eroding the control of their former aristocratic sponsors. The slaves' contributions served the purposes of the most innovative actors and sometimes thinkers of their times.[48]

Monarchs and the Problem of Merchants

In broad terms, during the millennia characterized by horse-based military control of the populations resident in the fertile river valleys of Afro-Eurasia (that is, ca. 3000 BCE–1000 CE), the unprecedented power of military and associated priestly establishments allowed them to extend violent conquests to the limits of their logistical capacities,[49] thereby straining infrastructures of transportation and communication built to consolidate power of a personalistic sort, locally. Conquest is always cheaper than consolidation of control. Empires are therefore historical processes rather than sociological structures. To fill the logistical gap opened by imperial success, merchants extended their local operations to become camp-followers in the field. They organized to transcend the growing distances involved and to overcome the anonymity of transactions with otherwise unaccountable strangers by developing commercial methods involving currencies and credit as well as systems of writing antecedent to literacy. But their credit-based commercial investments had greater inherent expansive potential than military plunder as well as greater sustainability, since their inventories and legal obligations (that is, their debts) endured through time and even increased in value in ways that armies and subjects did not. As a result, military rulers found themselves struggling to control the merchants whom their conquering exemplars had earlier enabled as commercial slavers. The classical empires of world history—from ancient Mesopotamia through China, northern India, Greece, Rome, and the military regimes of the Islamic world before the sixteenth century—cycled repeatedly through this historical dialectic of military expansion succeeded by commercial integration and an uneasy mutual interdependence and rivalry.

The slaving on which military conquerors depended created political problems for their successors as rulers. It enabled merchants and other ambitious challengers to acquire outsiders and to sequester them in personal retinues removed from the rulers' growing demands on local populations for taxes, corvée, and other services. By the middle of the last millennium before the current era, merchants in the commercialized areas of southwestern Asia adjacent to the Mediterranean Sea had accumulated assets in quantities that enabled them to create dependence among local farmers through indebtedness, enforced by the power of militarized regimes. To set these commercial strategies within the processes of the military successes of the preceding millennium, Sumer, the Assyrians, and later imitators, initially marginal merchants—always suspect and mundane hangers-on around the established "virtuous" claimants to deity, sanctity, and valor—had thrived on the plundering and captive taking of their military sponsors, not least through slaving. But they had thrived on and beyond the margins of the prevailing land-based military empires of the era, and they were more collaborative than competitive because they exploited contacts in remote locations and did not need the services of the resident population of farmers or access to the lands they cultivated. Being excluded from investing in production, merchants concentrated their wealth in cash, consumable commodities, infrastructure, and urban households, both the real estate itself and the people they assembled, including slaves, within the featureless exterior walls of these compounds.

Building incrementally on this wealth, they then used their cash liquidity to intrude on domestic elites' access to local populations, extending credit to peasants to relieve pressures put on subjects otherwise desperately beholden to and belabored by rulers or state priests. Merchants loaned grain they had hoarded from good harvests to peasant families to cover short-term deficits in times of famine, whether induced by failed harvests, foreign invasion, or imperial taxation. This balanced arrangement—in which merchants, enriched by their logistical roles in overextended conquests, invested their wealth in the local populations stressed by the same logistical challenges—prevailed in many other parts of Asia for two millennia, from *about* 500 BCE until about 1500 CE. Throughout much of agrarian non-Muslim Asia, particularly the Indian subcontinent, military rulers seem to have reached such accommodations with local landlords and with resident merchants. These balanced arrangements allowed merchants a significant but not overwhelming interest in agricultural production, and so they invested further in the form of cottage artisan production. Although these arrangements have often been classed with slavery as an institutionalized form of unfree labor, as historical strategies they are virtually opposing. As a historical strategy, debt bondage is one component of multiple, shared interests in distinct aspects of the lives and labors of resident agrarian communities, not the exclusionary control over the entirety of an isolated outsider that distinguishes slaving.[50]

But in the eastern Mediterranean in the last millennium before the current era, a dialectical and thus quintessentially historical elaboration of monarchy as a distinctive strategy of political authority countered the successes of mercantile slaving under the military/imperial umbrellas of the preceding millennium in southwestern Asia. My characterization of political systems as contextualized historical strategies gives a more differentiated, precise, and processual sense to the term "monarchy" than the general literature in political sociology, which focuses on power in an abstracted sense and as a result conflates widely varying strategies of exercising it. The distinction between abstracted power and contextualized strategies of creating and maintaining it parallels the contrast between slavery (as an abstract institution) and slaving that runs through this consideration of the problem of slavery as *history*.

In this historicized sense, the term "monarchy" refers to a singular, direct, and personalistic ideology of power, strongly correlated, if not exclusively associated, with monotheistic theologies. Monarchy consolidated the personalism of the patron–client politics of imperial composites to a single, universally shared, albeit remote and idealized patron. It contrasts with the ideological and practical remoteness of military regimes oriented toward the gods and plundering foreign lands. It thus turned external authority in the personage of the chief in a communal environment, representing the group as a whole to outsiders, to a benevolent patron of the individuals within a polity thus rendered unitary. The paradigmatic example is found in the strictly monotheistic Hebrew monarchy in Jerusalem in the last millennium before the current era. The historical question is how the context of mercantile slaving at that time and in that region challenged, and in the end contributed to, the consolidation of monarchy's distinctively singular political ethic.

The compromise between merchant creditors and their landed, military, and religious competitors was a fragile one. Merchants claimed the agricultural product of indebted peasant farmers and elaborated complex strategies of inducing default on these contractual obligations. Under such financial pressure, members of local farming families could recover only by conceding persons to their creditors. The more successful merchant creditors, operating essentially as loan sharks, grew wealthy enough to use the proprietorial provisions of emerging commercial law[51] to force the debtors they had created to sell themselves, individually or, more often, female dependents in their families to relieve their starving relatives both of potential mouths to feed and of further liability for such debt by the rules of collective responsibility.

Notions of personal private property afforded the opportunity to establish exclusive personal claims to such defaulters. They also occasioned yet another aspect of modern slaving that has become a trope of slavery seen as institutionalized. However, the historian must carefully delimit the relevance of the concept of commercialized, fungible personal property to these earlier times and other places. Traces of proprietorial interests in local debtors, as well as commercial transactions involving outsiders as slaves, appeared as early as several millennia ago in legal documents from Mesopotamia, but to construe these isolated commercial transactions or transactional moments as defining slavery at that early time would indulge the fallacy of origins in an extreme degree. It would treat an incidental aspect of the practice as defining. In fact, or rather, as contextualized historically, such state-guaranteed proprietorial rights over persons applied only to moments of definitive transfers of interest in individuals, local debtors as well as outsiders, between contracting strangers. But many other kinds of less individuating transfers of personal responsibility, allegiance, and dependency among groups predominated in moving personnel among families in the Roman sense of large households in ongoing balanced relationships with one another. Property in persons, in the modern commercial sense, was present, but it was far from pervasive, and it was significant primarily as a mercantile strategy to intrude politically on the prevalent, if also tenuous, claims of military rulers to legitimacy in communal societies by extracting debtors from them.[52] Such commercialized transactions in people could be regulated by public law, or more often by judicial enforcement of private contracts, within given political domains.[53] By the rule of historical change as incremental, the quite specialized documentation from this era represents only mercantile extensions of the range of other means of transferring people, all of them below the radar of the public laws that constitute our evidence.

We can hypothesize three outcomes of the general contest between merchants and militarists for control—via credit or coercion—without pretending that these three exhaust the possibilities of outcomes that historicized research on ancient Mediterranean slaving might reveal. The political sensitivity of successful slaving was greater when it added or removed mostly men to or from local populations. Young females whom indebted peasant families conceded in satisfaction of what they owed to urban creditors, once moved into mercantile households, did not fundamentally alter the delicate political balance between merchants and military rulers. However, during the middle centuries of the last millennium before the current era merchants in the eastern Mediterranean region seem to have indebted productive farmers to degrees that led to seizures and enslavement of enough of them that they diverted agricultural populations from the services and taxes claimed by military rulers. When merchants began to use debt to intrude on the productive, tax-paying population of males on whom rulers depended, the reaction of the home authorities, particularly in urban settings, was expectably restrictive.

Military authority loomed in the background of these mercantile intrusions on landed or other noncommercial interests from Syria to Palestine to parts of Greece. Rulers there repeatedly countered growing mercantile indebting and enslaving of peasants by asserting more direct, benevolent authority of their own. They thereby created a monarchical style of authority that, by reaching individuals personally as subjects protected by a good king, countered the similarly personal credit of the merchants. Monarchical authority thereby forgave commercial debt or limited its accumulation in the hands of merchants by intruding on the up-to-then primary loyalties of peasants to their own communities, whether seen as families or villages or tribes. To counter merchant commercial initiatives, rulers limited or forgave the farmers' debts to creditors.[54] These rulers, later and appropriately famed also as lawgivers, thus invented monarchy as a historical political strategy to push merchants to the margins of highly personalized polities, at no cost to themselves. The first half of the last millennium before the current era became an era of kings[55] in lands around the eastern Mediterranean, and direct, unmediated subjugation to monarchs, wrapped appealingly in the cloak of protectors and grantors of beneficent liberties, became the peasants' price of protection against the intrusive commercial strategies of mercantile slavers.

If one sets classical Greece against this background of Asian military empires and emergent kingdoms, the city of Athens (from whence comes a large but not necessarily representative portion of the information we have on slaving in that era) represented a triumph of mercantile interests. Athens in the fifth- and fourth centuries BCE provides the implicitly paradigmatic example of political consolidation around mercantile prosperity. In effect, military rulers had yielded political recognition and eventually participation to wealthy merchant challengers of the sort elsewhere, with greater expanses of territory and populations to plunder, kept relatively marginalized. In gaining participation in the polity, merchants converted it ideologically from a militarized externality imposed on peasant domestic communities and one excluding merchants to an inclusive (if only imagined) collaboration among the commercially affluent heads of large urban households filled with dependents, including slaves. It became the *polis* at the etymological root of what we have overgeneralized as politics of any sort.

Athens might be called a democracy of slavers. Great patrons assembled wives, clients, and outsiders of other sorts in large domestic aggregates of people. Affluence consisted largely in personal honor performed in significant part by surrounding oneself with dependent personnel in private households displayed in new public spaces. Dependents in superfluous numbers, including skilled and elaborately dressed slaves, became the currency of claims to individuated honor, deserving of respect among peers. Such participatory accords among the honorable, democratic in the Greek modeling of the strategy and republican at Rome, characteristically included the heads of the constitutive urban or urbanized households, familiar in the Greek *oeikos* and the Roman *familia*. Since these heads of household competed among themselves within the polity and also against the political collectivities in which they participated in a classic zero-sum game, the competitors could make absolute gains most easily by enhancing local cores of kin and clients with outsiders taken in as slaves. Merchants, who by then ranged widely throughout the Mediterranean, had direct access to the personnel and skills of the entire region. Concentrated back at home in Athens and in other commercial cities, they became the swarms of household slaves and other slaves employed in artisanal workshops that have puzzled historians of Greek democracy, and who caught David Brion Davis's eye for irony in terms of the progress they have been claimed to represent.[56]

With no less schematic brevity, I characterize the position of Rome in this array of the politics of slaving.[57] In that considerably more martial polity, by the time of the military conquests in the last centuries before the current era that built the empire, the contest for domestic control became a standoff between an incipient integrative corporate polity and the independent-minded, large military-aristocratic households that composed it. The earliest days of the city of Rome had a commercial character that evidently introduced most captives through trade; the resulting commercial elements of the city's laws, themselves of a public standing characteristic of the world of trade, therefore defined the slave in that limited context in proprietorial terms by their famous analogy with domestic animals, as a fungible thing (*res*). However, the historian does not reify a formulation that was in fact a legal analogy, specifying not the inherent nature of the enslaved but rather the commercial terms under which transactions in such persons might be settled. The Roman example adapted older proprietorial formulations of the transactional moments of outsiders brought in to live most of their lives as members of domestic households, well out of the public sphere of commercial law, and also beyond the range of much of the documentation of the era.

In the last century or two before the current era the wide-ranging and over-whelming armed force of Rome's military legions provided captives in massive numbers, sufficient to inflate to imperious scales the domestic retinues of the commanders of the armies. They invested the booty of their conquests also in rural lands for agricultural and livestock production for the city and staffed them in part with slaves, in a radically new application of military slaving to agricultural production.[58] The strategy of military conquests also allowed the generals at the heads of the legions to convert the urban republic to an imperial system to a great extent built through slaving. So central was slaving to the Roman imperial state that emperors assembled the great imperial administrative household, the *familia caesaris*, around slaves.[59] The values of personal valor and inherent or inherited honor excluded the merchants, whose slaving might otherwise, as it had done elsewhere, have created wealth of proportions threatening to the power of the generals.[60]

Even more schematically, but no less historical in its political dynamic, the slave-staffed Roman imperial palace combined these very old patterns of military authority, ideologically external to the underlying communal ethos of republican families, with an innovative civic inclusiveness of citizenship for the men who had left their home communities to join the legions to fight for interests they could effectively construe as their own.[61] The civic terms of citizenship substituted an aggregate public approximation for the personal communities these men abandoned. The new citizens of Rome proved to be a sometimes unruly crowd, suggesting the problems, in spite of bread and circuses, of attempting to create a sense of political community among detached individuals numbering in the hundreds of thousands.[62] The famous public immolations of slaves—gladiators and others—in the coliseums of Roman cities resurrected and expanded to colossal scales the very ancient strategies of consolidating senses of community in much smaller, more intimate contexts by immolation. Republican politics, no less than their democratic counterparts in Greece, thus made slaving a critical strategy both in gaining on one's rivals within the civic sphere without having to confront them directly and in balancing popular armies and citizenship against an abstract state. In monarchical regimes, in contrast, kings consolidated the defining singularity of their authority by limiting the ability of lesser figures in their realms, especially merchants, to build personal autonomy around retinues of outsiders over whom they could assert exclusionary authority. Monarchy and slaving, incompatible in principle, were in practice therefore always in tension.

Legal definitions of the standing of the people who entered the households of both the Roman civic state and the later Christian empire as slaves, and who eventually emerged as freedmen, have framed most of the discussion of Roman slavery. Laws are the working documentation of historians seeking slavery in Roman times. A historically contextualized treatment of these legal materials, usually discussed in the arcane and abstract domain of jurisprudence, would distinguish the dramatically changing political contexts that produced them over a time span of more than a millennium and in contexts ranging from a small republican polity to a populous city thriving on remote military conquests and maritime commercial integration, to a military composite empire, to an eventual monotheistic monarchy in Christian Constantinople. The earliest of these laws regulated the commercial terms through which merchants conducted slaving; late republican legislation attempted to manage the hordes of sometimes unruly captives dispersed throughout Italy; the bulk of the later imperial decrees, including monarchical-styled codifications, were essentially laws of manumission, not laws of slavery comparable to those constituting the modern institution. Unlike modern slave laws, which established masters' control over humans valuable as property, Roman law attempted to balance the competing claims of former masters and a more enveloping monarchical-styled regime to ex-slaves, freed in growing numbers as heads of households filled with slaves during the era of expansion later tried to consolidate diminishing domains by formally manumitting dependents to a semiautonomous standing as clients. The political question throughout revolved around the exclusivity of the slavers' claims to the enslaved, or formerly enslaved, relative to the competing claims of the sequence of overarching political domains through centuries of changes.[63] This variety of historical contexts and strategies demonstrates the futility of attempting to assimilate them all into a single, timeless Roman slavery (structured) as an implicitly static institution.

Slaving Contained: Politics in the Millennium of Monotheisms

After the late seventh century of the current era an uneasy, shifting balance between military rulers and mercantile challengers marked the greater Mediterranean region, most of it Muslim for the millennium following the disintegration of what had arguably been a political regime consolidated through centuries of military seizures of captives but that, like its predecessors, reached its logistical limits. The late eastern phase of Roman political consolidation, centered after the fourth century CE at Byzantium on the margin of southwestern Asia, recovered from the disintegrative tendencies of a military regime running out of conquests by tapping both the monarchical ideology of Christian monotheism and by enslaving the human resources of the accessible Black Sea region.

In the Muslim millennium, the politics of slaving played out in the context of a monotheistic culture, within which warlords—often ruling as sultans, secular figures without claims to religious authority derived from the Prophet (Muhammed, ca. 570–632 CE)—used slaving both to sponsor and to compete with commercial interests.[64] The overwhelming military conquests of the seventh and eighth centuries expanded Islam, the domain of peace, within which no believing Muslim could be enslaved, and put enslaveable populations of unbelievers, or "kaffirs," far beyond the range of ordinary raiding. Islamic warlords—like their predecessors in similar positions for millennia—cultivated mercantile sources to provide slaves to sustain regimes always vulnerable to challenge from Shi'ite heirs to the family of the Prophet, a formidable clerical establishment, populist Sufi *sheykhs,* and other claimants to the singular and therefore disputed legacy of Muhammad. Military rulers, powerful but merely in secular terms and thus marginal in the world of Islam, therefore surrounded themselves with eunuchs and other young males captured abroad, trained them militarily, and used them as palace guards to exercise, through them, a highly personalistic power against a strong clerical establishment always capable of rallying devout populations of peasants against excessive secular demands.

Merchants themselves were forced outward also by Islam's prohibition of lending at interest, which inhibited the opportunity of investing in local peasant debt. By the fourteenth century, the thriving commercial sectors of the vast Islamic *oecumene* reached from the Strait of Gibraltar in the west to the Philippines in the Far East. Secular Muslim rulers positioned their slave soldiers in sensitive capacities, which varied with the contexts in which they found themselves but almost never included basic agricultural labor.[65] Men of slave origin often were drawn into the highest ranks of the sultan's advisers, emissaries, and generals because their isolation from local politics and networks of patronage made them reliably loyal. The famous militarily trained *mamluk* slave palace guards of prosperous Fatimid and Ayyubid Egypt (tenth century through the thirteenth) and in military polities elsewhere in Asia and Africa were also loyal protectors of incumbent rulers against the threat of relatives ambitious to succeed them. Successors continued the practice, since as a dynastic line they needed slave palace guards to protect their military rule from the competing legal and moral authority of Islamic clerics as well as from potential challenges originating in commercial circles, not to mention brothers or other family challengers. Slaving bolstered secular power in a Muslim world otherwise submissive to the word of God.

At the same time, merchants throughout the Islamic world consolidated their positions by staffing their domestic households with slaves, mostly politically less sensitive females.[66] The recurrent historical dynamics of these processes of slaving included the contradictory consequences of initial military successes capable of producing slaves directly by conquest and capture, without mediation by merchants. When conquerors reached their logistical or geographical limits, they turned to purchasing the slaves at the hearts of their regimes from traders, in this manner enriching the very competitors who came to threaten them. The standoff between the contending merchants and militarists continued because merchants in the Islamic world operated primarily across uninhabited deserts and empty oceans beyond or between the populous agrarian zones of primary concern to territorial rulers and the clerical establishment. Slaving brought returns enough for all, so long as the slaves came from enslaveable kaffir populations in Asian hill country, islands of the southeast Asian archipelago, and sub-Saharan Africa, and merchants invested their profits in politically benign ways, that is, in domestic servants at home and commercial operations abroad.

The political risks of buying slaves from local merchants also inclined military rulers to favor foreign commercial sources as suppliers of the captives they needed. In the Muslim world, the politics of slaving thus favored the Christian and Jewish communities, tolerated legally as *dhimmi,* co-heirs to the monotheistic Abrahamic tradition and available to perform commercial services difficult to reconcile with the communitarian base of Islamic law. However, they were also excluded from acquiring politically sensitive interests in the great Muslim majority and from owning Muslim slaves, theoretically any captive acquired by a Muslim, who was required to convert her to Islam. The extrapolitical grand collectivity of Islam thus everywhere harbored non-Muslim communities, and its cities were intricate ethnoreligious composites that reconciled military rule with local commercial accumulation, particularly of women and girls as slaves.

In the twelfth and thirteenth centuries, Christian merchants from northern Italy responded to the commercial opportunities at the height of Islamic prosperity in the eastern Mediterranean, then centered accessibly in Fatimid Egypt.[67] Starting from economic positions quite marginal to Cairo and other thriving cities of the eastern and southern Muslim Mediterranean, and lacking comparable opportunities in Christian Europe, Venetians in particular recognized the opportunity in slaving for captives to sell in wealthy urban Muslim markets. In the fourteenth and fifteenth centuries, among their many other mercantile and banking strategies, they profited from selling (and eventually etymologically defining) ethnic Slavs from the Black Sea region to the Islamic world, in return for the valuable Indian Ocean spices available there. In an incrementally historical initiative, they extended their sales of Slavic captives to other cities and merchant households in the Christian Mediterranean. In a further historical, dialectical extension of this strategy, by the second half of the fifteenth century competitors from Genoa and elsewhere in the western Mediterranean supplemented these inflows of captive Slavs from the east with ventures out into the Atlantic and eventually enslaved Africans.

The succeeding sixteenth-century Atlantic extension of this deep-running sequence framed slaving in the Atlantic in an unprecedentedly unrestrained context of commercial initiative. Merchants, particularly ones foreign to the sponsoring, but in Mediterranean terms very marginal, Portuguese monarchy clinging to the fringe of the Iberian Peninsula, invested in producing sugar on previously uninhabited or depopulated islands in the eastern Atlantic.

Although repeating the deep historical pattern of merchants operating most successfully outside the populated territorial domains of Church and monarchy, Italian and German financial investors, for the first time on significant scales, extended uses of these new supplies of slaves from far western Africa from providing domestic servants for the urban wealthy to staffing agricultural production, for commercial purposes.[68] The commodity of interest was sugar. Elsewhere in Christian Europe, slaving had figured only marginally in earlier Italian cultivation of sugar cane on Mediterranean islands and shore, not least because the region was too poor to compete for captives with Muslim commercial markets, too Christian to enslave local populations, and increasingly too politically inclusive in monarchical styles that granted personal liberties to subjects of patron-kings to turn to outsiders to support royal power or to tolerate potential local opponents' seizures of people as slaves whom kings needed as subjects.[69] However, the early Atlantic was a political and legal vacuum, without competition from the continental landed and ecclesiastical interests that had inhibited mercantile elaboration of slaving in Asian and Mediterranean regions since the last millennium before the current era, It thus provided a propitious launching pad for two larger elaborations of this newly commercialized process of slaving, one in Africa, and the other—arguably no more pervasive—in the Americas.

A Note on the Enslaved

An inclusively historical approach to slaving necessarily takes into account the perceived worlds of the enslaved.[70] Conventional attempts to identify the strategies and initiatives of the enslaved center on outcomes more plausible to modern historians than to the individuals enslaved. In accenting, as these scholars do, slaves' public agency as resistance, or as sustaining communities separate from "the worlds the slaveholders made," or as devotees of iconic remnants of their African backgrounds in the European cultures of the Americas, as they do, they presume a number of modern, essentially North American perceptions, motivations, and strategies not present in the Old World or, for that matter, absent also in most of the Americas, most of the time. Resistance does not stand out in the narrative developed in this chapter, or in Africa and in the Americas.

The enslaved in the Old World were few in number compared to these in the modern Americas or in increasing portions of eighteenth- and nineteenth-century Africa. Unlike stereotypical gangs of men cutting cane in Jamaica, they were mostly women and children, who lived dispersed in domestic households, not interacting significantly with others who had also arrived through slaving. Their stories as active historical agents accordingly center on their attempts to make places for themselves within villages, communities of kin, and large urban households or in whatever face-to-face communities they might find themselves. Creating and struggling to maintain places for themselves, to belong somewhere, on terms more committed than the most contingent, were their logical responses to the disabling initial isolation of enslavement.

The uprootedness or deracination usually emphasized as a proxy for this experience refers to an absence. It is essentially a negative concept derived from the abstract perspective of the modern historian, in relation to what the enslaved had lost, not to what they experienced as slaves. The experience that overwhelmed the enslaved instead was profound existential isolation.[71] It is the slave's experience of being utterly and helplessly alone that historians must emphasize to historicize enslavement for the enslaved in the experiential contexts that motivated their actions. Though absolute lack of autonomous social connections left the enslaved vulnerable to whatever mistreatments they suffered, these were not defining; rather, what motivated them was avoiding the consequences of the underlying isolation. More important as a motivation for people who had been uprooted was their resulting vulnerability to and fear of further arbitrary transfers and hence to having to find yet other new places for themselves, starting over again, and yet again, living with the never-ending contingency of whatever relationships they might try to form, in the psychological and metaphysical senses of relationality. Even voluntary resettlement, as mobile individuals in modern times know all too well, is not easy even when it facilitates personal opportunity. How much harder were involuntary separation and relocation under the terrifying uncertainties of enslavement?

In Old World processes of slaving, the slaves' strategies of belonging or being retained were generally private affairs that the mostly women enslaved pursued within domestic entities, villages, and households. The historically interesting variability among their options arose from the differing cultural contexts in which they conducted such maneuverings and the intense rivalries they evoked, in doing so, from insiders to the communities in which they lived, what one might call the "legitimist interests."[72] The slaves in Greek and Roman theater are not political protestors but vibrant violators and exploiters of the intimacies of family life. The civically inclusive Roman imperial state was not a major exception, since asserting a public presence was a primary issue less for the enslaved than for the state itself. Slave revolts, the conventional but ahistorical emphasis that comes out of focusing narrowly on the master–slave dyad, lacked ideologies of freedom in a civic sense of state-guaranteed individual rights; even in the New World before the nineteenth century, rebel slaves had no recourse that might incline them to question slavery itself.

The Politics of Historicized Slaving

In sketching here these general dynamics of four or five millennia of slaving as historical strategies, I am not attempting to diminish the many insights of the skilled historians who see slavery as an institution of personal domination and economic or sexual exploitation. Masters dominated and abused the people they enslaved; some of them profited at their slaves' expense; and adult males raped young girls. But the same men also aggrandized themselves, gained from, and abused others around them, others who were not enslaved. For many, if not most, of the enslaved, their extreme vulnerability to maltreatment upon arrival resolved into vital, if usually humble and still vulnerable, positions in households and in workshops, in guarding insecure and therefore belligerent sultans in their palaces, and much more rarely on the small family homesteads and villages at the base of agricultural production. The captive men rowing galleys in commercial ports or diving for pearls or engaging in mining or sacrificed in gruesome public spectacles or disposed to other lethal tasks suffered all the horrors associated with slavery: extreme deprivation, whipped domination, and morbid social invisibility. But they died physically, slaughtered in imperial and commercial immolatory equivalents, including mining and diving as sacrifices to extreme wealth, of the rituals that had sustained the coherence of the earliest human communities.

However, these tormented men were the publicly visible exceptions to strategies of slaving that centered on females and children, "displaced, disoriented, dispersed, and domiciled" within the urban households of the wealthy and powerful. Not even the boys and men in these households were exposed to a public, institutionalized slavery of the modern kind. The Roman jurisprudence known (again, as so often, by modern analogy) as laws of slavery in fact consisted of laws of manumission, expressing the struggles of a waning imperial state to establish its own claims to taxes and conscription over former slaves that lords and patrons of powerful households had manumitted (into public space) to earn money for the support of their households. This contest illustrates that what distinguished the enslaved from other dependents was their political potential, the exclusivity of the control that their captors or buyers could claim over them, as outsiders, in the otherwise balanced composite politics of the communal ethos, of military imperial regimes, and merchant republics. Slaving thrived where politics were personalistic and plural, as in all of the historical contexts just named. Only when political authority became singular did monarchs and monotheism tend to exclude slaving from realms seen as unitary; in the pervasive political domain they claimed, slaving was a strategy that would enable the slavers to stand apart, leading back to political pluralism or to composite politics.

This politicized and therefore more historical approach to slaving embeds the abstracted master–slave dyad on which the modern historiography of slavery turns in the competitive contexts that both motivated and enabled a succession of interests marginal to prevailing practices—at first incipiently social late hominids, then ambitious individuals in strongly collective local agricultural communities, then military and associated priestly rulers external to the underlying agrarian populations on whom they depended, and eventually commercial and financial interests long kept marginal to military and ecclesiastical authorities at home. All attempted to gain personally by importing human resources from outside the contexts of internal politics where they competed at a disadvantage.

The strategies of slaving I have cited should be understood as defining these varying historical contexts only in the limited historical sense of becoming the politically efficacious, hence motivating of responses, uses of slaves amidst the great variety of strategies followed in every historical context. I am not attempting to characterize any of these broad periods as abstractly homogeneous in terms of the strategies of slaving I use to define each; slavers with many different interests, in many competing ways, and in all times and places appropriated isolated outsiders for purposes of their own, at the intended expense of the others around them. Similarly, the more established interests within these historical contexts had similarly diverse ways of engaging local communities, on varying terms of dependency.[73] Such a comprehensive approach describes how things were; my historical selectivity is meant to account for how they became, who changed the rules of the game, and how, by slaving. I defend the *historical* validity of the characterizations of the epochs I have offered here as distinguished by significant strategic innovations. In focusing on history, I am analytically interested in the innovatory strategies efficacious in the contexts from which they emerged. The strategies I emphasize therefore constitute incremental extensions of received practice, of unanticipated efficacies derived from momentary conjunctures of circumstances.

And all began in positions of marginality of as many sorts as there were coherent historical contexts (from the perspectives of those present, not of the teleological retrospective of the historian), stepped outside the local spheres in which they were playing losing hands to introduce outsiders through slaving. Under the elders, ancestors, and chiefs of the cultivating and reproducing communities of the world, younger men advanced their own positions within the communal ethos by bringing in women through slaving but wrapped their personal gains into complementing advantages for other members of their groups. Third-millennium BCE military exigencies in the temperate latitudes of Asia promoted individual valor, and war leaders appropriated captives from campaigns in remote regions to build massive and massively expensive personal power and monumental presence at lessened costs to local agrarian populations. When the spoils of plundering ceased to support these costly regimes, successor military and priestly establishments turned to merchants, by then much more efficiently in touch with still more remote regions, to provide continuing streams of helplessly isolated and therefore dependably loyal outsiders to staff imperial overlays on local peasant populations, thus maintained for their vital agricultural production and demographic reproduction. Slaving not only supported heirs to pretensions inherited from the past as dynastic lines grew increasingly marginal to their own changing times but also perpetuated the local communities who marginalized them.

In the longer term, warlords turned to merchants to obtain slaves to sustain military establishments running out of significant battles to fight—other than mutually destructive internal struggles among successors struggling to live up to exaggerated memories of their founding predecessors. This move led in dialectically historical fashion to unintended challenges from the merchants. Merchants, originally marginal to military raiding, took advantage of the warriors' growing dependence on their commercial networks to amass wealth in currencies and credit at rates faster than militarists could integrate the spoils of military domination of land and people. In time, merchants, as slavers, threatened to build up retinues of outsiders under their personal control on scales sufficient to compete for the services and produce of the local agricultural populations with older landed, military, and priestly interests. By the last millennium before the current era militarists and merchants had reached regional variants of this long-term historical standoff in much of Asia and northern Africa, where it prevailed until the nineteenth century.

In no instance had slaving attained the status of a legal, public institution, where the state presumed to intrude on communities of kin, peasant villages, great Mediterranean households, even the rural domains of Roman generals and senators, and the slaves of the ruling houses themselves. Rather, these private domains sheltered vulnerable and manipulable outsiders, who effectively sustained the composite structures of polities other than monarchies, whether formalized as democratic cities, republics, or empires. Patterson's "social death" turns out to have strategic political implications, differing in diverse historical contexts. Nor was the process then highly commercialized, other than in moments of acquisition. Even in the most commercially developed parts of southwestern Asia and the Mediterranean, its limited proprietorial aspect was supplementary to other means of transferring dependents directly among households. In the lives of the enslaved, the isolation and anonymity of being transferred from hand to hand like a thing was momentary or at worst intermittent, often a form of punishment for betrayal of the trust expected of a member of the household.

From the slavers' perspective, slaving enabled whatever degree of individual autonomy they could withhold from overweening collective/political/military authority; in increasingly commercialized urban contexts, slaves displayed wealth, performed services, and sustained competitors in the public sector. To the limited extent that authorities external to these large, slave-staffed domestic households interfered in relationships between slaves and masters living within the high, featureless walls of their compounds, they did so only through the masters, who represented these extended family collectivities to the world beyond. The polity itself was either a republican composite of these great households or an imperial authority external to them; in neither instance did it claim the direct access to individuals that eventually defined monarchs and that modern civic nations later claimed as participatory citizenship. The exceptions to this rule were the rare monarchies of the Christian Mediterranean, and eventually maritime western Europe; I account for their distinctive aversion to slaves in a succeeding chapter.

In contexts of so limited and alien a political sphere, personal freedom in the modern, civic, public sense had only occasional significance at best, and even then only for a wealthy few, in particular those with many slaves, who used them to assert themselves in the politics of the composite. The relevant standards of treating the enslaved were therefore ethical and personal, not abstractly legal; for respectable patrons these were matters of honor, and they applied to everyone in the domestic retinues of household heads, not alone to the enslaved. These obligations found expression therefore primarily in the reflections of the Christian and Islamic thinkers on the responsibilities of believers in a monotheistic God, in a vein that we now term religious in a sense that they would not have recognized, contrasting with the political. Slaves fell within the realm of personal, self-motivated, honorable responsibility that we regard as ethical. Reflections of the same ethical order and strategic effect in the secular literate context of ancient Greece to us appear philosophical.

These were the quite distinct realms of earlier times to which David Brion Davis attributed continuity in the "legal and philosophic concept . . . the *idea* of slavery" into the Atlantic era. But historicizing them, as I propose, indicates radical discontinuities of slaving in the Atlantic, and not in terms of race but in the unfettered commercialization and consequently expanding public sphere of law and contract in which the enslaved served, first, as collateral for the credit that entrepreneurs required to build enterprises producing agricultural commodities for sale. In effect, borrowers displaced the costs of servicing their debts from themselves and their families—as peasants in the classical eastern Mediterranean and elsewhere had long had to offer themselves in cases of default—onto enslaved strangers whom they could work to death to produce commercial products to repay what they had borrowed or, in the event of a need to liquidate, to sell the fungible human collateral itself.

Slaving, positioned within the political contexts of the times and places of marginal interests who used it to promote themselves and understood dynamically as a political strategy, often forced more established rivals to fall back also on slaving in self-defense, thereby motivating and enabling highly varied changes obscured by abstracted understandings of a singular institution of slavery. The sociological institution thus imagined freezes selected outcomes of the throbbing dynamics of human historical processes in time long enough to contemplate their logical coherence and nuanced implications. But institutions are also ideologies, and, when contemplated historically, ideologies are inherently deceptive, denials of change. They are defensive, often retrospective rationalizations created in belated attempts to preserve the failing stages of spontaneous, opportunistic processes that earlier had coalesced spontaneously at paces too fast to need, or to gain further momentum from, intricate analysis of selected elements of their logic. Ideologies are also retrospective public memory systematically elaborated to wrap the actual historical dynamics of the past in political priorities of the present. As history, these rationalized outcomes therefore explain nothing; they are rather what historians must explain.[74]

The historical epistemology I outline here is meant to tie some of the many and varied instances of Old World slaving together over a more comprehensive geographical range than the usual Athens-to-Alabama narrative, and to do so in terms of historicized dynamics of integrated incremental changes rather than in terms of static sociological comparisons of isolated cases, abstracted retrospective ideologies, or selective originary continuities.[75]

3

Slavery and History as Problems in Africa

In Africa, history and slavery present problems of a distinctive peculiarity, though one no less politicized than slaving elsewhere in the world. Modern historiography's preoccupation with change as progressive and the racial politics of remembering slavery, mostly in the New World, for a long time (and arguably still in some quarters) excluded the continent entirely from the conceptual domains of both slavery and history. These exclusionary modern lenses, trained on Africa largely from perspectives outside the continent itself, had little bearing on the particular priorities and historical processes of slaving in Africa.

In this chapter I review these background omissions of Africa from both slavery and history by way of framing a historicized sketch of history and slaving there. With these ahistorical conceptual obstacles problematized, we may place slaving strategies in Africa in the historical contexts that motivated the slavers, there and then, as anywhere else in the world. These strategies reveal historical dynamics parallel to those introduced in the preceding chapter for other parts of the world. Slaving in Africa served as a strategy of militarization and then of commercialization, though in contexts specific to Africa: first, however, it had served as a strategy of creating and maintaining an ethos of community, and then, in the last few centuries, increasingly in ways that implemented the same militarizing strategies of Muslim and then

European slavers, effectively outsourcing Asian and European militarization and violence to people in Africa.

Accordingly, readers will not find an integrated narrative history of Africa in this chapter. Its chronological structure does not follow all the specific outcomes of strategies of slaving there but instead tracks the distinctive motivating contexts that challenged people in Africa to slave, and hence of the slaving strategies themselves. The generality of these strategies implies no historical homogeneity in Africa, any more than those outlined in Eurasia in the preceding chapter. Africa was a place of uncountable diversity and locality; in fact, one recurrent strategy of slaving highlighted here was African communities' calculated development of complementing distinctiveness.

At a similar level of abstraction these and other African historical strategies contrast with the axioms of modernity, including the modern West, and so, to problematize history and slaving in Africa, I accent them. Since this sort of generalized contrast is cognate with, but not identical to, the exclusion of Africa that modern history inherits from Hegel, and may also evoke the political sensitivities of race and civilization, it sometimes tempts defenders of Africa's intricately humane and experiential diversity to blur the strong distinction I am drawing between the heuristic analytical contrast I employ and an essentialized attribution of yet another demeaning differentiation of Africa, which I reject. I hope the following explication will leave even wary readers convinced that my historical—not abstractly structural—approach ends up integrating Africa by revealing parallels between history and slaving in Africa and history and slaving elsewhere in the world, both the ancient world sketched in the preceding chapter and the modern Americas sketched in chapter 4. We are the same, but different; and, as I assume here, we can also be different, and still the same.[1]

Historicizing slaving in Africa is thus the extreme version of the historiological challenge of understanding strategies of slaving different from both the familiar modern model of black men producing white commodities for white men and the politics of slaving strategies in the military empires of Asia and of the cities of the Mediterranean region before the sixteenth century. In Africa specific kinds of marginal individuals, no differently positioned from their counterparts elsewhere, had slaved, in their own ways, from the beginning of their histories. Their histories were also the beginning of human history itself, since Africa appears to have been the home of the late hominids whose descendants invented community, language, and historical strategizing. As circumstances in Africa changed, their successors adapted slaving to the challenges of emergent eras there, but in ways distinct from the militarization and commercialization that framed the better-known strategies of slaving in agrarian river-bottom Asia and eventually Europe. This chapter outlines what I hope will be a history that acknowledges slaving in Africa in the strategic, epistemological sense obligatory for historians.

For Africa, as for the rest of the world, I thus continue to move beyond contemplating slavery as an implicitly static institution. My purposes go beyond the tendency of the literature on Africa to phrase the problem of slavery there only negatively, as lacking features of the modern American institution. Rather, I want to render African slaving familiar, as just another set of recurrent historical strategies (plural) to which people in positions of specifiable marginality there resorted, like others nearly everywhere in world history prior to the latter part of the nineteenth century, in most world areas until the middle third (or so) of the twentieth, and in a few until now.[2]

Some Basic Premises

In chapter 2 I contextualized slaving in a very long term narrative of the succession of marginal interests who deployed captive outsiders to gain leverage over the ways in which they and more established competitors collaborated or competed. The aboriginal use of slaving to create human society itself eventually led to a broadly Old World struggle between elaborated and adapted, but similarly communal, domestic groups forced to live in militarized, costly, broader political (that is, no longer face-to-face) collectivities. The members of these extended families, peasant villages, or elaborated households viewed most such polities as external to the intimate, ongoing, enveloping, face-to-face human engagements within them.[3] Africans militarized later and so proceeded with alternative strategies based on and integrated into the underlying ethos of community based on familiarity.

In Africa these existential groupings retained the defining metaphors of kinship, as they primarily valued and reproduced people, largely autonomously in terms of the lands on which they lived and the products they drew from them. Organized at this collective level by men, their principal external connections were alliances with similarly kin-structured neighboring groups, known to anthropologists as lineages, to obtain the unrelated women whom all needed as wives in order to reproduce their communities through time. When they collaborated on larger scales, they preserved these primary reproducing communities in internally differentiated political combinations that I term composites, distinguishing these polities as supplementary to the primary focus of the component groups on maintaining themselves through the generations. These political composites elaborated overall authority primarily to represent the collectivity to outsiders, through personages whom I term chiefs. Though these representatives are often glossed simplistically in the general literature as kings, chiefs did not rule internally, except as authorized by councils or other assemblies of representatives of the components of the composite. Historically these polities must be understood in quite specific terms, not as unitary or singular states, with comprehending identities, but as situationally contingent collaborations among these primary groups of kin. People identified themselves in terms of this political option as only one among the many other networks that they also cultivated.

The kingdoms and empires ubiquitous in conventional accounts of the African past claiming to be historical were in fact rare, and where they existed they were built around the deep tensions they created with the underlying communal ethos. In these respects, their externality to underlying communities differed little from that of the military imperial systems of ancient southwestern Asia. The conventional premise of the civically defined modern unitary Weberian state, as routinely misapplied to Africa, forces us to distinguish African politics with the language of networks or other similarly a- (if not anti-) political-sounding methods of strategic collaboration, in order to denote the compositional, as distinct from integrative, strategies of political collaboration common in Africa.[4] In fact, they were all polities, in the sense of strategic collaborations among groups (not individuals) otherwise unrelated, none of them more natural or inevitable than any others. They were all, in a word, historical strategies, contingent constructions in specific contexts of times and places.

The distinction between states as abstract entities and these other equally political strategies—but collectively negotiated rather than individuated, personal rather than abstracted, and experiential rather than imagined and institutionalized—is crucial to understanding how slaving in Africa was a strategy no less political than anywhere else in the world. In fact, given that Africans, more than those in militarized and commercialized parts of the world, valued people primarily, slaving there was essentially political. Africa, far from its longtime invisibility in terms of slaving and history, becomes the distilled essence of slaving as an efficacious historical strategy, long before Muslim and European merchants came to Africa to exploit the tensions of the communal ethos that the residents of the continent had preserved.[5]

Ahistorical Africas: Racial Lethargy and Antiracial Legacies

In spite of the considerable achievements of my colleagues during the last half century, slaving and history remain problematic in the historical literature on Africa primarily as reactions to European initiatives in the Atlantic, with allowance also made for intrusions by other, earlier outsiders, Muslims from the north and east. I began this chapter by referring to the paradigmatic American outcomes of slaving as "background omissions of Africa from both slavery and history," that is, to Africa as having neither history nor slavery. Taking a step beyond these exclusions, I criticize the premises operative in maintaining them.

First, the exclusions of history, since the intellectual framework here is relatively familiar to most readers and disposed of relatively easily. It is familiar because it is the Hegelian heart of the progressive vision that pervades the modern historical discipline. Africanists refer to Georg Wilhelm Friedrich Hegel (1770–1831) primarily because they find his specific exclusion of Africa from his (otherwise) "Universal History" of civilization an easily destructible straw man. For Hegel, only civilizations that were products of the moral civility achieved through writing and large-scale, inclusive states, and associated military force and monumental expressions of their presence and precedence (if not also the costs of their coerciveness), represented progress toward attaining the virtue that seemed, in his time, to be the civic genius that was allowing early nineteenth-century Europeans to dream of unprecedented power throughout the world.

Hegel defined the essence of his Universal History by what he also celebrated as the distinctive, and therefore historically unrepresentative—indeed, ultimately unique—standards of what was then becoming the European nation-state. Since no Europeans had the slightest inkling of substantive alternatives, African or other, the contradiction passed unnoticed. They remembered only their own recent experiences with monarchy as a past to be escaped. In this progressive construction of history, Africans appeared to represent only all that Europeans were not, or nothing that Europeans were becoming: in the historicized terms of time, they were people trapped in the primal, if not also primitive, eras of savagery that Europeans had moved themselves far beyond. This progressive logic of history temporalized growing, but still dim, awareness of the diversity of contemporary humanity around the world. But rather than accommodating the diversity that was becoming apparent, Hegel in fact attempted to temporalize "inversity" (to coin a word that ought to exist). His idea of Africa was based not on information or on a positive appreciation of differences, but on imagined inversions of how Europeans were coming to think of themselves. Their own conversion, incomplete by any accurate appreciation, looked better in comparison to an Africa radically dichotomized.

In particular, Hegel's fantasized Africa lacked states, at least as he understood them as custodians of progress, leaving Africans only with tribes, by analogy with the Germanic groups in northern Europe who had troubled the ancient

Romans exemplary in his era; tribes carried connotations of logically and morally negative statelessness, which the word still retains. Nor had Hegel's Africans had any meaningful contacts with the surrounding parts of the world regarded as civilized, implying geographical isolation. This insistence on Africa's isolation took ancient Egypt out of Africa, claiming it for the West, even as Napoleon claimed it militarily for France. Isolation, not inconveniently, also rendered insignificant, if not invisible, the pervading contacts through European slave trading in Africa that peaked during Hegel's lifetime.[6]

The maturation of Hegel's allegedly progressive legacy as a historical discipline narrowly and insistently nation-state–centered left the first generation of professionally trained historians interested in Africa—Edward Wilmot Blyden and others in Africa in the late nineteenth century, and quintessentially W. E. B. Du Bois, Leo Hansberry, and colleagues of African descent trained before the First World War in the United States—to play by these then-unchallengeably dominant rules of the historical game. These modern creators of a historical Africa played well enough the intellectual hand they were dealt, concentrating almost exclusively on the earliest, largest, most militarized, monument-building moments in Africa's past that they could identify. They reclaimed as African the then-romantically celebrated ancient Egypt (third to first millenniums BCE), or at least Nubia, from its recent Europeanization; against the background of the imperialist age in which they lived, they also revealed tenth- to sixteenth-century CE empires in the sub-Saharan regions of western Africa known as the Sudan and highlighted the mysterious monumental stone structures (thirteenth to fourteenth centuries CE) at Great Zimbabwe in southeastern Africa. They framed Africa's past in terms of parallels with, or even precedents for, the progressive early twentieth-century narrative of Europe's global military triumphs. Their vision of militarized monumentality still thrives in current world history texts as the touchstone of their lamentably limited references to Africa.

When Du Bois and his colleagues turned to the fateful era of the slave trade that followed, they treated it as a history of descent from these ancient, and also implicitly isolated, heights of militarized grandeur in Africa. Beginning with European explorations and exploitation in the sixteenth century, as they saw it, contacts with an overwhelmingly powerful outside world steadily eroded Africa's ancient glories. In this pointed inversion of the progressive dismissal of Africa from Universal History in Europe, Europeans had achieved little that was not based on or at least anticipated by precedents in Africa. But they nonetheless wiped out the gripping achievements of Africans, far-seeing paradigms for modernity before its time, and all the more poignantly because the black builders of such states must have constructed them, however unknowingly, in defiance of hostile modern racial stereotypes of their incapacity. The intrusions of ungrateful barbarians from Europe had tragically cost later Africans the opportunity to build on the promising foundations laid down by their ancestors. Africa's subsequent contacts with the rest of the world, via the slave trade and ultimately imperial military conquest, were a decline and fall comparable to the tragic loss of the glory that had been Rome.

Versions of these classic attributions of modern accomplishments to ancient Africa continue to appeal today, since they seemingly rescue Africans from the dismissive racial stereotypes under which we all still labor. It may be a narrative ready-made for introducing Africa comfortably, seemingly respectfully, into a global history for youthful beginners barely aware of the world beyond their own personal, very contemporary, and only hazily national contexts. But it thereby also accepts (by playing off) precisely the modern, often implicitly racial, distortions that exclude Africans from their own, independently motivated history, arising, as it must, from Africans' own, alternative understandings of what they did. To generate history in Africa, one must abandon these forced analogies to modern European standards of progress and start from African contexts, from understanding how people in Africa acted on the meanings they attributed to the circumstances in which they found themselves. Unsurprisingly, their perceptions were largely in terms significantly different from what our own historically unique moment of modernity would lead us to expect.

Modern racism further limits our ability to see either history or, particularly, slaving in Africa. Politicized racism emerged simultaneously with progressive history as the popular doctrine of social and political exclusion that matched Hegel's philosophical dismissal of Africans from his Universal History. With regard to more recent historians' reflections on slavery, the continuing centrality of race to the cultural politics of modern nations—especially in the Americas—has conditioned the role (*sic:* singular!) attributed to Africans, as if they were a single, implicitly racialized group. These Africans themselves, although imagined as homogeneous, as historical actors in fact share only this attributed racial caricaturization. It is a modern idea, which acquired meaning only in the wake of Atlantic slaving in the nineteenth century, when people of African descent, mostly outside of Africa, invoked it as a dignifying construction of the denigration they were suffering in the Americas and elsewhere as "negros" or "blacks. " Its strong accent on (racial) solidarity, however useful culturally and politically, has no utility whatsoever in understanding how people of many carefully distinguished communities in Africa might earlier have thought of themselves or what they might have done, and particularly not in the times that concern me here, before and during the Atlantic trade in slaves. Given the fundamental historical association of slaving with change, it is not surprising to learn that the era of Africans' more and more intense commercial engagement with outsiders, which the Europeans knew as the slave trade—roughly the seventeenth and eighteenth centuries—was one of profound change in Africa and that modern Africa proceeds now within frameworks built then out of slaving.[7]

Thinking of the self-consciously differentiated historical communities in Africa only as unidimensional Africans creates the problem, for understanding slaving there, that its imputed racial unity implies that no one there could or should, morally, have been involved in "selling their own people." But the comprehensive and inclusive homogeneity of race is entirely today's issue.[8] It draws on modern, not inappropriately defensive racial solidarity among diasporic Africans to project similarly mutual and intense loyalties into the African past, asserting an ancient, common, racialized identity on a continental scale. By extension, this racial association also underwrites recent animated controversies as to whether people in geographically African pharaonic Egypt were black.

Such absolute unity by definition excludes the possibility of internal enslavement, since slaves must be outsiders, both in conventional sociological definitions and also in the historical terms developed here. In attempting to contemplate the possibility of slavery within an attributed community that—in an age before global racism and in a place where it did not develop— Africans did not imagine, historians would stumble upon an ethical oxymoron: all of them being blacks, they cannot be others to one another, susceptible to enslavement. Against the politicized background of the subject of slavery today, the idea of slaving within Africa would have to acknowledge divisions there of a depth that could have led some to sell others, allegedly of their own people, to outsiders like Europeans, equally racially defined. Admission of so heinous a crime is a truly dangerous threat to modern idealized solidarity outside of Africa, since, on the prevailing cultural premise that minorities are potentially flawed until proven flawless, the slightest failure to live up to the humanitarian pretensions of the majority culture stirs suspicions of disabling deficiency, not just among some or a few but among all of those excluded as "those people." In comforting contrast, the failures of the majority to practice what it preaches go unnoticed.

To raise even the possibility of slaving in Africa treads on delicate popular sensibilities on the continent itself no less than outside of Africa.[9] The first generation of modern historical research in Africa missed these tensions entirely. Working in the optimistic decade of nationalist independence in the 1960s, they had access only to the public documents of the colonial era, in which colonial regimes had every reason not to discuss at any length the embarrassment that the legacies of slaving in Africa constituted for the pretensions of their perceived civilizing mission. In the glare of the nationalist unity of that time, divisions of any sort among the fully equal citizens of new African nations faded into the historical shadows. Further, Africans of that generation were themselves survivors of wrenching, late nineteenth-century displacements of the populations of most parts of the continent. These displacements had left majorities of the citizens of the new nations in Africa immediate descendants of at least one enslaved parent or grandparent. Ancestry remained important, as it defined the communal ethos in which most Africans lived. In response to questions from insensitive outsiders like Western historians, representatives of lineages, households, and other solidary communities presented descendants of enslaved ancestors as integrated members of these groups. African scholars among these historians knew better than to ask.

The question was too sensitive to raise because within these same communities, where most Africans derived their primary identities, the descendants of the enslaved were excluded from core positions and routinely reminded of their moral and political marginality.[10] Only with gradual opening of the administrative and judicial records of the colonial period in the 1970s and 1980s did historians gain access to evidence of the extent to which slavery pervaded Africa's modern history, as well as slaving its past.[11] And only in very recent years has slave ancestry become a matter of public discussion, as second and third generations of citizens of independent African nations have begun to invoke the theoretical egalitarianism of the modern nation-state against ongoing disabilities inherited from slaving.[12]

Abroad, the subject of slaving in Africa acquires overtones of alarm if one includes it among the multiple factors that converged, tragically, to motivate and sustain the Atlantic trade in enslaved Africans. However, those sensibilities, American as well as African, however relevant to modern politics and ethics, are not historical. A historical approach to Africa, working from the sensibilities of people in Africa in their own times, allows us to come to terms with circumstances there—including, and eventually prominently, contact with outsiders, and not only Europeans—that make it not only possible but even unavoidable to consider slaving as a salient strategy of Africans, no less—and also no more, *under similar circumstances*—than of anyone else. If the silenced problematics of slavery and history in Africa are linked in their conventional obscurity, so also are they connected in what they reveal about slaving as a historical strategy anywhere in the world. And so, too, do they, however tragically, include Africans among the ambitious, change-oriented contributors to the largest scales of world history, also through slaving.

Historical Strategies in African Contexts—
Maintaining Diversity

I emphasize the recurrent resort, in Africa no less than elsewhere, by insiders marginal to currently dominant interests to acquiring isolated, and hence at least momentarily vulnerable, people from outside the dynamics of the society—or community, or social formation, or any sort of aggregate of people competitively engaged on an ongoing basis over the distribution of limited resources, or for control of the cultural idioms in which they compete, by whatever term social scientists might theorize these historically coherent entities. History is dialectical; one's own actions motivate one's competitors' reactions, and vice versa. Historians therefore must systematically problematize these contexts of meaningful human interaction. Interests marginal within such historically coherent spaces appropriate the outsiders' *presence and potential*, or the *products* of their efforts, for purposes of their own, always doing so at the expense of others in the community, and in Africa eventually at the expense of community itself. From the collective perspective of a community, by definition viewing itself as pure, slaves are contaminants, literally foreign bodies, social irritants that activate the human equivalents of immune reactions to expel them.[13]

A historical accounting of slaving in Africa begins by positioning the master–slave dyad in contexts of community quite unlike the modern civic societies that implicitly frame the slave's vulnerability as social. Africa's history of slaving reveals circumstances that have offered many ways of excluding imported outsiders other than by invoking the analogy of things to claim them as personal, hence fungible property [14] under the commercial law of a polity, whether ancient empire or republic or modern civic state. Phrasing the contrast between Africa and the recent West in terms of these differing cultural routes to the convergent ends of isolation and control puts readers on notice that I will not be contrasting slavery in Africa as mild or benign (or other current ethical contrasts) in comparison with conditions in mines and on plantations in the New World. If all roads lead to Mecca, so too do all experiences of helpless, baffled isolation lead to living hells of parallel intensity, and not transitory ones. In communities where origins and antiquity count for more than current comfort or even personal prestige or authority, social assimilation *to* a group does not lead to ethical inclusion *in* it. In Africa's additive historiology, there was no escaping slaving in one's ancestral past.

Historical Africa could not have been more different from the homogeneity imposed on it by progressive implicitly racial history. In terms of how people there thought of themselves, it was, in fact, a place of calculated diversity and consequently also of multiplicity. Africans contrasted themselves in collective terms as insiders and outsiders to stronger degrees than we modern crowds of miscellaneous individuals struggle to attain, even momentarily.[15] So, human historical strategies in Africa, by definition, arose significantly from living with, even cultivating, differences with others, starting with the descent lines that defined lineages. These distinctions varied in degree with changing frequencies and intensities of contacts with outsiders—the multiplicity and immediacy of neighboring communities or enemies—relative to themselves. This division of the perceptual world in Africa into collective insiders and outsiders recurrently adapted and thus maintained the ethos that in chapter 2 I described as communal.

The fundamental diversity of human existence, though denied or decried by the modern epistemological premise of homogeneity,[16] lies at the heart of the historical dynamics of slaving in Africa. Diversity in Africa may be no greater than elsewhere in the world, in some objective sense, but it was (and still is) affirmed there collectively, to motivating degrees comparable in intensity to modern ideologies of homogeneous individuality, whether inclusively humanistic or excludingly racialized. Africa's differentiated communities are not of the primordial (implied primitive, immutable) tribal sort emphasized in contemporary media, where the adjective "tribal" modifies only nouns like "conflict" or even "genocide." Outsiders to African studies, aware of these pejorative overtones, nearly always resort to a polite euphemism, like ethnicity, to attempt to acknowledge growing academic and popular awareness of Africa's historical diversity, but they do not thereby historicize what they leave as still-homogeneous, epistemologically illusory (and ahistorical), structural figments of the modern imagination.

Accordingly, to account historically for the motives behind slaving in Africa I will not invoke the fifteen hundred or so modern languages of the continent (that is, not counting innumerable others in earlier eras)[17], or, to avoid the unfortunate connotations of "ethnicity," their "cultural" correlates, or any of the other stereotypes of local homogeneities that ethnographers and other well-meaning liberals invented as nonpejorative replacements for the tribal collectivities that colonial rulers demeaned as primitive survivals from a timeless past. In Africa today, thoroughly modern political factions designated as tribes have strong meanings for people, and more so now in modern nation-states than formerly, but these ethnicized strategies are outcomes of the continent's recent history rather than inherited and inherent causes of occasional chaos. Ethnicity is useful historically only to designate contextualized strategies of creating communities efficacious not in excluding or exploiting others but in joining together situationally to seek the mutual benefits of complementary differentiation.[18]

That is, rather than denying the inherent, historical diversity of humanity, as the ideology of modernity does, and then struggling over claims to define its necessarily single normative standard, Africans cultivated individual diversity within multiple worlds that complementingly invoked—though only situationally, thus (again) historically—many specific ideological commonalities. Depending on immediate contexts, these ranged in scale from small lineages on through various residential and occupational identities (including bearing and nurturing children), to large abstract, anonymous ethnic collectivities mobilized for purposes of dealing with outsiders, including inquiring colonial-era ethnographers. Linguistic collaborations expressed these multiple identities to varying degrees, as people worked out specialized habits of speech for these specialized purposes, ranging from esoteric codes of secret societies to technical jargon among technicians of iron smelters or animal husbandry to what colonial outsiders eventually created as standard languages, by weak analogy with the singular, standardized modern languages of their own European backgrounds.

Successful individuals in these multiple historical contexts were, in the linguistic analogy, multilingual. They claimed, by performing them, memberships in as many of these differing communities as they could, including the shadowy ones we designate as ethnic, moving strategically among them, depending on where they saw momentary personal opportunity. People with fewer such options, that is, people less well connected, might be relatively immobile and vulnerable. Strong groups tried to incorporate individuals who brought in as wide a range of skills, backgrounds, and contacts as they could, and they thought in terms of transferring personnel for the purpose, by marriage and adoption. Individualism was anything but absent within the communal ethos I described in chapter 2. Rather, individuals pursued personal ambitions by building networks of partners and patrons, or clients, and as multiplistically as possible. Success consisted of being related in some way to everybody with whom one might conceivably come into contact or need, ideally in more ways than one, and thus having both claims on and responsibilities to them.[19] Personal ambition was admired, so long as it involved everyone else, openly; one advanced by contributing to the collective welfare. What was feared was its perversion, isolation and selfish, secretive greed. That is to say, what modern times celebrate as individualism Africans condemned as witchcraft.

Africa in World History

In Africa, as in the rest of the world—since Africa has been very much a part of the world since long before historical times, slaving served not only the early effort to create communities in the ideological/ethical sense but also to maintain the ethos of collectivity while simultaneously and dialectically advancing the personal agendas of all who subsequently challenged it. Thanks to forty-odd years of accumulating research,[20] historians in Africa can now present a coherent narrative in sufficient detail, and with enough confidence, to serve my rather broad purposes in this chapter, starting at the beginning, with the slow and anxious shift from appropriating evolutionary advantage to seizing the historical (that is, purposive and social) initiative. People in Africa began to collaborate in historical ways at about the same time that descendants of earlier African hominids did elsewhere in the world: perhaps twenty thousand years ago.

To assess the utility of slaving in initiating changes that marked the broad epochs in Africa that followed,[21] I cannot presume the same familiarity with them that I take for granted among readers of my assessment of these processes in better-known parts of the world in chapter 2. By way of setting my analytical stage, I delineate the following:

> Consolidating broad linguistic communities and corresponding technological strategies in four major variants ancestral to the four families of languages spoken in Africa today, from the dawn of historical action until roughly seven thousand to five thousand years ago. These consolidations broadly corresponded to the wetter and drier environments of the continent in the relatively propitious grasslands and woodlands south of the enormous area that was then gradually desiccating to become today's Sahara Desert.
>
> Taking these basic strategies south, as continuing desiccation encouraged growing populations to move toward wetter equatorial regions, adapting their cultural heritages—and in one significantly enabling instance in the region of the lakes of upland eastern Africa combining them as they engaged and then absorbed most of the hunting-gathering people they met as they settled there, from ca. 3000 BCE until the first half of the first millennium CE;
>
> From that era until the last century or so, they worked out more specific economic and correlated cultural strategies, where they settled, that became classic in Africa, in the same sense that modern Western civilization looks back to the ancient Mediterranean (and in the same era) as elaborating the principles in terms of which their heirs have thought ever since, even as they have also modified them continuously to engage emergent contemporary circumstances; these may be mapped linguistically and provided the frameworks for colonial-era ethnographic definitions of tribes.

These broad epochs of history in Africa paralleled those of the Eurasian world in historical significance and in timing. But they differed in the specific strategies, as people in Africa did not suffer the high costs of militarization that characterized Eurasia from perhaps the third millennium before the current era, except locally and belatedly. As a result, even in moist, flat, alluvial plains like the inland delta of the upper Niger River they managed to preserve small, face-to-face communities of the sort I have designated as domestic, often in metaphors invoking the intense terminology of intimacy and personhood that we characterize as kinship.

From the time the African frontier of southward settlement closed about fifteen hundred years ago (that is, ca. 500 CE) until 1900 or so, these face-to-face communities of familiarity, kinship, and affinity were anything but traditional, in the sense of static. Rather, they adapted their legacies from the past to meet a sequence of emerging challenges, using slaving to build new groupings of personnel adapted to new purposes, beyond (but never abandoning) the underlying focus on female fecundity and the fertility of the lands where they lived. They began by intensifying the distinctiveness of each settled community relative to its neighbors by specializing in the resources of their lands, the microenvironments, where they lived. They cultivated complementing environmental identities and engaged in increasingly elaborated exchanges of the products distinctive to each with others around them. Where they formalized these arrangements on larger scales, they drew on a variety of techniques to maintain the local, rich diversity they had cultivated; these were the political and economic networks I refer to as compositional. They consequently succeeded in preserving what I am calling their ancestral communal ethos, in contrast to the homogenizing dynamic of European and Asian monotheisms and correspondingly singular models of secular monarchy, in which everyone was considered alike in the eyes of God and eligibility to enjoy the favor of the sovereign.

Africans also preserved their experiences of these strategies—literally the experiences, not memories of them removed in time—through an epistemology of change that might be called additive, in contrast to the progressive logic of modern history. Progress is substitutive change because it rests on a linear concept of temporality, in which one must abandon pasts to move on through a series of ephemeral presents toward some ever-receding future, a Never-Never Land of not yet because one never gets beyond one's present to reach it. In Africa, by contrast, the present does not leave the past behind but updates it by compiling a string of presents through what we view as time into a temporally composite awareness of self.[22] Life is diverse and compound, temporally as well as socially. For example, the cultivating communities moving south into central and southern Africa in the eras before the current one assimilated the foragers whom they met not by converting them to new ways but by adding their ways and their very selves to their own communities;

two millennia later, their heirs continued to pay their respects to the ineradicable precedence and ongoing presence of the "little people."[23] The present is the accumulated composite of the elements of the past viewed as valuable and hence preserved. Africans have demonstrated an enormous ability to assimilate the modern world in precisely these terms, though not without strain, through always-updated and ever-current "tradition."[24]

Africans thereby preserved a communal ethos and interdependent mutuality—hence its classical standing—in contrast to recurrent assertions of individualism based on resources introduced from outside the ethical communities at the cores of most cultures there. Assertive individualism in fact probably became historically significant among Africans—that is, a motive and strategy that enabled the people who effected the principal lines of cumulative change—at about the same time that Europeans affirmed it as a historical ethos in the seventeenth century, as opposed to the much older monotheistic premise of individual salvation as a matter of the soul. The Enlightenment in the eighteenth century would mark this watershed of modernity in Europe, and in Africa it was commercialized slaving that enabled similar challengers to the communal ethos. Then, particularly recently, Africans adapted collective practices to create secure, or at least shared, refuges from the perils of the modern world, in which most people in Africa have been able to compete as individuals only on decidedly disadvantageous terms.[25] But in Africa the autonomous individualism celebrated in the West remained an anomaly rather than becoming an axiom. The tensions commonly construed around the individual and society as being mutually exclusive exist also in Africa, but the terms of the dichotomy were reversed. European colonial authorities distorted and condemned African reliance on communal loyalties as being atavistically tribal, and Africans condemned members of their communities who tried to profit personally from the colonial world as witches.

Alert readers will have noticed that this broad periodization of Africa's past parallels the timing of the major epochs of conventionally progressive history that Europeans have employed to describe (self-congratulatingly and teleologically enough) their own ascent from barbaric antecedents to an originary classical era of their own and on to modernity itself.[26] After an apparent and inexplicable lapse from the presumed path to modernity during the millennium between the disintegration of Roman military strength and the Renaissance revival of its secular learning, long described only negatively as a dark or middle interlude, the metanarrative of the march toward modernity resumed, with its initial phases described negatively and teleologically as early modern, that is, anticipating what people in the sixteenth and seventeenth centuries hadn't yet become. The modern epiphany of full human individualization and freedom, however limited the ability to realize the promise of those ideals may be in practice, is so resounding that it has been proclaimed as the end of history as a dialectical process or, to convert the twentieth century into a triumph over all other possibilities, declared deviant. Even its critics, still styled negatively (and as always, thus vacuously) as *post*modern, have no substantive way to describe themselves, other than what they want to have moved beyond but have not, quite.

I elaborate the African parallels to this familiar periodization not only to frame the historicity of Africa's past for readers unfamiliar with it but also to emphasize Africa's integral place in world history. Beyond the contrasting tendencies (and they were tendencies, historical creations, not differences in any essentialized sense) in contexts, and hence in historical strategies, Europe and Africa, and Asia, were all parts of a single broader historical process realized experientially in its many particular regional and local manifestations. Europe's versions of this historical dynamic were no less peculiar than Africa's. In both regions, as well as in all others, people marginal to each of its epochs used strategies of slaving to confront and to take advantage of the dilemmas of their times.

Methods and Meanings

One final preliminary observation, for readers who may wonder about how historians can know about the pasts of people who left relatively few written records of the sort on which document-based progressive historical method (but not its epistemology) has depended since its invention in the nineteenth century: the evidence of meanings in Africa's past, particularly for its earlier eras, is significantly linguistic. All those fifteen hundred or so modern languages may not be useful as markers of timeless tribes, but they are revelatory of the sequences and approximate timing of successful and therefore enduring innovations that differentiated them all from only four breakthroughs to syntactic speech some twenty thousand years ago (particularly when correlated with more directly datable archaeological evidence).[27] People in the past talked creatively about the things they did that they found most efficaciously intriguing. How they construed what they were doing, even if in multiple, competing ways, particularly whatever was new, notable, and debatable, left verbal tracks in new words that their heirs preserved. A spoken record of strategies that conduced to continued success, or echoes of them, thus survives in present speech. Historians may therefore read back from how people talk now to what worked among predecessors long ago. Analysis of the semantic fields of terminological innovations or innovative terminologies gives us not only direct evidence of what ancient people did but also some basis for inferring why they did it, how they thought about doing it, or at least how those who prevailed construed themselves ideologically. Since these processes are collective they can't be faked; one can lie with words about particularities, but the words don't lie about whatever it is that is important enough to lie about. Linguistic sources could not be more revealing of meanings in the collective lives of people in the past. Since meanings and intentions are the starting points for historical understandings of human actions in the past, our ability to sequence linguistic innovations in Africa creates the framework for inferring dialectical historical processes there.[28]

Beyond written documents, which historians in Africa may consult for at least the last millennium in quantities far greater than most nonspecialists would suspect, oral traditions similarly track collective assessments of the creation of significant social components of African compositional polities, past and present.[29] By the African principle of historical change as additive, the new does not obliterate the old, and memories of successful historical strategies may be as enduring as the strategies themselves. As a fortunate result for historians, orally transmitted memories may allude to innovations far back in time, apparently as much as seven or eight centuries. The modern historian mines (literary theorists might say "deconstructs") the words uttered not as an individual's direct observations, transmitted as documents might have been copied through a succession of individual repetitions, but as highly interpretive collective memories, historical and ideological creations no less revealing than Western historians have now discovered their European and American equivalents to be.

Within the outlines sketched from these sources, historians can fill in further nuance by deconstructing twentieth-century ethnographic descriptions to sense not their contemporary coherence[30] but the incongruity of their various components, assembled cumulatively—that is, historically—over many years as innovative responses to varying novel circumstances at moments in the past. Meanings that today are incongruous with one another or implicit ideals inconsistent with contemporary practice coexist as independent adaptations of earlier practices that were significant in the past at different times.[31] Fortunately for modern historians, Africans' additive historical epistemologies often described novelty by adapting ongoing presents to legacies they had preserved from the past through metaphors of continuity and integration rather than, as European progressive history has done, wiping them out by invoking metaphors of comprehending and substitutive change or achieving a comparable sense of continuity by selecting ancient origins teleologically from the past, and thereby distorting it. The effect of appealing in Africa to tradition, rather than emphasizing innovation with accompanying selective forgetting, was to preserve metaphors of relevance to former times. Critical methods can distinguish the modern adaptations and applications of them that historians may observe and then sequence the residuals from the past as historical processes.

The same additive principle applies to the well-known (some would say "notorious") interdisciplinarity of early African history; the field truly is what Wyatt MacGaffey once called "the decathlon of the social sciences."[32] The characterization is acute in two ways, one good news, the other less so in an epistemologically historical sense. The not-so-good implication of MacGaffey's comment is that it accurately characterizes the relatively structural, social-scientific character of the field, overwhelmingly so at the time he made this remark, and sometimes so still today. The more promising implication is the number of different perspectives that the various disciplines available allow historians to draw on, provided they do so in a historically valid way. Historical validity in method derives from recognition of the perspectival quality of history as experience, its consequently fundamental multiplicity, and the many distinct aspects of the contexts that may motivate participants in them to act in diverse ways. By this standard, historians must not attempt to reconcile data produced in one discipline—say, archaeology—with data from another—say, linguistics—or try to match, say, documents and oral traditions or even documents from Arabic and Christian sources. Reconciliation in search of a single, verifiable truth has been the modernist methodological accent that has characterized the discipline until very recently. In fact, each of these sources, all historical products in themselves, has its own distinctive voice, and the historian must recognize their selectivities and then their compatibilities rather than seeking straightforward confirmation of one in any other. Historical method, like Africans' approach to adapting older communities to novel political challenges, is compositional. Diverse knowledges fill out complex historical contexts.

Slaving in Historical Africa: Early Times to ca. 2000 BCE

Historians of Africa now have sufficient density of possibilities, even probabilities, based on these radically independent and thereby also increasingly revealing sources that they cohere around a plausible broad narrative, several thousand years in depth, of slaving as a historical strategy. Much of the insight into the possible (plausible?) beginnings of slaving in creating coherent communities presented as a global process in chapter 2 in fact come from African materials. Here, by way of shifting the focus to Africa, I will merely localize those points in specific contexts there.[33] In terms of the communal ethos I've emphasized, the key strategies were and continue to be directed at forming collectivities and then, in reaction, for individuals marginal to these groups to attract and integrate personal dependents who might allow them to secure positions more central in them: wives were the most accessible and (re)productive dependents of this sort.

Children, the ultimate objective for anyone aspiring to honored ancestor-hood, were not always easy to conceive, and infants suffered very high mortality, were challenging to raise to responsible adulthood, and even as adults yielded veneration only over the very long term. Clients could be of moderately greater efficacy and more immediately so, but, as in the acquisition of legitimate wives, obtaining them required maturity and resources largely controlled by the collectivity. Consequently, for young or unsuccessful men eager to escape delays of maturation and the drag of communal responsibilities on personal ambition, slaving's yield of isolated outsiders, especially females in contexts of reproducing communities like lineages, was more effective. Groups dedicated to strategies other than reproduction, especially ones involving mobility—say, military bands or trading parties traveling by canoe or caravan—tended to sustain their numbers and hence their activities by recruiting boys and men through slaving. In the broad historical context of Africa's communal ethos, commercial and military strategies were innovative; slaving once again was the recurring strategy of choice to effect significant change.

All the more so because in Africa wealth was people, and people were power. This aphorism, a favorite among Africanists, contrasts the integrated communal ethos in Africa and its ethnicized occupational complements with the modern reliance on money and machines as wealth, which we use to sustain ourselves as individuals, as independently of others as possible. The entirely relational African calculus of position, with no escape into material representations of individuated status,[34] was politically a zero-sum game: one gained personally only relative to others, that is, at others' expense. Opportunity, cherished by moderns as universally available, open, and apparently cost-free, is not in fact open simultaneously to all; some have to settle for the promise, with fulfillment displaced into an always-receding future. We now lament the practical difficulty of achieving this ideal of self-confident self-sufficiency, though we cling stubbornly to the illusion by celebrating the tiny minority who realize the dream and ignoring rampant evidence of the loneliness and isolation that success in these terms exacts.

Africans explicitly affirmed the experiential truth that "no man is an island."[35] They recognized the personal costs of individualism as illness, emphasized its destructiveness to social solidarity, even its threat to collective survival, and strongly discouraged even trying to attain or, as they saw the matter, risk it. However, since people in Africa were no less personally competitive than any of us is now, one would expect to find no fewer ideological obfuscations of individual ambition there than the illusions that we revere among ourselves as opportunity. The resulting communal ethos did not celebrate our ideal of individualism but affirmed and enforced the always threatened loyalties to the collectivity. Among these, the idioms of kinship, among many others one could cite, stand out in Africa. Isolated outsiders taken in as slaves within the group where they found themselves would accordingly be qualified by metaphors of affiliation to (as distinguished sharply from membership in), often as wives or as children or wards, in order to lessen the risks of their otherwise exclusionary connection to the individual who had brought them in.[36] If, to ambitious individuals, slaves were opportunities to gain at the expense of the collectivity, to the groups they thus challenged slaves as excludingly dependent were threats.

One immediate implication of contextualizing slaving in Africa within this ethos of community is that the resulting affiliations neither constitute slavery in the modern, institutionalized, exclusionary sense, nor contrast productively with freedom, as personal autonomy guaranteed by civic governments. All members of and affiliates to African communities are parts of and thereby also subject to the theoretical consensus of the whole, contrasting with our sense of less-than-totally voluntary collaboration with other individuals as subjugation. The relational places slaves occupied in this collective social context we can contrast with modern institutionalized slavery—as restraint by and dependency on another individual beyond societal consensus, which in modern contexts takes the form of abstract government-guaranteed legal protections of individuals. But in historic Africa, where nearly everyone belonged in collectivities of one sort of another, all were also subordinated to some community. At the same time, as individuals they were both subordinate to others—as clients to patrons or wives to husbands—while correspondingly also superordinate along the dimensions of other relationships they were able to create. Everyone therefore sought to build as many connections, of as many dimensions, as possible. The chief, for example, was defined not by singular personal authority but by the most plurally and centrally related person in a community, the one capable of channeling everyone's concerns, particularly ones widely shared, to spiritized collective authority envisaged as common ancestors or predecessors.

Against this basic valuation of belonging somewhere, anywhere, preferably in as many places as possible, and hence being protected on negotiated terms by kin or a patron or potentially valuable to in-laws as a spouse, slaves were isolated. Rather than nestled in the security of an acknowledged position in a supportive, structured community, slaves were vulnerable appendages to them, initially connected only through individual members. They were correspondingly valuable to their single patrons because they lacked competing connections to patrons or protectors within the group or to the group as a whole. Since the strongest position was to belong everywhere and to have multiple ties of varying qualities, so as to always have at least one and preferably more than one available or operable connection on which to draw, in whatever circumstances one might encounter, the weakest position (since alone no one survives) was a new slave's hanging onto the group by only a single human thread.[37] In Africa, the patrons' interests lay in keeping people under their exclusionary authority rather than disposing of them, and this inclination to retain slaves rendered irrelevant the modern notion of an individual owner of a human held as a negotiable asset, in contexts in which capitalist debt made their fungibility a priority for owners, always potentially in need of liquidity in their assets.

The feeblest position in which one can exist in a communal ethos was the subordinating singularity (not subordination itself) of entering an alien community alone, through slaving. In the genealogical idiom of descent, the slave was the individual without ancestors, the person without responsible local relationships. In an environment in which claimed antiquity of belonging is very much present and therefore asserts entitlement to contemporary respect, slaves acquired through capture or purchase were the "most recently arrived."[38] Looking toward the future through the lens of this genealogical calculus, such appendages were not entitled, either, to recognized progeny and hence were eternally denied eventual ancestorhood or superordination (that is, honor or respect) of any sort.

Since personal standing in African communities—often in European languages phrased as respect—was relational, multiplistic, and situational, children born to enslaved women by fathers of local ancestry had genealogical claims in the communities where they lived through paternity but faced a gaping ancestral absence on their mothers' sides. Depending on whether marriages into the community in subsequent generations added more local ancestries, grandchildren and great-grandchildren of an enslaved female ancestor might acquire more local connections, potential protectors, and more secure positions. Descendants of slaves married to other slaves within the community remained marginal. But for those who married in, the genealogical gap, although it might recede, never disappeared. It became relevant to fewer situations, but under pressure on the group as a whole it became the disability of last resort, leaving even people who were prominent and prosperous in normal times potentially catastrophically vulnerable to exclusion from dwindling resources or even to expulsion or disposal. The genealogical disability of enslavement in Africa and the corresponding advantages to communities claiming them were no less enduring or heritable than the matrilineally exclusionary civic status of slavery eventually defined in the United States.[39]

Given the high value of ancestorless outsiders in communities of shared descent, the history of slaving in Africa followed the ways in which communities as wholes, as well as individuals within them, resorted, in differing ways, to outsiders to build up numbers and hence wealth and power to struggle among themselves and with one another in reaction to a succession of changing contexts. The specific strategies, in their initial stages always—by my definition of history as incremental—marginal, were largely opportunistic responses to momentary novelties. Novelty is by definition unplanned and uncoordinated and perceived only fragmentarily. Incipient change opens contexts to challengers to exploit for personal advantage, particularly for ones in disadvantaged, marginal positions. The generic initial contest, tens of thousands of years ago, would have been incipient communities capturing the loyalties of late hominid random individuals through intensely emotional collective ritual immolation of "captives of the community," as sketched in the preceding chapter.

After routinization of the successes of these strategies as the communal ethos, during the era of growing aridity in Africa some twenty thousand to twelve thousand years ago and consequent generalized population pressure,[40] ritualized immolation of captured enemies would have continued sporadically in comparably formative or fragile moments of building communities on bases other than the prevailing, institutionalized strategy of reproductive kinship. These community-creating resurrections of publicly performed and participatory bloodshed recurred at moments of desperation, a kind of convulsive catharsis of stress experienced collectively.[41] These moments, although no longer involving slaving as such, have continued in military, political, and commercialized modes into recent times, right down to contemporary mass genocides and slaughter and child soldiers set to maiming and killing of their own families by way of condemning them to very precarious places in gangs where they are brutalized and themselves threatened with death by systematically erratic and abusive leaders.

Weak parties throughout the world trapped in confined circumstances have turned to human slaughter at critical moments of collective, hence public, survival. Under external constraints they cannot displace violence into unifying plundering of others or into the military expansionism that consolidates political loyalty by generating wealth from abroad for internal payoffs or other incentives. Ironically, or tragically, modern globalization has enveloped the world within national boundedness and in this way inhibited these usual historical strategies of building community, all of them involving slaving. Correspondingly, the vulnerability of modern individualism has intensified individual anxieties, tending to produce implosive reactions rather than external plundering. Historical examples from Africa include late sixteenth-century Angola, where desperate refugees from the chaos of drought and the initial phases of Portuguese-supported raiding for captives to enslave formed efficaciously cohesive bands around extreme rituals of "cannibalism," culminating in public and ritualized infanticide by a female leader, who thus performed an absolute inversion of the presumption of maternal reproduction at the core of the communal ethos in the region.[42]

A parallel wanton, ceremonial, public consumption of slaves' lives marked the agonistic formative decades of early eighteenth-century Dahomey, one of the major military regimes that emerged from the chaos of Atlantic slaving in western Africa. The efficacy of immolation may be assessed by the eventual survival of the Dahomey polity, in spite of pervasive militarized violence in the region, until colonial conquest in the 1890s. The Dahomey polity rested on an unprecedentedly militarized ethic, one by definition external to the underlying communal ethos of lineage reproduction. In this fragile political context, warlords converted ad hoc battleground leadership into an institutionalized monarchy by lavishly slaughtering enemies captured, reportedly by the thousands, in so-called (by the British) annual customs. These mass immolations became famed in the Atlantic world because European slavers seized on their spectacularly calculated brutality to defend their own purchases of other captives, with claims that enslavement in the Americas, no matter how harsh, could be said at least to have saved innocent victims from even worse fates in Africa.

In terms of Dahomean political ideologies, however little the local communities subject to Dahomean warlords might have had in common otherwise, they could appreciate the power and protection they shared as witnesses to the fates of such radically externalized outsiders as the slaves the regime slaughtered.[43] Dahomean warlords in those decades confronted intense military pressures from rival polities, particularly powerful bands of cavalry warriors in Oyo, the major military confederation to the northeast. Blocked from continuing the external plundering that had supported the founding generation of Dahomey warriors, their successors the mid-eighteenth century perpetuated violence through in this involuted form. As military access to outsiders reached its logistical limits and systematized raiding for slaves receded into the remote interior in the later 1700s, the Dahomean heirs to this authoritating violence attempted to maintain the political integrity of their regime by still further involution, condemning internal political competitors as traitors or witches subject to sale into the Atlantic; they replaced the outsiders immolated to create a polity with insiders expelled to purify and maintain the presumed existing body politic.[44] The problematic of slaving in Africa, as elsewhere, was significantly political.

Change as Collective Continuity: Defining and Maintaining Ethnicity, ca. 2000 BCE–500 CE

Succeeding these immolatory slaving strategies of ancient origin (but of ongoing and renewable utility also in later parallel historical contexts of political fragility), local communities succeeded during the following ten millennia or so—from ca. 12,000 to around 2,000 BCE—by differentiating themselves collectively from their neighbors and by recruiting personnel into defined and continuing communities in as many ways as possible, including slaving. Beyond a primary emphasis on politicizing reproduction through various combinations of unilineal descent, which establishes unambiguous claims of only a single – maternal or paternal – side to children born of parents belonging to two such groups, these descent-defined communities also acquired isolated, vulnerable aliens. Slaving became one strategy among the many that Africans elaborated to develop and display the specific shared characteristics as markers of collective identities that colonial ethnographers later characterized as ethnic. That is to say that "ethnic" or rather, since they were not inherent qualities but calculated strategies of historical differentiation, ethnicized stereotypes were designed to display uniformity and solidarity to outsiders. Performed homogeneity also masked the intricate internal differentiation that held the group together around the mutually supportive relationships thus created. Their external contrasts were similarly complementary, not inherently conflictive, as modern media inevitably make them out to have been.[45] Internally, women brought in from outside through slaving, beyond adding to the reproductive capacity of the group, added potentially usefully distinctive experiences elsewhere to groups' carefully composed diversity.[46]

The historical ethos of slaving to maintain the communal environment of Africa was the inverse of slaving's association with progress in the linear historiology of modernity. In African thought, the historical responsibility of the living generation is not to push forward beyond its inherited present but to hark back to an imagined originary ancestral standard of harmony and balance, both within a community and also of the community as a whole in the context of its neighbors. This historiological ethic might be characterized as restorative, in contrast with progressive. The dynamic of historical change does not move whiggishly forward toward human perfection but drifts recurrently away from idealized integration and coherence to experienced dissolution and dissension. Historical actors in Africa must maintain their communities' solidarity and balance against ongoing disruptions from outside, that is, against change itself, as well as from the all-too-human tendencies of those within toward selfish greed, jealousies, and betrayal of the consensus that constitutes community. Africans know and accept the risks of novelty,[47] and tradition and antiquity are the collective standards of countervailing validity.

The expected predictable, structured relationships with neighbors depended on each reproducing community's defining and performing an identifiable façade of homogeneity. But, as with all historical processes, success led to stress as these strategies of constructing ethnicity eroded the circumstances that had rewarded their initiators. As time passed, groups that had consolidated in relatively open and easy circumstances of initial settlement grew in the numbers of people they assembled. Then they faced the necessity of intensifying the effort required to preserve the broad characteristics their fewer founding ancestors had shared spontaneously. As larger populations found the lands defined by earlier generations confining, they intensified their exploitation of them; life became more laborious, and heirs to inherited practices had to modify them.

One method of facing (internally), or rather denying (externally), these contradictions of change was to pass off the ignoble and often unpleasant but growing drudgeries of daily life to newcomers irrelevant to the antiquity and continuity of the locally born heirs to the group's collective identity. Slaving accordingly allowed full members of the community to continue to live or perform its defining, hence prestigious, inherited character. And so communities respected as potters or smiths or cattle lords might live up to their reputations by displacing cultivation or the carrying of water or gathering of firewood to vulnerable newcomers dismissible as originating in slaving. The external ethnic stereotype of homogeneity ideologically obscured the status of those actually able to live up to the collective legacy as a dwindling minority. We readily recognize the explicit parallels here with the cultural devaluation of slaves in the Americas, allowing Spaniards of humble standing in comparably corporative environments in Spain's American Indies to live like gentlemen by surrounding themselves with enslaved natives, and then Africans. In the nineteenth-century American South, honor became the equivalently dubious, fragile claim to respectability among indebted agricultural entrepreneurs struggling to live up to standards of agrarian gentility articulated, most famously, by Thomas Jefferson. In Africa, where ethnicity expressed one component of the radically less individualistic political culture, slaving may be said to have enabled the strategy of ethnicization itself to survive the historical challenges brought on by its own efficacy in supporting the growing populations that defined success in contexts based on human reproduction.

Throughout world history innovation has tended toward intensification of effort, and hence of greater toil for most, until the productivity gains from technology in the nineteenth-century North Atlantic. In this sense, other collectivities have also used slaving to mute the demands of history itself, recruiting outsiders to counter the otherwise erosive effects of earlier individuated initiative at the expense of whatever groupings they find themselves pressed to defend. The restorative African historical ethic expresses its explicit recognition of this dynamic by displacing innovations uncharacteristic of inherited identity but necessary to support the larger numbers of people who were the products, and definition, of earlier successes. Slaving in Africa was thereby integral to strategies of managing change, no less than the changes in the other parts of the world that Davis described as progress. But in Africa slaving reconciled novelty with a historiology of continuity. It may also be said, in all cases, African and otherwise, that slaving serves to maintain the gains of the few by displacing the burdens these would otherwise impose on the many onto outsiders who do not count in the moral calculus of the community. For modern westerners, the exclusion of slaves obscures the high costs—in effect, enabling the illusion—of progress. In modern times the enslaved also were involuntarily used to support the coalescence of nation-states as ideological—or political—collectivities imagined as homogeneous.[48]

In Africa, and again no less than elsewhere in the world, the morally charged communal ethos became an amoral collective ideology, marked more by what it concealed than by what it revealed about actual changing historical experiences. As internal differentiation between haves and have-nots increasingly divided these more and more territorially confined, nonetheless growing, and hence increasingly ethnicized communities, the declining proportions of the people heir to earlier strategies found themselves constrained to convert an initially successful historical strategy into the succeeding phase of denial of changing circumstances. Insiders entitled to privileges found themselves marginalized, in despised positions once displaced onto enslaved outsiders. The privileged few found it in their interests to mute their advantages to maintain the sense of solidarity with others supposed to be the same, and so ethnic ideologies grew to exaggerate external differentiation in relation to growing internal disparities. Internally they muted tensions, once again by displacing change—novelty perceived as inconsistent with the originary inspiration—onto outsiders.

As these ethnicized communities, nominally homogeneous but in fact sharing primarily a language sufficiently defined to mark insiders and to exclude outsiders as soon as they opened their mouths, distinguished themselves three thousand and two thousand years ago, they also consolidated themselves by exchanging personnel, mostly women, among themselves through marriages or other arrangements regulated collectively and thus legitimated. In times of conflict, groups took captured enemies as hostages, to hold temporarily and collectively against the prospect of returning them to their own, neighboring groups, in the interest of restoring the mutually beneficial engagements and maintaining their differentiated identities. In its collective engagement, this strategy extended relationships conducted in more tranquil times in terms of marriages into and through the inevitable moments of conflict.[49] Interdependence at this historical phase of growing integration both within and among intensely communal groups converted immolation of captive enemies to conditional internments of affiliated outsiders. The strategy of slaving moved from forming collective sensibilities around shared guilt in autonomous groups to maintaining the collectivities established in more confined spaces and to negotiating interests among them.

Slaves in Africa were well within, but explicitly not of, the groups that incorporated them to preserve—for declining proportions of quintessential insiders—ethnic characters formed in earlier, easier times when they became no longer sustainable by the strategies they preserved, at least as ideals, or rather ideologies, if not as practice.[50] At the same time, the collective identities that slaving in Africa preserved became increasingly politicized, as they grew in scale and as exchanges among them intensified. This strategic accent on what one might call restorative slaving would have prevailed broadly until the end of the era in Africa I have called classic, notionally around 500 CE. The efficacy of slaving is thereby evident in abundant recent ethnographic examples. Saharan Tuareg, or at least the small minority of blue-veiled aristocratic males astride high-bred white horses among them, managed to continue to present themselves as pure pastoralists long after (and well into the colonial period) they in fact came to depend on the labor of the despised agriculturalists among them, whom they acquired as slaves.[51] On the margins of the Kalahari Desert in southern Africa, Tswana cattle lords overcame the contradictions of basing comparably (ethnically) stereotyped prestige on maintaining large herds in very dry terrain by dispersing them widely, concentrating the people (wives, children, and other dependents) they assembled from such dispersals in viably moist and confined locations, and integrating modern Christian and democratic civic political strategies by displacing the inevitable dirty work onto the struggling foragers from the desert known as San.[52] In what is now southeastern Nigeria, Igbo maintained intensively agricultural local communities around highly ritualized male cultivation of yams throughout centuries of commercialization by displacing other, less prestigious aspects of social and cultural maintenance onto slaves.[53] From then on, collectivities—or rather, only the dwindling minorities within them able to live up to their ethnic posturing—resorted more and more intensively to strategies of slaving through a sequence of new historical circumstances that increasingly challenged both the communal ethos and the local autonomy of such groups. Outsiders naturalized as inherently others accordingly became enslaveable by attributed character rather than neighbors enslaved only occasionally and incidentally, and even then primarily redeemable.[54]

Kings as Marginal: Slaving as a Strategy of Composite Political Integration, ca. 500–1600 CE

Over the succeeding millennium, ca. 500–1600 CE, these strategies of community definition and maintenance, including slaving, succeeded sufficiently in integrating larger populations and in intensifying differentiation among them that the resulting communal ethos became a significant means of mobilizing even larger groups to compete over relatively constant and increasingly limiting pools of accessible resources.[55] Presumably, few relished living in this atmosphere of growing potential hostility, and so local and regional sets of groups devised a rich, diverse array of supradomestic methods of regulating tendencies toward conflict: that is, constituent local agricultural communities formed polities of composite or compound sorts. They were confederative networks rather than unitary in character, like centralized monarchical states, or homogeneous like the imagined communities of individuals constituting modern nations, at least theoretically. We should not confuse these African political strategies of incorporating diversity, or the utility in them of slaving, with the usual, even insistent, characterization of them in the historical literature on Africa as kingdoms or even empires. History traces strategies, not ideological structures, and particularly not this quite modern modeling of politics.

This compositional political strategy follows from the historiological premises already introduced. Additive African attitudes toward change consolidated the preceding local communities of many sorts politically by preserving them rather than replacing them with the sort of homogeneous polity implied by such terms as "kingdoms." Monarchies are singular, not compound; they are also composed of individual subjects rather than communities, similar (and theoretically homogenized) in their shared personal allegiances to a single ruler. In contrast, in Africa political strategies of composition added a level of recognized shared authority to their constituting components. These central figures embodied the whole and represented it primarily to the world beyond. Internally they were subject to the prior, constituting components of the polity, often represented in a council with powers to name and to replace the figurehead. The politics of gaining access to this externalized symbol of unity—thought of as separate from the ongoing primary world of reproduction and marriage and other alliances—were intense and constantly negotiated. Balances of power within them alternated between the council and the chief-delegate according to the changing urgencies of needs within and challenges from outside. In times of threat from external enemies, the figurehead, or literally often the personification of the whole, emerged as war leader. In times demanding reunification among feuding internal factions, they acted as prophets or as mediums for contacting unifying ancestors. In this historicized sense, these personages were more contingent reserves against disaster (that is, disintegration) than authorities of a pervasive presence and power. Growing contacts with merchant outsiders presented opportunities for such literally internally marginal figures to aggrandize their personal power, which they implemented by slaving.

Like people in earlier militarized polities external to the primary domestic communities constituting them in Asia, Africans employed slaving to preserve political systems of this composite sort into the ethnographic present or recent past, which is how historians know a great deal about them. Or rather, if we abandon the obsession in the historical literature with treating Africa by limited or false analogies to modern, implicitly national states, we see how politicians in Africa constructed and operated coherent polities not as abstract, imagined institutions but as constant, face-to-face negotiations among experiential communities. Then we might understand the historical efficacy of political slaving in Africa as a further way of updating and integrating local collective strategies of reproduction in broader, more intrusive historical contexts of integrating outsiders through militarization and commercialization.

These African "middle ages" (as sometimes characterized, though not without more than muted overtones of progressive teleology), notionally from 500 to 1500 CE, were thus an era of innovative political consolidation among the communities constituted earlier, in which slaving served both the challengers to and the defenders of inherited communal integrity. Confederative politics, on the one hand, added political incentives for local groups to build up their respective numbers to compete on the larger scales of emerging political integration, in this way intensifying slaving strategies of the sort that had long maintained community continuity through the currents of time. On the other hand, expanded political integration also displaced the supposed enslaveable barbarians to more remote, unfamiliar communities beyond the expanded sense of politicized community thus formed. The political *pax* reduced local opportunities to acquire captives of enslaveable alienness, in favor of slaving by large, long-range, militarized expeditionary forces of the polity, or, at a still further extreme, through traders able to conduct goods and prisoners over inter-regional scales. The historical dynamics of military expansion in Africa were no less contradictory than in Asia.

Politicized security meant that, while the relatively low, only occasional, incidence of hostage taking and even slaving among neighbors probably decreased, incentives grew simultaneously to intensify slaving externally to degrees that ultimately transformed the institutions required to support it. A metaphor of electrical voltage highlights the potentiality of such historical tension—meeting emergent challenges with only inherited inadequate, because by definition outdated, means to meet them—to motivate significant change: the historical flashpoint[56] comes at the moment of a circumstantial appearance of new means of acquiring isolated strangers from beyond the no-longer-viable range of social, political, or cultural accommodation and of redeemable captivity. The potential for this historical lightning of change to strike becomes all the greater because the costs of political consolidation on these scales grow beyond the capability of the ordinary farmers and others protected by them to sustain them. The historical context becomes labile, susceptible to sudden, unpredictable change. In the face of impending chaos, human resources from increasingly inaccessible alien populations become all the more necessary to conserve what they and preceding generations had attained.

Schematically, four such means of slaving reached historically efficacious levels in different parts of Africa during the millennium or so after ca. 500 CE. Integrative opportunities arose first, opportunistically enough, through consolidation of relatively individuated personal networks formed through commercial contacts. In African communal contexts, commerce distinguishes contingent encounters among individuals beyond the range of, and hence independent of, the ongoing multilayered group-to-group exchanges long enabled by complementary neighborly ethnic and (unilineal) genealogical differentiation. Individuals could support themselves beyond the range of their home communities by specializing in such commercial contacts, becoming traders.[57] Individuated mobility, rather than the prevailing communal stability, became their game. As such, they were strangers in the perceptions of the domestic communities they visited and not morally responsible for the integrity of the groups they visited. Such itinerant merchants' contacts in remote locations allowed them to remove (among other *things* separated from their human creators and contacts) captive outsiders or members of communities deemed undesirable and hence dangerous. So long as the numbers of these hazardous human materials remained modest, such undesirables could be exposed as witches and expelled to groups far enough away from their home areas that buyers could effectively control them, isolated and culturally disabled as they arrived.

This hypothesized contact between local residential groups and mobile traders describes instances when such enslaved people were taken in by communities or in the name of the collectivity and not claimed outright by individuals within them, consequently generating the subtle dynamics of slaving internal to the communal ethos described in chapter 2. Such acquired aliens were not numerous enough to become the norm or a routinized means for their captors to effect cumulative change. They became parts of the collective patrimony, along with its lands and other inalienable assets, effectively capitalized real human property, though affiliated to the group rather than members of it. Women acquired through slaving were qualified as wives or otherwise designated in terms of the internally structuring categories of kinship and affinity. They were the kind of people, slaves in their origins, whom later European ethnographers, insensitive to the considerations of descent motivating the Africans they observed, recognized only negatively and paradoxically as unsalable slaves—one of the clichés of ethnographic observation—in their own narrowly commercial and, in the context of the slave trade, self-serving terms.[58] But for Africans, relational origins, not alterable material conditions of life or personal achievements, defined slaves perpetually as adjuncts without ancestors and as lacking integral positions among those who belonged more fully, by inheritances independent of their patrons.

At least from early in the last millennium before the current era regional traders in western Africa developed dispersed communities specialized in moving the complementing products of the Sahara Desert and the grasslands to its south.[59] Other traders in the vast riverine network of Africa's equatorial forests developed parallel networks in the first millennium of the current era.[60] Judging from strategies that later mercantile communities followed, these trading groups would themselves have grown by taking in and training the alien people they acquired, like themselves strangers without connections in the domestic communities they connected to one another.[61] Traders resident in these diasporas were independent aliens in the communities where they lived, though not incorporated by their trading partners as slaves and with the substantial strengths of their networks. Rather, they explicitly maintained the marginality that seems to have motivated slavers in context after context throughout world history,[62] so that they could deal with sellers and buyers at arm's-length. Rather than being obligated to distribute whatever they might gain from transactions among kin or clients, they could accumulate assets for themselves, hoarding both material commodities and people as retinues of dependents.

At that point they were on their way to becoming traders who staffed retinues of their own through slaving, independently of the surrounding reproducing communities. These assets, human and material, they could invest in staffing further exchanges rather than in consumption or integration in the community by distributing them to build and confirm relationships. In a communal environment, slaving was traders' primary means to individuation and capital investment, in wealth in people.[63] Material assets they conveyed from sellers to buyers. Human assets they integrated into quasi-communal collectivity, called houses, filled with loyal personnel of slave origins, trained to protect and transport goods.[64] But they were strategic collectivities, commercial enterprises rather than ethical communities. It is worth emphasizing, to anticipate later changes in the European Atlantic, that the complementary differentiation of the African communal ethos left production in the hands of the resident reproducing communities, among whom diasporic merchants lived, linked affinally by marriages; a major change in the Atlantic was European merchants' move there beyond exchange to invest in production itself. European Christians in the same millennium had similarly segregated capitalist accumulation in communities of exclusively and excludingly Jewish descent. The parallels recur between Africans' and others' historical strategies.

The African traders, by connecting producing and consuming communities over considerable distances, stimulated groups formed around reproducing strategies to produce material, incipiently commodity, surpluses beyond what they could store or redistribute and consume among themselves. Merchants both stimulated and enabled further ethnicized specialization and differentiation among these communities, and on growing scales of both space and specialization. Communities that departed from their inherited domestic character in order to survive in changed times thus opened internal gaps between their central and their increasingly marginalized members. They blurred the threat that growing internal differentiation brought to collectively claimed heritages of homogeneity by incorporating other outsiders to perform the tasks that violated the collective character that some had had to abandon in order that the wealthy and powerful among them could preserve it for themselves. Merchants held prime positions to acquire and deliver the outsiders, for whom they simultaneously also promoted growing needs, thus stimulating slaving in a self-perpetuating dialectical process. Traders grew by recruiting their own personnel through slaving, and by the same means they provided alien personnel to resident communities of producers and sellers. To the still limited extent that these dynamics prevailed before, say, the seventeenth century, slaving propelled direct exchanges of specialized commodities for the people who produced them. This exchange was an African uncommercialized version of the economic exchange that flourished later across the Atlantic, as Africans raised the children who were sold to become slaves in the Americas to produce commodities that financed further slaving.

The second means of gaining regular access to enslaveable aliens in the era 500–1500 CE developed out of contacts with specialized and well capitalized merchants from the fully commercialized and individuated Islamic economic sectors of the Mediterranean basin and the Indian Ocean. After about the eighth century, consolidation of the Muslim œcumene throughout both these vast regions brought commercial credit, the historically significant (that is, enabling) aspect of these contacts, to the domestic economies that slaving up to then had partly preserved in both western and eastern Africa. Incrementally, as historical change always proceeds, such local slaving put local African merchants in touch with large, external markets for helpless, isolated captives, particularly women.[65] Consider the enabling potential of large quantities of trade goods introduced into the domestic networks of personal obligation in Africa, where distributions of material wealth as gifts otherwise established enduring connections and community. This external credit financed unprecedented amounts of debt, that is, in degrees of human dependency within communities in Africa. But the debt was commercial, that is, personal, not collective, with resources introduced from beyond the local networks of intricate, balancing reciprocities. Further, debts from mobile strangers were to be repaid, or terminated, rather than retained to create and preserve relationships. From the perspective of African collectivities, one concluded exchanges with itinerant strangers rather than with resident neighbors as sales canceling the mutual obligations otherwise implicit in transfers of personal or collective wealth. African communities were no less vulnerable than Asian peasants to commercial debt.

Outsider merchants competed with one another commercially by offering trade goods on credit to individuals eager to advance within their communities. The African debtors, if they could, paid off their obligations to itinerant outsiders with commodities, mostly extracted; if they could not, again as peasants in agrarian Asia also did, they conceded dependents. Those dependents could be children of the community, if necessary, since by the prevailing doctrines of collective responsibility the group as a whole was liable for its members' commitments to outsiders. However, if an individual debtor exercised exclusive control over dependents of slave origin, these adjuncts would be less of a loss to the group as a whole and hence be the first to be conceded. African traders taking dependents in these circumstances were potentially interested in keeping the people they acquired as clients or as members of the commercial communities they were building. But African traders were intermediaries, in debt also to external creditors of their own, and they were in positions to dispose of the people they acquired in exchange for further material resources, or, in highly organized commercial economies, ultimately for currency. People enslaved in these commercialized circumstances had become liquid assets in a sense closer to the modern notion of personal, fundamentally fungible property in humans, isolated consummately in the constant potential for disposability in which they lived.

We must therefore observe a clear distinction, as Africans did, between people maneuverable within frameworks of domestic alliance or through political networks, where the communal ethos accorded them degrees of respect and security, and the highly contingent status of others vulnerable to disposal to strangers, or, as Europeans saw their status, saleable. Transfers of the former were conditional, potentially reversible; they maintained relationships. Sales were definitive; they severed relationships. The increased liquidity in human holdings that commercial credit promoted, the accent on transferability (or sale of personal property), and the endlessly recurring isolation for the enslaved would become an overriding aspect of slaving in the highly commercialized Atlantic.[66]

Trade goods offered on credit enabled speculators within the domestic economy, even otherwise marginal upstarts, to acquire personal dependents in anticipation of doing business with outsiders on individually liberating terms like these. Commercial credit enabled young men marginal to the ethos of community and already inclined to evade the restrictions on youth rooted deep within its generational hierarchy by slaving. Stockpiled dependents acquired through slaving were the prototypes of the isolated people whom later African creditors, working with European merchant finance, routinely accumulated to hedge speculation in commercial debt contracted in much greater and eventually transformative volumes. In this manner, from the seeds of slaving as a strategy of personal gain in communal contexts grew the competitive and eventually pervasive resort to debt provided by Europeans in the eighteenth century, paid off in people, in the most commercialized parts of Atlantic Africa to construct political and military power in towering proportions.

The dynamic, escalating processes of commercialized slaving in collective contexts thus highlighted in their eventual, starkest form had first gained momentum in Africa half a millennium before the first Portuguese probed tentatively along the continent's Atlantic coasts in the fifteenth century. Over the two or three centuries from ca. 800 to ca. 1100, diasporas of traders from Mediterranean North Africa, many of them Muslim, though less well financed, had developed commercialized transactions all along the southern edges of the Sahara Desert in western Africa. They had incrementally extended anomalous and occasional, only incipiently commercial local and regional exchanges to routine borrowing from Muslim sources of commercial credit based in the desert and in North Africa. Individual speculators south of the desert built up inventories of captives in anticipation of selling them, or invested their gains from dealing with foreign creditors in personal dependents of alien origin. Some managed to surround themselves with retinues whom they could mobilize to assert themselves personally within their home communities or to pressure their neighbors.

To characterize these slavers in terms of the recurrent global historical patterns of slaving, they were individuals marginal to the communal ethos but with effective numbers of slaves under their exclusive control. They could not only build trading houses of their own but also establish political power of a personal sort, that is, outside the existing networks of collaboration that the communal ethos deemed legitimate. By the time thirteenth-century Muslim travelers began to record their impressions of these African political systems, warriors whom they regarded as rulers were claiming individual autocratic power militarily, with horses, primarily by surrounding themselves with retainers of slave origin. Slaving, as it had millennia earlier throughout ancient southwestern Asia and the classical Mediterranean, became the means by which powerful individuals south of the Sahara, styled rulers but operating strategically as warlords, imposed themselves on the otherwise collective ethos of composite politics with varying degrees of arbitrary force, often outright violence, exercised through retinues of slave origin. The third strategy of slaving in Africa, as elsewhere, thus contributed to creating and maintaining personal power of a distinctively military character.[67]

From the ninth century onward, these overlords—in Ghana (Wagadu), Mali, Songhai, and other polities less well known—created the "empires of the western Sudan" famed in conventional narratives of Africa's past. However, the imperial analogy to European ideologies of monarchy only very inaccurately represented the African communal contexts and the compositional political strategies and the slaving necessary to support warrior regimes largely independent of the underlying resident communities. Their commanding aristocracies relied on wide-ranging military plundering of others to create and maintain their autonomy. The relatively personalistic political networks these African warlords created by slaving contrasted strongly with the integrated, but impersonal, and theoretically homogeneous civic political communities that we think of today as states, which inherently exclude slaving within them. If not as early as Ghana (before ca. 1050), certainly the later rulers of Mali

(ca. 1250) and other, later competitors to the east imported substantial numbers of horses from north of the Sahara Desert to deploy as military mounts,
and they used the mobility the horses enabled, as well as the overwhelming
force they could deliver, to consolidate unprecedented degrees of personal
influence over regions vast by any standard. They systematically raided for
captives among vulnerable agricultural populations living beyond the areas
they controlled, and nominally protected.[68] Many, if not most, of the slaves
these cavalry raiders seized were retained to staff the considerable infrastructure—economic, police, administrative—needed to maintain the households
and personal networks they thus consolidated, relatively independently of
the farming communities whom they protected from the depredations of
rival warlords. The warriors thus supported themselves through slaving more
than using local populations for direct support through tribute or taxation.[69]

These warlords sold considerable numbers of these captives to Muslim
merchants from the Sahara to pay for the horses that gave them such military
power. By the sixteenth century the resulting arms race had escalated to degrees
that provoked the outsider populations threatened by cavalry raiding and
enslavement to flee to defensible locations, where they formed new communities of refugees. Thirteenth- to fifteenth-century Benin (in the forests near the
Gulf of Guinea) was a militarized defensive reaction to and extension of these
commercialized strategies and their militarized consequences. However, the
protection from cavalry attacks that forests offered prevented militarization
with horses there; hence the historical process of militarization in Benin was less
mobile, being built around defensive walls, and based on collective, communal
mobilization of manpower. The Mossi of the remote, dry headwaters of the
Volta River come to mind as other examples of militarized fugitives, and there
were many others.[70] These cavalry-based warrior strategies of slaving, unique
in Africa in that era, were a fourth strategy of reaching and capturing people
of sufficient alienness that they were routinely enslaveable, therefore also in
numbers that made the warlords' reliance on them significant and cumulative
in effect.[71] These warrior regimes increasingly took up the Muslim religion of
their mercantile backers and breeders of military horses—the international
arms dealers of their era—and used Islam's tolerance of capturing and enslaving
so-condemned unbelievers as legal justification for their systematic political
uses of slaving.[72] The mass conversions to Islam that have succeeded one
another throughout western Africa since then began as vulnerable unbelievers sought protection by clustering together under the banners of the faith.[73]

As the Portuguese simultaneously felt their way down western Africa's
Atlantic coastline in the fifteenth century, slaving as a militarized political
strategy had already incorporated *most* people in western Africa in new,

more intensely and defensively politicized aggregates, defined increasingly in relation to war, not reproduction: raiders, refugees, Muslim believers protected from Islamic raiding, unbelievers vulnerable to raiding, and merchant purveyors of the captives whom the raiders seized, most of them also Muslim.[74] Increasing proportions of the people living within each of the contexts so delineated owed their presence wherever they were living to prior removal and to proximate (social) origins through reincorporation, that is, through slaving. Origins in these new collectivities, and the ethnicized identities they created to consolidate and defend them, came to express not the continuity of the reproducing groups into which people had been born but their recent, individual, shared experiences of involuntary uprooting and transfers from heterogeneous backgrounds through calculated strategies of slaving. Ethnicity grew as the ideology of identities shared among relative strangers, collectivities no less imagined as communities than modern nation-states. As a historical strategy, it was an ideology rather than the inheritance from a shared past as asserted by traditions of origin. Paradoxically, political integration at this transcending level—and its neo-ethnic expressions—arose directly and in multiple ways from the individuation of capture, or flight, and self-defense. As is often the case, the restorative tenor of African historiology represented as most ancient what was in fact most recent, and the urge to portray unity to threatening outsiders obscured the centrality of slaving to the internal strategies of creating it.[75]

Atlantic Credit and the Corruption of the Communal Ethos, 1600–1900

The fifth, and transformative, phase in the historical sequence of slaving strategies in Africa developed in the seventeenth century from dramatically increased introductions of commercial credit along the continent's Atlantic coasts. Credit in these enabling proportions did not reach Africa with the mid-fifteenth century probings of underfinanced Portuguese but only in the later 1600s, when Dutch and English merchants introduced trade goods in much greater quantities. So general a sketch of the historical process of slaving in Africa as I undertake here cannot pause to delineate all the incremental steps along the path that African borrowers followed as they used the goods imported to assemble and retain retinues for purposes other than the inherited emphasis of the communal ethos on reproduction. The significant aspect running through them all was that they increasingly focused on personal rather than collective authority, power rather than representation, and increasingly assembled people through slaving rather than through reproduction.

To proceed responsibly, historians need to reason along the lines of the intentions of the people in Africa who desired and acquired imports, thus moving beyond the conventional understanding of this tragic period in Africa's history largely in terms of such abstract and animate externalities as the slave trade. The Africans' side of the story centers on men marginal to the prevailing communal ethos, men who primarily bought imports, on credit, to acquire and retain people whom they could control as personal wealth and hence also as power. What the Europeans saw as the era of the Atlantic slave trade, the initially marginal Africans engaged directly with them saw as an era of opportunity in acquiring imports from the Atlantic to buy into their historic collectivities, to exploit the tensions of both the communal ethos and the composite polity. They could not have anticipated the tragic disintegration of these African values that followed.

From these strategic perspectives, the issues in Africa centered on who could get their hands on the trade goods that European merchants offered on credit and whom they could use them to attract and on what terms. For the succession of marginal interests in various regions in Africa who engaged European merchants, the Europeans' abundant resources of commercial credit were means of increasing the numbers of people over whom they could exercise personal control as well as the degrees of the control they could impose. They tried to minimize the proportions—half, or less?—of the people they consigned to the Europeans to obtain the imports they needed to keep others. They began by distributing the imported goods, often borrowed from European merchants or their African agents, through the local networks of domestic affiliation and dependency and—as became necessary—also beyond them through commercialized contacts.

Later in the seventeenth century in both western and central Africa, European commercial credit inflated these domestic strategies to intensities that propelled competition to violent levels. Borrowers had more goods to enlist or capture or buy people than they could find people to attract or acquire. The violence of this competition provoked refugees to form militarized regimes, costly as any others elsewhere, that protected the populations within their logistical and administrative reach. To sustain the costs of these regimes over generations, successors turned to predatory raiding, with human resources obtained by capturing the inhabitants of more remote but reachable areas. The slaving states of this era, centered on the eighteenth century, are prominent in the conventional histories of Africa, though primarily as unproblematized states. They included the Fuuta Jallon in far western Africa and Segu in the valley of the upper Niger River, Asante, Dahomey, Oyo, and Benin along the lower Guinea Coast, and Lunda and the so-called Ovimbundu warlords in western central Africa.

The limited space of a single essay precludes detailing the dynamics of these incremental transitions from militarization for protection from early slaving to its all-but-inevitable extension to offensive raiding for captives to support costs of militarization no less overwhelming than those of earlier warrior regimes in southwestern Asia,[76] or later repetitions of the process in southeastern Africa in the late eighteenth and early nineteenth centuries. The general pattern concentrated violence in a localized frontier that moved inland from the coasts throughout the seventeenth and eighteenth centuries.[77] By the early nineteenth century, the primary raiding had reached its geographical and demographic limits: the margins of the Sahara in western Africa and the very heart of the southern parts of continent. Warfare then become implosive, in multiple senses. The warlord regimes sustaining themselves by raiding for captives were raiding one another rather than expanding at the expense of vulnerable, less organized populations. Driven by the growing escalation, some were turning to imports of modern weapons to keep ahead of their rivals.

But the greater, less violent implosion exploited the denser populations built up nearer the coast by retaining female slaves. As the frontiers of slaving violence receded far into the interior, merchant sectors of the coastal regions were becoming strong enough to assert control of the military legacy of the now-strained warlord regimes. European mercantile interests not infrequently supported these moves, as happened in Dahomey in the 1830s and elsewhere in collaboration with African mercantile communities, like Asante's growing involvement with Hausa traders from the Sokoto caliphate. In Angola in the 1750s, Portuguese-linked merchants installed the successor to the warlord regime in Kasanje, the main slave-supplying polity east of Luanda.[78] Later oral traditions recalled this man as having abandoned the relationships that constituted the composite structure of Kasanje; he was the first in the long line of warriors who "kept his trade goods in his compound" rather than distributing them to consolidate his composite regime.[79]

Where merchant groups gained the political initiative, they distributed imported goods locally on terms of credit that obligated debtors far beyond their means to repay, other than by conceding dependents of their own. This commercial strategy of slaving—in effect, a loan shark operation—repeated the pattern of intrusions of southwest Asian merchants on indebted peasant populations three millennia earlier, but without the protection that monarchical patrons in the eastern Mediterranean had provided to peasant subjects and with the full militarized power of the political regimes to back it. In nineteenth-century Africa, the slavers had gained political authority and military power and so distorted the legal processes they controlled to enslave the people whom they claimed to protect.

So many people in Africa had been uprooted by slaving and retained as slaves by the nineteenth century, that the populations nominally subject to these slaving lords had no more than marginal positions at best in the underlying resident communities. However, the African restorative historiology meant that the discourse of community survived as an ideological shell. Slaving had intensified from a means to build personal political power independently of the communal ethos to a means of assembling subject populations of otherwise isolated, politically marginal individuals, thus challenging the ethos itself. The community survived as an ideology because it made collectivities liable for the debts of any of their individual members. Individuals marginalized by these processes turned to them to gain within by borrowing without. Motivated to excess, they could eliminate their rivals by exposing them to seizure and sale. Those exposed to such risks in turn engaged in slaving themselves to accumulate slave dependents whom they might concede to the extortionate world in which they lived. And when they failed, as they were systematically pressured to do, the internal tensions generated led communities to search within themselves for the human greed to which they attributed the dissensions, even victimization, they were experiencing—and which, by the inherited standards of the communal ethos, they were also charged with restoring. They depleted their numbers further by condemning their own members as witches and selling them to slavers only too happy to relieve struggling communities of suspicions of the disloyalty they were provoking.[80] The African experience of slaving, internalized through debt distributed through existing channels of theoretically reciprocal loyalties, rather than more open violence against outsiders, thus became betrayal on every level. At this ultimate stage of commercialized intensification, in the idiom of collective solidarity, the individuation of commercialized slaving had created a plague of witches.

The history of slaving in Africa sketched in this chapter stresses that the value of the newcomers to their masters could reside in either their sheer presence or in what they might produce, depending on whether the slavers sought advantage in terms of altering relations within the community in their favor—in which case sheer presence counted—or later outside it by commercial means—in which case product prevailed in ways closer to the modern Western stereotype of slaves as belabored. Presence counted more than product also in the commercialized phases of slaving; with debt looming, small groups of kin inventoried large numbers of people, acquired by purchases with the imported goods they had borrowed, in anticipation of forced foreclosure. An implication of this contrast is that commercial contacts, with strangers to the community by definition, were strategically cognate with slaving, dangerously so from the perspective of the community's tranquillity. This distinction between assimilative presence and instrumental productivity is an observer's abstraction; with witches everywhere presence was also instrumental in containing them. By the nineteenth century in central Africa, where the ethos I have termed communal has prevailed even into modern times, communities distinguished the enslaved people they retained, designating them differently from those whom they acquired with the intent of selling them.

As history, each of these steps represented an initial intensification of strategies of slaving that had previously enabled success: bulking up a relational community with outsiders, as slaves, enabling individuals within it marginalized by this process to attempt to recover their positions, winning the struggles among component communities that characterized every succession to the central positions in composite polities, and then confronting the consequences of paying off the external debt they had taken on to do so, while simultaneously facing growing costs of defending the gains they had made. The costly second stage of maintaining early, low-investment gains occasioned violence, competitively so, and in the eighteenth century militarization was pervasive. As militarization reached its logistical limits mercantile suppliers gained accordingly, as earlier in Asia. In the late eighteenth and early nineteenth centuries they converted the collective responsibilities of the lingering ethos of community to collective liabilities. Historical processes in Africa were no less incremental than anywhere else in the world.

The inflationary impact of European credit came not only from its absolute volume, large as it became by previous standards, but also from its overwhelmingly rapid rate of growth. Given time—and I will risk the hypothetical counterfactual, since it involves timing, and time is central to my emphasis on understanding history as process arising from slow, incremental extensions—established authorities in Africa might have channeled smaller quantities of imports through their existing networks, if and as populations grew proportionately, and if and as they had had time to invest in infrastructure. Given time, they might have diverted enough of the assets they gained into productive technologies and into monetized economies and thus attracted productive workers by means other than violent extraction. But Africans enjoyed no such leisure. As it was, the unprecedentedly rapid rate at which the much larger financial capabilities of European merchant-capitalists flooded Africa with credit, particularly after about the 1670s, exceeded the ability of established interests to expand the human resources they controlled and direct their efforts to pay for the trade goods they received in commodities. In chapter 4 I will consider slaving in the Americas in this same context of growing European, particularly British, financial capacity.[81]

As collective debtors to the exploding financial capacities of Europe, Africans built short-term commercial capacity rather than investing in infrastructure and production for the longer term. They therefore turned first to low-investment extracted commodities—gold, ivory, dyewoods, tree gums, and other accessible hunted and gathered exports—to pay on the deficit in their balance of payments with the Atlantic. Capturing people to sell was an incremental extension of these strategies of extraction, as Africans drained existing supplies of the commodities they extracted and as demand in the Americas for captive laborers grew. In the competitive rush to survive the scramble for European credit, ambitious individuals—merchants and chiefs authoritative primarily outside composite polities, or marginalized or alienated members within them, including women seeking escape from their patriarchal aspects, refugees from the raiders (themselves often turning raiders in order to survive), and eventually people who themselves had originated as slaves—motivated by their positions on the margins of these domestic collectivities, seized opportunities, often violently, to improve their positions by slaving.

And their slaving in turn worsened the positions of many more. Their successors depended more and more on acquiring and distributing imports to maintain positions they had inherited without other means to maintain them. Under these pressures, commercial competition repeatedly spilled over into violence, and the violence produced captives, who made slaving the preferred or most efficacious route to accumulating the dependents who constituted power. By the nineteenth century, warlords were absorbing entire, formerly autonomous rural communities into the retinues of slaves who surrounded them, some deployed in raiding, more employed to extract or produce commodities, and many assembled in new commercial collectivities built around transporting the new range of bulky commodity exports, including palm oil, groundnut oil, ivory, and wild rubber. As the increasing quantities of imported goods depreciated against constant (or locally depleted) supplies of people available as dependents, African slavers trapped themselves in an inflationary spiral of borrowing more to acquire less. Importers from the Atlantic faced a vastly expanded sequel to the deficit balances of international payments to Muslim merchants that had escalated slaving in the western Sudan during preceding centuries, coincidentally with the resort of Italians in the Renaissance Mediterranean to slaving to cover their own trading deficits to Muslims in the eastern Mediterranean. The tragedy was a historically revealing and humanly terrifying example of the unintended consequences of slaving. Adopting means external to the old communal ethos to seek respect within it, financed by European commerce, ultimately eroded community integrity, leaving ethnic solidarity and mutually balanced kinship as hollow

ideological covers for rampant individual ambition, aggression, and accumulation through slaving.

Africans' primary uses of captives to build human retinues rather than
connections generated their sales of other people to Europeans as a strategy secondary to sustaining the internal process. Sugar in the New World
and commercialization in Europe extended an emerging Atlantic economy
centered on African gold and American silver to acquiring people in Africa,
as slaves, also as a secondary option, for interests in Europe marginal to the
main Atlantic game. During the era of growing commercial credit from the
Atlantic, the violence in Africa arising from competition to control supplies of
imports produced more captives than even the slavers could support from the
human resources they commanded. Contrasts in ethnicized terms hardening
within lines formed out of growing conflicts lessened the moral problem of
such slaving in Africa, and little or no sense of ethical responsibility extended
to aliens more inventoried than integrated, even marginally. Even less did
African communities attempting to preserve their integrity by expelling suspected witches regret the losses of those whom they expelled.

Through processes too complex and varied to attempt even to sketch here,
the excess people ended up being sent off toward buyers at the coast. Women
and children could be controlled more easily than men, and—beyond the
other considerations in play, particularly the ability of mature females to
reproduce—slavers made the obvious choices: they sent young men off in
proportions that produced the nearly two-to-one male majorities among the
captives who ended up being taken across the Atlantic and kept the females
in a losing pursuit of the communal ethos of reproduction they had lost. The
Bobangi, a large and prosperous nineteenth-century trading collectivity of
canoe men along the middle Congo River explained as much, when they attributed the sterility of the women they had bought, caused by the venereal
diseases rampant in the region, to the anger of the communal ancestors whom
they had abandoned in pursuit of individual wealth.[82]

Conclusions—Slaving, History, and Africa

Slaving as history arises from motivations generated within a historically
coherent collectivity, around competition for unequally distributed internal
resources, and thus from the ongoing tensions that ideologies (that is, historicized structures)[83] are created to contain. Efforts directed externally gain
momentum because they opportunistically exploit other imbalances and hence
energies and historical dynamics without. As in the other parts of the world
outlined in chapter 2, slaving in Africa had long been a significant means

by which marginal figures effected internal changes with external human resources.

In Africa, the axis of marginality lay along the dimension of the collectivity's suppression of individual (male) ambition and personal accumulation. From the twelfth century, commercial credit from Muslim North Africa financed militarization in sub-Saharan western Africa, which African warlords managed by raiding for captives, some of whom staffed their personal regimes and others of whom they sold to the international arms dealers who supplied the imported horses at the core of the military escalation. The cascading warfare they set off along with the corresponding commercialization predisposed others and the trading diasporas supporting them to engage the underfinanced Portuguese when they appeared in the fifteenth century. The Dutch and English later introduced much greater quantities of European mercantile credit, which intensified militarized strategies of slaving in Atlantic Africa to epochal proportions as the terms of the exchange moved in their favor, throughout the eighteenth century. European credit became a principal means by which ambitious individuals succeeded, drawing more and more of the personnel of domestic communities of the continent into the commercial world of the Atlantic.

Or rather, to restate the process in terms of African historical dynamics, slavers in Africa captured and integrated isolated strangers into new pseudocommunities by increasingly violent means and eventually by commercial methods of indebtedness backed by the force in which they had invested. In Africa's restorative historiology, they converted the ethos of community to an ideology obscuring their fundamental violation of its reciprocities, applying it more and more to collectivities—some ethnic, others political, and more and more of them fundamentally entrepreneurial—consisting of people whom they had acquired by slaving. The further intensification of slaving for internal purposes in the nineteenth century, long noted by historians as a bitterly ironic extension of slaving to commodity production occasioned by British suppression of exports of people to the Americas, was thus not a transformative change but merely a further incremental development of African strategies of slaving dating to the beginnings of history. Militarization and commercialization in Africa had stimulated slaving in a process that paralleled earlier interactions of merchants and warriors in Asia and Europe. By the time European colonial authorities in Africa attempted to estimate the proportions of people in the generation living in 1900 who had been captured or traded in the most commercialized areas, slaves were large majorities, in a few areas approaching 80 or 90 percent of the population. The militarily dominant Sokoto caliphate in what is now northern Nigeria harbored the largest number of slaves living under a single political authority anywhere in the world.[84]

The contextualized historical dynamics of slaving that underlie this book rescue Africa from the obscurity to which the conventional presumptions of progressive historiology have condemned it. However much these historical processes are not what the contemporary politics of race and slavery may lead some to wish to read, I have gone out of my way here to indicate some of the parallels between processes of slaving in Africa and those in the more familiar Asian and European contexts introduced in the preceding chapter. The same dynamics will emerge again in the final chapter, on slaving in the modern Americas. Referencing the African domestic contexts of the sorts sketched at the start of this chapter, historians no longer have to imagine Africans as passive victims of European aggression in an Africa homogenized by modern racialist and sometimes still racist imaginings of a continent thereby rendered without slavery—and also, not coincidentally, without history in any autonomous, dynamic, dialectical register. Far from the innumerable passive victims in Africa, with only a few active agents reduced to externally oriented collaborators, at an epistemological level African historical energies pursued through slaving in fact enabled the processes usually conceded to outsiders in varying phrasings of such abstractions as European expansion and the Atlantic slave trade.

However difficult these African processes may be to accept, African buyers of European wares delivered nearly all of the captives sold for transport to slavery (mostly) in the Americas. My notes here only hint at the great volume of incontestable documentation of the tragedy. Further, Africans who sold enemies, aliens, suspected witches, criminalized political rivals, debtors, and others who posed the threat of individuation in a communal ethos had reasons for doing so, personally and in the short run, that we can recognize— however much we also lament the deep longer-term human collective costs that proceeded from the unintended consequences to the whole of what they gained as individuals. That is, historians understand any process as broad and multiplistic as Atlantic slaving historically primarily in terms of the local processes that motivated its participants. The local processes are, in turn, understandable historically only as fully contextualized in, and thus enabled by, the transcending cumulative process.

For people who sought to accumulate dependents in a continent that valued people above all, credit from commercial economies in the Mediterranean area, then in the Indian Ocean region,[85] and eventually by European merchants in the Atlantic became a prevailing means by which marginal interests got the jump on more established predecessors, to eventually implosive intensities. They engaged equally marginal merchants from Islamic lands, then marginal Christians from the Atlantic as well as others from the western Indian Ocean, to obtain commodities that they used to acquire what they cherished most: people of all sorts, increasingly including slaves, first by violence and then by commercial debt. It is a general pattern of world history that domestic economies, like those in Africa, long on people and short on goods for them to consume, transfer the people they have on hand when they come into contact with commercial economies, which are countervailingly long on commodities and short on people to produce and consume them. The historical dynamics of slaving in Africa, doubly difficult as they are for conventional history and modern memory to acknowledge, constitute a problematic essential to understanding the European slaving strategies in the Atlantic that we know better, or at least think we do. The following chapter on that Atlantic context, particularly in the Americas, includes Africans and other Old World strategies of slaving in ways that, again, allow us to think further about slaving in a historical register.

4

Problematizing Slavery in the Americas as History

In the Americas, history and slavery are problems, in many senses: moral, political, and epistemological. It is the last of these conceptual senses that organizes the material in this chapter. History and slavery both seem familiar. We know too much about them, or think we do. But, as products of both, we are compromised as historians. We live in and with them. So they are politics; politics are ideological; and ideology, as earlier chapters have argued, is meant to obscure the diversity and dynamics of the experiences and motivations that create historical processes.

In chapters 1 and 2 I argued that we don't know slaving on a global scale if we only project what we think we know about slavery in the Americas onto other places and earlier times. And what we think we know about slavery in the Americas derives not from either masters' or slaves' actual experiences of it and with it but primarily from the polemical metaphors that abolitionists and masters developed to create the "institution" here, principally in the United States and only in the middle of the nineteenth century, and then debate it. But the antebellum United States was a very distinctive, even unique, historical context, the most modern (though still formative) civic political culture in the world. The familiar terms of "slavery as an institution" therefore do not describe strategies of slaving that prevailed elsewhere, including what slavers did with those whom they enslaved, or what the enslaved did for themselves.

This chapter argues further that "elsewhere" also included most parts of the Americas as well as aspects of the antebellum United States itself.

This chapter extends these world-historical dynamics of slaving to historicize our usual structural perspective on the Americas, drawing on that very general sketch to chart what I think are the conceptual challenges we all face in problematizing slavery as history. It also applies to the Americas the underlying, very long-range dynamics of slaving as a historical process outlined in chapter 2. It provides the context of Atlantic finance that enabled commercialized slaving in Africa and concludes by suggesting how the historical dynamics of Africa also enabled the Atlantic processes usually Europeanized as the slave trade. It also indicates how resources introduced from Atlantic commercialization intensified these long-term dynamics in the Americas in parallel with the processes of slaving in Africa, and at the same pace. The methodological—or, better, epistemological—critique of social science methods that runs throughout the book, applied to the Americas, suggests that we don't know either slaving there or slavery as it became in the antebellum United States, if we compare it—as has been conventional—only in terms of such relatively timeless, ahistorical, and imagined abstractions as the United States with the Spanish colonies or Brazil or sugar plantations in the Caribbean. This chapter thus presents the example of slaving as yet another critique of the prevailing ahistorical nation- or empire-centric logic of the modern discipline of history as a whole.

The historical problematics of slaving in the Americas arise instead from the sequence of varied strategies of crafting the novelty of a series of radically commercialized extensions of slaving in the Americas and then attempting to manage the monstrous, unanticipated contradictions these innovations created. The incremental steps or adaptations in this process run from the cities of late-medieval Iberia to sixteenth-century New Spain, to early seventeenth-century production of sugar (I am not saying "plantation agriculture") in Brazil, to the mature plantations of the eighteenth-century West Indies. Farmers declaring themselves gentlemen in North America, as well as others, made a separate series of adaptations of their own through these earlier centuries, leading to the antebellum politicization and institutionalization still enshrined in popular culture today and to the neo-abolitionist tone of nearly all the academic literature. They built changes on legal and other legacies from the initial phases of slaving in all of these areas, but always within local contexts of the long-term process of Atlantic commercialization. The first generation of the enslaved followed no less historical strategies of adapting elements of their backgrounds in Africa, but succeeding generations worked from the American contexts into which they had been born, no less than did their masters. The highly theorized master–slave dyad, its conflicts thus contextualized, was also a resource on both sides. The politicized caricatures of the slavery we think we know as an institution do not go far in revealing the fundamentally changing ways in which would-be masters in the Americas and those whom they enslaved there encountered one another through time. The problem of understanding slaving and slavery in the Americas is, again, a historical one, and significantly a political history at that.

Critique of Comparison as History—Cases, Races, and Labor Systems

The historical dynamic missing from the familiar comparative analysis of slaveries in the Americas is a classic casualty of what in chapter 1 I characterize as the social science or broadly sociological approach to an institution: it abstracts selected aspects of human experiences from actors in their historical contexts and freezes these outcomes in time. This static approach is not promising as history. The logic of comparison requires that the historian first isolate from all other variables examples of a concept presumed comparable, thereby suppressing or analytically neutralizing the contexts that provide the history's explanatory power; historical connections are backgrounded as analytical noise. In the case of modern slavery in the Western hemisphere, abstraction and isolation create logical problems of a particularly disabling intensity, since the makers of the cases compared were in fact not isolated from one another but rather continuously and consequentially engaged. The dynamics of slavery in North America were in significant ways by-products of those in the West Indies, French and British, as well as of those in Brazil, for example, and slavers in Brazil were working in economic and, later, cultural frameworks emanating from slaving in the North Atlantic.[1] The isolating quality of making comparisons suppresses the increasingly engaged—or mutually contextualized, even mutually constituting—historical connections among the several principal strategies of slaving in the Americas.

A second ahistorical limitation of formal comparison—and there is no point in comparing informally since doing so produces only incidental juxtaposition, not controlled analytical insight—arises from the reductiveness necessary to sort the rich variety of historical fruits, that is, the internally varied and even competing strategies in all historically coherent entities, into conceptual baskets filled uniformly with, say, Brazilian apples and North American oranges. Historically speaking, one must compare like context with like context, and circumstances in Brazil and North America did not correspond remotely to this logical premise, either internally or over time. One may attempt to meet this condition only by selecting an arbitrary, limited aspect, however considered and rationalized, of whatever one intends to compare, thus necessarily emphasizing only a single shared element or aspect, however valid, among the infinite moving parts—potentially motivating components—of all the contexts to be considered. But then one has again abandoned the contextualization on which history draws as a central element of its epistemology.

In the Americas, a presumed framework of western European law, for example, or its specific application of a public principle of individual proprietary ownership elaborated from an analogy taken from Roman jurisprudence of the slave as like a thing,[2] ignores the fact that the Romans developed the analogy in a political context very different from the ones to which it was applied in the Americas.[3] The idea of property serves well enough this very limiting purpose of comparing what became increasingly selective and rhetorical adaptations of a Roman legal principle, but it takes no account of the historical circumstances of slaving to which these were being adapted, also historically. Accenting these historical aspects of the abstractions that the comparative method attempts to compare makes clear its discounting of the specific and differing motivating elements of many distinctive historical contexts. Comparison contrasts isolated outcomes of historical processes rather than elaborating the historical contexts that motivated the people who created them. A historical emphasis on contextualization takes into account as many as possible of the contrasting components of these specific times and places.

A common alternative categorization of slavery in the Americas, but one no less abstracted, treats slaves as people denied the waged status of the free labor that emerged gradually in the eighteenth century in limited parts of the North Atlantic. This implicit typology of abstracted systems of labor—indentured servitude, peonage, share cropping, and so on—serves a similarly narrow purpose, one no more historical than comparing cases. It is substantively negative, using an idealized model of comprehensive modern wages as an implicit standard and judging all other arrangements as deficient in comparison. This negative concept immediately raises analytical problems in most parts of the Americas in the past, since it assumes the fully monetized and highly theoretical premises of modern economics. Most of those regions employed numerous, varying methods of mobilizing labor other than slavery, some of them more collective, others more individuated, and in less commercially integrated areas well into the twentieth century. The Americas were generally a debtor region to European creditors so long as Americans persisted in slaving, and this chapter elaborates the strategic reasons that cash was uniformly in short supply. "Unfree" is thus not only an essentially negative and internally diverse, and therefore not substantively analytical, category of labor into which slavery is collapsed, but it also rests on an essentially ideological characterization of wage-labor practices that in fact approached the theoretical model only to varying, but universally limited, degrees.[4]

One of my primary purposes is to distinguish slaving, based on introducing isolated mobile individuals, from the other ways of mobilizing the resident and reproducing communities that this typology classifies undifferentiatingly as unfree. The origin of these enslaved people outside the relevant labor market is their singularly distinguishing feature from other laborers mobilized, on whatever terms, locally. Comparison of slavery with other human relationship classed as labor arrangements, unfree or not, further presumes that slaving is directed at the essentially productive ends the others do in fact share, and even further that their products are intended for sale into the commercial economy as commodities. Other than in the modern Americas, with rare and notoriously unsuccessful exceptions, slaving was in fact distinguished by its application to ends other than basic agricultural production. It was substantially political, not economic.

Globally, these other strategies of mobilizing and controlling local labor have varied contextually and thereby historically through time and space, the differences among them reflecting varying local degrees of commercialization or the amount of cash available to utilize as a strategy to entice, indebt, and thus control production. Investors otherwise focused not on labor itself but on product. The historical dynamic accordingly turns on the deficit of cash in the economy as a whole in relation to needs for product or for militarization. All these alternative arrangements, unlike the autonomously domestic political economy of Africa before the nineteenth century or the idealized independent family farmstead of the North American frontier, appear in contexts involving partial commercialization. In such contexts, cash is short in relation to demand for product. Brokers of many sorts attempt to acquire a share of the available commodities by interposing themselves between local producers and the cash returns available elsewhere for their products, basically grain in Asia and Europe, though supplemented by artisanry or animals or gathered resources, and exotic goods that merchants with commercial contacts in the remote sources of these goods offer for sale, only for the cash they need to pay their own suppliers. Like slaving, these strategies develop primarily in contexts of rapid economic growth, where demand exceeds supply and the cash available to incentivize production. In addition, they are all historical strategies understood best in terms of managing change itself.

These historical circumstances of surging economic growth and lagging means of commercialization applied in force to the Atlantic economy from the sixteenth century into the early nineteenth. Consideration of these contexts of uneven changes in this historically analytical mode thus reveals yet another aspect of the fundamentally modern, highly commercialized, and therefore limiting premises of studying slavery primarily as a form of labor. In the modern Atlantic, slaving proved to be a strategy adaptable to the uniquely commercialized context there, although, like most historical strategies that succeed, its very successes reframed these contexts in ways that first institutionalized its consequences, to defend them even as they became intolerable, and then terminated the institution created.

Among the other forms of mobilizing labor on the margins of more limited commercial sectors of the world's economies, in Africa bondage by indebtedness took the form of pawnship, or rather claiming humans from debtors lacking personal proprietorial resources to offer as collateral. In the communal ethos, no one had personal property to commercialize. So groups offered members, or adjuncts, to neighbors as wives, hostages, and, as they turned to commercialized strategies, as pawned security for loans of imported goods. In agrarian Asia, with its vastly greater stocks of internationally monetized precious metals, merchants used formal cash debt, but military rulers there, caught in the costly contradictions of supporting themselves by plunder, hoarded silver and gold to display the grandeur they claimed and imposed collective obligations in kind, characterized as tribute, or in service, characterized as corvée. In thirteenth- and fourteenth-century western Europe and later in central and eastern Europe, including Russia, landlords such as local military lords and ecclesiastical estates resisted weaker commercializing impulses by holding peasant communities on their lands with the variety of quite specific legal restrictions on residence loosely grouped as serfdom.[5] These arrangements for tying peasants to the lands they worked reflected a kind of truce among landholders not to poach on one another's scarce resident populations and also a collective way to restrict their access to growing opportunities to earn cash in growing commercial sectors in nearby towns.[6] Enserfment, like slaving, was the historical strategy of marginal interests, in this case landowners excluded from a cash economy and retaining labor to produce commodities to buy into it.[7] As a strategy of controlling product, it differed from peasant indebtedness by its resort to force (phrased as law) in contexts relatively lacking in cash.

The distinctions of caste employed in Hindu southern Asia rank residential communities in terms of differentiated responsibilities for production and corresponding advantages for the composite as a whole, also without structuring strategic transactions in cash. They are fundamentally collective in the ethical sense developed in this book, phrased in sacralized and naturalized terms of bodily essences. They differentiate, but not with regard to the single normative standard of monotheisms or modernity; they are ranked categories equivalent to the less-ranked complementary differentiation in Africa according to descent and, eventually, also ethnicity. They serve only secondarily to mobilize the labor of some for the personal benefit of others; they are thus unfree only in the quite distinct sense of limiting individuals' access to status and knowledge assigned to complementing collectivities defined by birth. As highly differentiated complements, they secure socially necessary services directly among the human collectives they create, without the intermediating circulation of cash. They are therefore not competitive in the modern sense of individuals contending over cash, the single standard in an integrated commercialized economy of bargaining strangers. In parts of the Upper Niger River valley in Africa, less thoroughly ranked but equivalent communities defined more by proprietorial knowledge than by material means of production have been designated in the terms of ethnicity applied pervasively and loosely to the entire continent. Similarly complementing differentiation finds parallel expression in terms of Islamic, or sectarian Muslim, sacred knowledge.[8]

In the Hispanic Americas, land-rich but cash-poor colonial farmers and ranchers imposed varying obligations on local communities lumped generally under the concept of peonage to mobilize them for commercial purposes.[9] Enslavement of Native Americans elsewhere in the hemisphere was the extreme example of these, in the more commercialized and therefore internationally indebted sectors of the economy. Slaving again contrasted with other strategies of engaging unfree labor, as it was the resort of debtors attempting to invest in increased commodity production rather than investment of creditors in the product of peasants.

In more fully commercialized environments, similar local control may be attained by excluding nominal employees from the cash returns by means of sharecropping, involving little of no cash, or, in contexts of still greater liquidity, payment in scrip limited in fungibility to company stores in company towns operating on credit to cover sub-subsistence nominal wages. Finally, wages also sustain dependencies, though we voluntarize the relationship ideologically as attracting or incentivizing local workers. The attractions are in fact relative or, in historicized terms, contextualized; these strategies work only where the people thus mobilized as workers have been deprived of access to the local resources they need to survive by themselves. Wages also depend on having currency available in the local economy in amounts sufficient for diversion from its primary utility in facilitating commercial relations among merchants to commercializing the daily lives of resident populations, as consumers as well as contributors.

All of these methods of covering financial deficits brought by attempting costly commercial innovations in production or, in the case of military governments, in political integration of conquered territories are long-term arrangements imposed, with degrees and techniques of compulsion varying by time and place, on local, resident communities. This characterization of the abstract forms of unfree labor in terms of historical strategies effective in a range of specific contexts, varying in terms of commercial resources available, and relative to opportunities created by historical change suggests the limited utility of including slaving in a single logical (or, better, ideological) category of unfree. Rather, slaving was and continues to be a historical strategy directed at appropriating external human resources for private internal gain, thereby evading precisely the internal rivalries that created these other ways of competing with limited cash for local human resources. As an economic strategy, slaving is the resort of the competitors most marginal to the game.

As it happened, nearly all of the outsiders in the Americas who were publicly held as private property and who were thereby worked and supported, however minimally, without payment in cash in order to concentrate spreading but scarce currencies in other parts of the Atlantic economy came from Africa. This circumstance has offered a third, racialized framework for misleading comparisons of slavery. I have reflected earlier on how comparative studies in the Americas tended to tangle up race with slavery almost indistinguishably, particularly in initial historical treatments in the 1940s and 1950s.[10] In fact, identifications of individuals by their affiliations, their human relationships, varied with both times and places throughout the Americas, particularly early on; like relational identities in Africa, identities in the Americas were situational and relational. The same individual, depending on the context, might claim to be a volubly loyal subject of a European monarch, a devout member of a congregation of faith, a client of a powerful local patron, a family man or a devoted mother, a countryman or shipmate. But these personal connections applied infrequently to enslaved Africans, and so most were categorized individually in the superficial, hence abstract terms of their strikingly distinctive appearance to people who did not know them personally. In the United States, imported Africans were eventually categorized as black, and their American-born children were forced into the same somatic social convention as the category acquired legal definition and discriminatory political force in the nineteenth century. Color elsewhere in the New World was less politicized and correspondingly less polarized; individuals were differentiated much more personally and situationally rather than preemptively and categorically.

These extremely particular historical experiences of varying degrees of racialization, in this abstract sense, provide no viable basis of comparing, like with like, throughout the hemisphere. They were nonetheless subsequently reduced to timeless national characterizations, all as deviations from the most peculiar form, nineteenth-century North America, taken as the norm. Beyond the ahistoricity of these linked stereotypes (like any stereotype) of race and nation, the tendency to racialize slavery rendered all but invisible the critical initiating step in slaving in the Americas, the widespread enslavement of Native Americans throughout both hemispheres before the eighteenth century and continuing in some areas through the nineteenth century. Racialization further and, in the context of the historicization probed in this book, fundamentally provoked doubts about the comparability of slaving anywhere in the world that lacked a racialized context (not aspect!) with slavery in any part of the Americas.[11] Racialized slavery was not least disabling in attempting to understand slaving in Africa.[12]

This logical neglect of the explanatory potential of contexts and change led, in the fourth and final instance, to the classic but highly ahistorical and subsequently problematized explanations of variability in slavery throughout the Americas, not in terms of timing or of the dynamic pan-Atlantic processes under way, but in terms of presumed inherited continuities, usually from cultures in Europe. A favored early variant of the logic of cultural comparison cited prior medieval Portuguese familiarity with North Africans, heavily racialized as Moors, as the originary source of a racial openness attributed to later people of Portuguese backgrounds living in Brazil in very different contexts, including massive numbers of Africans held as slaves.[13] The most elaborated and celebrated formulation of this racial trope confused English cultural coloration of Moors, of whom they had little direct knowledge, as blacks with Iberian emphasis on the Muslim religion of local people of many somatic hues, whom they knew very well. This theory reduced the complex cultural world of medieval Iberia to modern racial obsessions and, once again, confused race and slavery in Brazil and elsewhere. The logic of cultural continuity or cultural determinism mutes the historicity of the strategies of both Africans and Europeans by misattributing agency to abstract cause, blurring the separate historical processes of slaving and racializing, and displacing the motivating context in both time and in space.

Beyond those highly problematic elements of comparative illogic, the national stereotypes on which it rested depended on the ahistorical assumption that none of those Portuguese learned anything significant after about the thirteenth century, which had also, conveniently enough, been the date of a Castilian, not a Lusitanian, codification of Roman-derived law that mentioned slaves. The mere mention of slavery in these legal terms invoked, without further systematic consideration, the entire chain of stereotyped associations—racial, economic, and others—of institutionalized modern slavery. Among Anglophone historians these tropes resonated with almost equally long-standing English suspicions of the innate conservatism of their longtime Lusitanian allies, an essentializing sort of logic closely parallel to racialization. A very loose string of ethnic stereotyping thus collapsed slavery and race into a single, enduring "institution," all but unchanging across oceans and over centuries.[14]

And then, having confounded race and slavery, followed the famous series of analogous attempts to untangle the two in the English context by looking for anteriority: did slavery appear in the documentation before race? or race before slavery? Taking chronological priority in an extremely local moment in a minor corner of a vast Atlantic context – Jamestown in the early seventeenth century – as determinative, which of these abstractions might have caused the other? This method sounds historical, but the logic was in fact resolutely originary and essentially asserted continuities: whichever could be found earlier must explain all that happened later. This search for origins fell into the additional ahistorical trap of seeking simple causation by sequencing decontextualized abstractions, even lifting wordings out of their textual contexts, in whatever selective references to coloration or laws of bondage (not restricted to slavery itself) could be found. The attempt to distinguish slavery ended up yet again blending slaving with other historically very distinct processes, practices, and projections of negative unfreedom.

This quest for origins reflected the most ahistorical features of a logic I rejected in chapter 1 as the "idol of origins."[15] But within the implicitly static logic of the comparative framework its appeal was so overwhelming that economic historians extended its emphasis on continuities to two other paradigmatic associations of slavery in the Americas, the sugar plantations on which some, likely most, Africans were forced to toil and the cane that they cut and crushed and boiled to *mascavado,* which others drained and packed in casks for shipment to Europe.[16] Among economists inclined toward model building (their behavioral equivalent of structures or institutions) it became conventional to start the story of slavery in the Americas on plantations and then to seek their origins in the small quantities of sugar cultivated on a few Italian manors in the eastern Mediterranean since the thirteenth century. Historians found there the first evidence of Christians adapting Muslim techniques of growing cane and producing sugar that they had learned in Palestine during the Crusades. Here is a particularly strong and not ancient statement of the logic of continuity in this stable, integrated, and thereby ahistorical institutionalization of a complex or system of sugar, slaves, and plantations:

> Neither slavery nor the plantation system were new when they emerged in the Lesser Antilles and elsewhere in the Americas. . . . Sugar plantations had been

developed in the Mediterranean and on the islands of the Atlantic coast of Africa before their reemergence with the rediscovery of the Americas. Indeed, their previous history helps explain the rapid expansion of slavery in the . . . colonies. . . . [T]he conditions of production were not based upon a new set of innovations in the New World.[17]

Here, sheer momentum seems to explain a great deal. This statement of the pervasive premise of continuity, extended from national cultures to agriculture, applies the inherently static logic of comparison so strongly that it attributes the rapid growth of slave-produced sugar in the New World to prior experience with sugar in the Old World, thus contradictorily attributing change (in location and scale but not in structure or dynamics) to a teleological unfolding of inherent potential. The obvious alternative is the historical one, which stresses the novel contexts in the not-entirely-coincidentally designated New World—but then one would have to contextualize strategies and trace their adaptations to novel contexts. Comparisons of this sort are fundamentally ahistorical in their explicit reliance on precedent, their systematic neglect of contexts, and their resolute focus on institutions that are retrospective intellectual constructs of the analyst more than the dynamic creations of historical actors proceeding from ephemeral and contradictory meanings and motivations of their own times.[18]

The basic premise of my effort to historicize slaving is that one can't tell the story in terms of selective originary (or ideologically claimed!) continuities from Europe, whether Roman legal formulations,[19] or sugar, or, once we include Africa in the historical dynamics of the Atlantic, in the form of the African cultural practices of the enslaved.[20] The pervasive temptation of this ahistorical ideologic, which has thus overwhelmed all historical aspects of the subject, must derive some of its persistence from its most perniciously permanent bio-analog—the geneticized continuities generated by racializing the identities of the actors, whether as races or as racists. The study of slavery thus once again circles back into the dark penumbra of contemporary racial politics with which I began chapter 1.

The epistemological effect of identifying variations in comparative terms, whether as sociological cases, in typologies of labor systems, as essentialized race, or as cultural analogs and anticipations of modern nations, was to acknowledge that the definition of slavery selected was at best partial since it always seemed to come up short in so many other respects. Historians working in this comparativist vein did not actually isolate whatever they treated as slavery from the historical contexts that accounted for differences, ideological or economic. So they tended to background as incidental whatever didn't seem to fit, as merely historical aspects particular to one place or another, which was to say analytically insignificant. Such dismissal of context evaded rather than exploited the engaged, contextualized, dynamic historical definition of slaving on which I am insisting. Particular circumstances were incidental only to the dominantly sociological structures, single (presumed) isolated aspects of the rich and contradictory historical realities of human lives, abstracted in static forms in order to compare them.

Comparative histories, having thus defined slavery exclusively and excludingly as a public legal institution protecting private property in people, characterized racially and as excluded from a commercial economy taken as otherwise comprehensive, then considered variations in the degrees to which the English in North America or the Portuguese in Brazil or the French in Saint-Domingue implemented these predetermined characteristics. This procedure, resting on laws constituted by governments, reified changing contexts as enduringly cultural. In fact, these distinctions projected modern national entities teleologically back in time. As variables explaining differences in the presumed unitary institution of slavery, they were conceived in self-defeatingly but correspondingly timeless terms. A historical approach turns instead to the varying momentary and historical circumstances and processes that seem repeatedly to have generated similar—or rather, parallel—resorts to slaving far beyond the modern Americas. The opportunity I want to pursue in this chapter is to look afresh at the Americas as realizations of these recurring processes of slaving, as contextualized in the larger historically distinguishing process of creating modernity; that is, how Atlantic interests marginalized from the principal strategies of financial accumulation in the seventeenth and eighteenth centuries commercialized slaving to keep their hands in the game.

Money and Monarchy as the Atlantic Master Narrative

As I move toward specifics of the historical processes of these strategies of commercialized slaving and its unintended consequences, I appreciatively acknowledge that historians of parts of the story of slavery in the Americas have begun to converge on local and particular historical accents. They know Europe and the Americas much better than I ever shall, and their works have encouraged me to take the plunge sketched in this chapter, as they have illuminated aspects of their fields obscure to nonspecialists like me. Prominent among them is Robin Blackburn's *Making of New World Slavery,* a brilliant, nuanced, comprehensive integration of comprehensive reading around the theme of the novelty of the New World's and slavery's (more than slaving's) critical contributions to the historical process of moving Europe, and eventually the world, "from [what the American edition calls] the Baroque to the modern." Ultimately, credit for seeing an integrated vision of the process goes to the famous Trinidadian scholar and politician Eric Williams, whatever the crudeness of his first approximation of regionally transcending historical thinking of this sort—once again, the price paid by a pioneer.[21] Others are moving in parallel directions, though usually on more local scales, and I intend no lack of appreciation in not mentioning them all here by name.

To begin: the same shortages of cash that provide the motivating contexts for other forms of unfree labor framed the adaptations of Old World domestic and political slaving that developed in the modern Atlantic. Leaving aside alleged continuities of culture and cultivation from the Mediterranean, the medieval Iberian background and the initial phases of Portuguese slaving in Africa provide relevant context by framing the initial strategies of New World slaving as motivated by the marginal positions of contenders in the politics of formative Christian monarchies in sixteenth-century Portugal and Spain.

If we abandon the usual transcending pseudonational cultural continuities, slaving in the New World, as distinct from Old World slaving in the eastern Atlantic, is readily seen to have gathered its initial dynamic as agents of the Hapsburg king in Spain captured Native Americans to create the formative phases of tapping the evident riches of an entire continent, in tentative ways particular to the fiscal limitations of sixteenth-century monarchies in Europe. To consider strategies far less coherent than what were later rationalized as colonies, one would also break down the ethnocultural and teleological cliché of Spain into the varied interests competing within a monarchical domain that was still a work in progress. One would certainly not consider nineteenth-century Spanish sugar and coffee in Cuba, which were quite distinct adaptations to much later and much more thoroughly commercialized conditions in the Americas, Africa, and Europe. Sixteenth-century buyers of Africans in American territories were strategically and politically distinct from the people who captured American natives, so that these multiple instances of slaving must be understood as competing strategies of contending interests. Then in Brazil, Portuguese and Dutch-based collaborators elaborated the enslaving of Africans on larger scales to produce sugar in circumstances particular to the early seventeenth century, in no small part the novel political context created by the union of the Spanish and Portuguese crowns (1580–1640), but not on plantations in the classic, later sense. The archetypal plantation strategy developed its unique features and key elements of the ideology that became the paradigm for modern studies of slavery only later, on the sugar islands of the Caribbean that the British and French were busy adapting to the specific economic challenges they faced in the eighteenth century.

In North America, colonists developed no-less-differentiated strategies of slaving in the early seventeenth-century Chesapeake, along only gradually institutionalized lines that historians still puzzle over designating as slavery under the prevailing paradigm.[22] These early practices assumed more institutionalized forms in the 1670s, acquired a significantly more African tone in the 1720s in the Carolina Lowcountry (and to a lesser degree also in the Chesapeake), and became politically significant between the 1770s and 1807, above all in the Chesapeake, with the maturation of growing numbers of American-born people held as slaves. In the succeeding two decades under the early Republic the legal distinctions acquired racial connotations, and not entirely coincidentally.[23] By the middle of the nineteenth century, people held as slaves in the antebellum years, almost entirely American-born, passed through the highly institutionalized and politicized paradigmatic moment of slavery as it is framed in the academic literature and in public culture.[24] These latter-day paradigms incorporated politicized caricatures as construed in both abolitionist and proslavery ideologies as much as they reflected the actual strategies on the parts of either the masters or the slaves of the time. All these changes occurred within a political culture—the primary consideration in the contextualized way that I want to historicize slaving—that itself assumed uniquely modern features in the Americas, and earlier in the United States than elsewhere. The key ideological dimension of the emergent national collectivities of that era was presumed homogeneity, in fact only legal and civic, and then only for some, but extended morally and racialized. The ideology of nation excluded enslaved blacks from the otherwise inclusive territorialized entities that people were struggling to create. Slavery institutionalized had become radically anomalous, and eventually abominably so.[25]

To rephrase this narrative in the language of the historical epistemology I am proposing: slavers behind each of these strategies on the hemispheric scale, from Brazil to Birmingham, were working in increasingly defining and also confining national-ideological contexts, each of them distinguished by the legacies that the generations inherited from their predecessors. In fact, the conventional historiography has long highlighted these contrasts, but only ahistorically, as an unintegrated set of separate regional narratives, presented comparatively, and thus contrastingly, rather than as the coherent sequence of incremental historical adaptations that they in fact formed: Brazilians adapted what planters had done in São Tomé and other eastern Atlantic islands off the African coast in the sixteenth century, and the Dutch extended their own modifications of Brazilian practice to the eastern Caribbean in the 1640s but did not subsequently change the framework there within which they continued to slave. English planters and then the French elaborated at the end of the seventeenth century what the literature typically stabilizes as a plantation complex or system in the larger islands to the west and took it on again to the North American mainland. Different contexts of place and of time provoked adaptations of each of these legal and cultural heritages to growing commercialization throughout the Atlantic. The literature has converted the retrospective ideological representations of waning moments in this historical process to continuity and then compared them.

My historical accent would shift the analytical emphasis to the ways in which Brazilians and the early English operated within a sixteenth- and seventeenth-century context of Spanish preeminence and extreme scarcities of financial capital, to how Dutch-based merchant networks in the early seventeenth century brought capital to fund productive agricultural slavery and subsequently maintained a niche in the midst of larger, ultimately wealthier and more powerful competitors, and then to how British financial innovations at the end of the seventeenth century funded the classic large, eighteenth-century sugar plantation in the Caribbean islands, as well as to how North Americans competed only at significant fiscal disadvantage with their nominally English brethren in the islands, and to how the French in the eighteenth century tried to use slaving to come from behind to compete with a British economy growing with the aid of gold from Brazil that London was acquiring through Portugal. A historical emphasis thus falls on integrating each of these moments in changing contexts of the others and on the incremental strategies needed to effect these changes. The significant long-term historical initiatives were built on American specie and then on Dutch and British techniques of mobilizing the financial resources it underwrote. Those with the money were the leaders; they set the pace. The slavers were those without it, those marginalized by the growing financial power concentrated in London, Paris, New York, and Boston, sometimes as channeled through Lisbon and Havana, and trying to catch up: merchants in outports like Glasgow, Bristol, Liverpool, Nantes, Brazil, and Rhode Island. One must also take into account the even lesser financial capacities in Africa as the continent fell into debt over the same four centuries, as financially marginal merchants in Europe collaborated with marginal men there.

The very different kinds of people throughout the Americas who resorted to slaving in differing ways over the course of three transformative centuries created communities of slaves far more dynamic and internally differentiated than the, once again, paradigmatic but homogeneous American stereotypes of blacks held in perpetual bondage. Even more reductively, characterizing these people primarily as slaves renders them historically inert as the least dynamic (because defined as "dominated," hence passive), most tautological characterization of all. To historicize these enslaved Africans we must recognize them as the women, men, girls, and boys they were in relation to one another when they crossed the ocean, some of them literate Muslim scholars, hailing from changing regions within Africa, skilled healers and experienced military veterans, and held through enslavement in the Americas under the most varied circumstances.

We must further grasp the challenges faced by all but the initial cohorts in entering already established quasi-communities of their predecessors and then in establishing and defending places for themselves among old hands, independently of whatever their masters might fantasize about them. The personal experiences of the people from Africa trapped in these processes also changed, again, to stay with my Brazilian example, from the first few who arrived there in the late sixteenth century, often via Portugal—skilled, baptized Catholics, often female, and integrated into their masters' households—to later cohorts of males who arrived, at varying times and finding varying specific circumstances from region to region in Brazil, in numbers large enough to sustain semiautonomous lives within their shared vulnerability to the arbitrary wills of the people who owned them. They differed also from still later successors from other parts of Africa, seen in Brazil as Minas or Bantu and attributed identities different from the personal experiences of any of them at home. Others might not arrive in numbers sufficient to claim new cultural communities of their own in reaction to the older American ones created by their predecessors, however African these might have been designated in contrast to the Catholic culture that their masters dichotomized as Portuguese.

On the historical level of personal experiences, enslaved individuals passed through a series of no-less-ephemeral moments, from isolated helplessness upon arrival on through constructing new para-communities of their own within slavery. Among these, they exploited the paternalistic ideologies that Brazilians of Portuguese backgrounds adapted (I am not saying inherited) from the domestic aspects of their ancestors' lives in Iberia and their predecessors' practices in Brazil. The strategies of the enslaved essentially focused on belonging, on retaining whatever human connections they might form, however opportunistically against the profound instability of their lives under enslavement. The many strategies of belonging that the enslaved carved out of their vulnerability to renewed removals, in ways differing through the centuries and throughout the Americas, constitute historically contextualized alternatives to resistance as the primary option left to people defined as dominated.[26] Trying to avoid repeated dislocation and re-isolation was the African-derived motivation that drove new arrivals to constitute new associations to which they might cling, as distinct from other more political strategies that American-born slaves elsewhere, and later, derived from their primary experiences of radically different immediate circumstances of growing up in families dispersed by institutionalized slavery.[27]

The remainder of this chapter once again sketches slaving historically, this time in the varied contexts of the increasingly modern Americas:

1. by focusing on who changed what in the sixteenth-century Atlantic (my context of time and place) relative to Europe in the fifteenth century, then who else, again later in seventeenth-century Brazil, and yet again who else in the eighteenth-century Caribbean (and also in the English colonies in North America as well as in the French Antilles and the Spanish Indies), and then still again, with intensifying local/national dynamics, in the nineteenth century;

2. all taking into account changes in different parts of Africa, since for most areas (the United States again being the exception, after about the 1770s) the strategies of managing the people whom the Europeans in the Americas were attempting to control as slaves were premised on maintaining constantly renewed majorities of new Africans among them;

3. since the Atlantic economy supported assemblages of enslaved males in the Americas in numbers sufficient and placed them under work routines separate enough from the lives of their masters, that these modern strategies of slaving enabled the enslaved in the Americas to create viable communities for themselves, within slavery—a nearly unprecedented outcome;

4. finally, with the distinctively balanced sex ratios in North America generating a unique multigenerational context of life under slavery that ultimately made them historical agents of the demise of their would-be masters as slavers.[28]

Slaving in the Americas Historicized: Problems of Finance

The space available here once again limits me to following only one or two suggestive threads in the intricate web of strategies through which a succession of characters marginal in Europe and in the Americas—as well as those in Africa identified in chapter 3—brought all too evident outsiders into rapidly changing contexts around the Atlantic world. Each of the initial strategies, all short-run solutions reached under pressure, left heirs to them with problems—unintended consequences—that very few, or almost none, of the originators had faced, again no less in the Americas and in Europe than in Africa.[29] To recall my opening invocation of David Brion Davis's "problem of slavery (in western culture)," I intend to foreground what in the early 1960s he backgrounded as the "economic functions and interpersonal relationships . . . for which [h]e [then] lack[ed] satisfactory data."[30] Four decades later, the vast subsequent outpouring of Atlantic-scale literature, including history and slaving in Africa, allows us to fill in those contexts. Beyond the changes in intellectual and ethical orientations in Europe that Davis elegantly elaborated, my emphasis on slaving around the globe now highlights the novelty of the public slaving that emerged in the Americas, and, for the first time on a historical scale, also collective experiences as slaves of the Africans taken there. What European slavers, American masters, and the Africans they enslaved did on their own are all essential to understanding the historical process of engagement that, together, they drove.

The motivating, enabling strategy of slaving in this Atlantic era was financial, essentially an extension of the long-standing commercialization of the means of acquiring slaves through purchase in Eurasia and parts of Africa to commercialization of the purposes of holding them. The primary slavers in Europe and the Americas, no less than in Africa (or throughout human history), were marginal to the contexts in which they lived, and so their positions changed in the course of the radical transformations that slaving on Atlantic scales brought to all three continents. However, they all operated on the fringes of a quest by others more powerful than they for the specie that financed the integration of an Atlantic economy of unprecedented scale and rates of change.

The Atlantic, as economy and eventually as catalytic historical space, was built in one of those commercializing contexts of limited monetization historicized in the preceding comments on the abstract typology of unfree labor. Facing shortages of cash in the Mediterranean, a quest for sub-Saharan gold had motivated the fifteenth-century European monarchical interests sailing along African coasts, where mercantile adjuncts resorted to slaving as a back-up strategy to supply existing urban markets in southern Europe for captives. In the later sixteenth century, Spanish silver from the Americas, again firmly under monarchical control, financed the extension of this maritime transport of captives from Africa to transatlantic dimensions. Again as a by-product of this search for specie, Portuguese sugar producers in Brazil integrated Africans into production of agricultural commodities on unprecedentedly large scales. From there, the Dutch used new techniques of merchant finance to carry the technology to English Barbados. English monarchs then chartered the companies that financed the conversion of that island from family farms to large plantations worked by numerous Africans brought there as slaves, as well as minor extensions to the North American mainland in the eighteenth century. Brazilians amplified their African sources of slaves in the eighteenth century to pan and dig gold in Minas Gerais, and the French monarchy provided fiscal subsidies to complete the cast of major European players who financed the growth of slaving to its peak volumes in the last third of the eighteenth century.

Through the seventeenth century, African gold and Spanish silver provided the financial liquidity that financed the trade, supplemented later by gold from Brazil and by modern strategies of finance in Britain. The slavers, in Africa and the Americas in particular, resorted to slaving as their Plan B, borrowing working capital to buy their way into the main game of accumulating specie or, increasingly, mercantile and bank notes payable therein. Africans, for their part, sold gold; they did not monetize the metal. No European bought slaves in Africa with gold or silver coins until American buyers at the very end of the trade in the nineteenth century, and so in financial terms the triangular trade from Europe to Africa to the Americas and back to Europe was a means of converting secondary products of European manufacture to labor saleable in the Americas, ideally sold directly for specie itself but usually only for an interest in agricultural commodities that, back in Europe, could be sold to realize cash or fungible near-equivalents.[31] In a commercializing world, financial resources—first specie, then compounding categories of paper obligations—replaced warfare as the efficacious historical strategy of choice. Cash marginalized older assets held in the form of land or its human occupants or both, and so slaving became the strategy of competing to join the accelerating race to commercialize.[32]

The strategy of commercialized slaving succeeded, in the unanticipated form of more than ten million Africans landed alive in the Americas and their descendants, all held there in slavery. These people and their owners created similarly unanticipated political problems for the monarchs in maritime western Europe, who were attempting to consolidate their political positions with commercial versions of the strategies of external plundering that, for five thousand years, had supported imperial warlords in Asia. The masses of slaves created other problems no less political for their masters. Monarchs and masters then turned to public law to supplement private discipline to manage these unintended demographic consequences of Atlantic slaving, creating the public institution on which the modern understanding of slavery rests. Slaving, once defined legally as a public institution, could then be terminated, abolished, by politically accessible means, by public authority, by government fiat. The particularities of converting slaving from a private means of evading public control to a public institution subject to political control forms one central narrative of this chapter. The implicit politics of slaving as a strategy became explicit.

To start by historicizing the process of adapting slaving to commercial ends, one may begin by noting key incremental innovations in the late medieval Mediterranean, but not by emphasizing slavery there. To anticipate consequences that eventuated in modern slavery in the Atlantic in this way would presume the outcome as a premise. Rather, the historian emphasizes the context of successful slaving there, at that time. The slavers, principally northern Italian merchants, were attracted to markets for valuable outsiders, Slavs or Africans, in Muslim cities, not to mention parallel urban opportunities along the Christian shores of the sea. The growing commercial towns on both sides of the Mediterranean were much wealthier than rural estates in the cash-generating opportunities that interested merchants, and they needed domestic staff as well as municipal service personnel, not least galley slaves. Urban markets, with cash, constrained use of slaving as a source of labor for rural agricultural production, without it.

In addition, there were the politics. At the time neither Christian nor Muslim merchants had penetrated the landed ecclesiastical and military-aristocratic domains in control of their peasant residents, themselves none too numerous at the end of the fourteenth century in the lingering demographic wake of the Black Plague (1347). The context was a prime example of the motivating general standoff among these three broad, competing interests in Eurasia over the preceding two millennia. In Christian Europe, the Catholic Church reinforced exclusion of merchants from buying into these domains, whatever the legal entailments of land and residents, by prohibiting usury. Law thus inhibited the buildup of unsustainable rural debt payable in currencies that might otherwise, as was common in non-Muslim Asia, have culminated in seizures of debtors as slaves or in enduring bondage for debts.[33] In much of continental Europe, the primary local merchant communities—as contrasted with the international bankers and merchants of Italy—were severely marginalized, culturally and religiously, ethnically suspect as Jews. The uncommercialized countryside left commercially oriented entrepreneurs confined (parallel to the ways I've described both for Africa and for ancient Mesopotamia) to channeling investments into urban property, staffed by slaving, and only marginally able to recruit personnel to intrude on the rural agricultural base of the productive economy.[34]

These mercantile interests, mostly Italians and also some central Europeans, found precisely these opportunities to invest their growing financial capacities in production itself in the early sixteenth century in the much less politically constrained contexts of manageably small, uninhabited islands off Africa's shores in the eastern Atlantic—the Canaries, in fact depopulated by slaving, Madeira, the Cape Verdes, and eventually São Tomé (the last three populated only by slaving).[35] Critically for my emphasis on political and economic marginality as both motivating slavers and also enabling them, in the early sixteenth century these islands were unclaimed by or beyond the development capabilities of merchants' domestic (aristocratic, ecclesiastical) rivals in Europe. The lack of political competition in these remote and hence risky environments offered a viable opportunity for merchants to invest in the cultivation of cane for sugar on significant scales. However, without some sort of reasonably liquid collateral to protect their financial interests, investors could not venture the large capital outlays for the necessary land improvements and equipment, beyond the military protection of these island assets that the Portuguese monarchy had its own strategic reasons for supplying.

The rising cash values of captive Africans as slaves in the cities of post-*reconquista* Iberia, at least as much as their immediate utility as producers of sugar on Atlantic islands, made commercialized rights of ownership in captives acquired on the adjacent mainland a significant strategy of claiming human potential as personal property. In turn, proprietorial rights in enslaved people created collateral for the credit required to launch a new, costly productive enterprise in the islands.[36] Historically speaking, contexts counted more as enabling considerations than eventual outcomes, even ones intended. The critical extension of commercial slaving from households in Iberian cities to production in the islands of the eastern Atlantic was not a radical innovation but another incremental extension of older strategies, updated to the novel open context of the Atlantic. The resulting reduction of people to property was also new in fateful legal terms: commercial law prevailed over whatever Roman-derived laws of slavery a consolidating monarch in Iberia two centuries earlier might have proclaimed, with primary application there to the claims to conquered resident populations of competing conquering warlords.[37]

Over the next two centuries, this radically novel commercialization of human relations in the eastern Atlantic as well as the parallel processes in Africa helped to finance economic growth at rates so rapid that they strained the process of accumulating sufficient and sufficiently liquid capital in Europe to fund them. And all the more so, given the marginality of the innovators in the Atlantic who were attempting to implement commercial strategies abroad to challenge military and ecclesiastical regimes at home. Integrating a vast Atlantic economy cost too much to leave resources of specie free to invest in currencies circulated as the wages that might have enticed rural labor in Europe or Africa away from strategies of agricultural production established within other relationships of dependency. By phrasing the process of strategies of capital accumulation in this historical way or by the legal sleight of hand that converted social relationships to personal capital,[38] I highlight the radical novelty of converting the once-intimate relation of slavery in collective Christian European households to personal property in the Americas, negotiable for cash and, as such, defined and protected publicly. One important innovation lay in the ambivalent treatment of slaves in Mediterranean Europe as real/entailed/household/family property, bundled inextricably with family or other collective estates, as distinct from the much more liquid, negotiable, fungible, and personal assets they eventually became in the Americas.[39]

As personal property in the Atlantic, slaves displaced from the human environment of the household into the soulless domain of commercial markets extended another, no-less-ironic quality of Old World practices of slaving: its privacy. But the contexts that distinguished private from public had changed. In the Old World, slavers secluded the people they enslaved in collective households from monarchical and other external claims on them. Given the political dynamics fundamental to strategies of slaving, both the increasing numbers of slaves in the Atlantic and the increasingly pervasive political contexts of monarchy there could not help but intensify this distinction. Slaves became the private property of the individuals whom kings claimed as subjects but not directly subject to kings. Slavers gathered unprecedentedly large numbers of slaves in the Atlantic islands and eventually assembled even greater demographic densities in the Americas, where their remoteness from European monarchical authority posed the usual logistical problems of overextended military rule. The usual problems of political integration were intensified by the context of historical processes of kings in Europe, attempting to use revenues from the wealth that slaves produced in the Americas to strengthen their monarchical power at home, over aristocratic and ecclesiastical rivals. These contradictory political processes created tensions that only violence could resolve. The late eighteenth-century phase of these processes in the Americas and the North Atlantic, subsequently known as the Age of Revolutions, relieved that tension, only to transfer the elemental contradiction of public, institutionalized slavery to the even more sensitive formative nations in the New World that it left behind as its residue.[40]

Atlantic proprietorial claims to Africans as personal property thus elaborated the entailments of late medieval family-based or otherwise corporate landed families' and master artisans' lands, workers, and skills for purposes of similarly commercial investment through socially accountable orders, guilds, apprenticeships, and serfdom. These European forms of collectivity had paralleled what in Africa I have termed the "communal ethos" in their primary focus on controlling production by controlling its producers, and at the same time. In the sixteenth century, Spanish law had initially extended the legal strategy underlying these entailments to the complex of commercial assets assembled on first-generation plantations in the Spanish Americas—cane-crushing mills, land and improvements, especially irrigation, and human beings—to include New World slaves as real property within a legal sphere of indissolubility.[41]

However, in Spanish towns elsewhere in the Americas, the personal, non-proprietorial bonds derived from Old World premises of domestic intimacy and integration continued to prevail.[42] These specific legal extensions of a strategy of organizing human affairs around abstract precedent are the alleged continuities usually attributed, in an unproblematized originary vein, to the specific Catholic culture of Europe. As history, however, it is important to accent their early timing, the sixteenth-century moment at which subjects of monarchs in Madrid and Lisbon were struggling to adapt their experiences of household slaving in the Old World to the unprecedented and growing scales of the commercialized, productive slaving in the Americas. To indicate only one unexplored example of these challenges, buyers of enslaved Africans in the Americas had to accommodate the female premise of Mediterranean and Muslim slaving to the large numbers of males whom they assembled in the Americas and put to hard labor in mines, fortifications, and canebrakes.

Historians must also problematize the political implications of the means, namely, commercial credit, by which slavers effected these changes. European credit underwrote Atlantic slaving. Debt was the enabling strategy in the Americas, no less than in Africa. The prominent public aspects of debt in monarchical domains in the Americas intensified government interest in captives who had, until then, been essentially secluded in private households. However, monarchies in sixteenth-century Spain and Portugal were hardly more than emergent dreams of their creators, who, like nominal rulers of other composite (corporate) polities in Asia and Africa, had to be wary of merchants using commercial means to build private retinues of their own that were beyond the reach of kings.

In the Atlantic, selling collateralized Africans to royal subjects on credit, in remote regions, held a lighted match to a potential political tinderbox. Merchants capable of finance on Atlantic scales had the capacity to grow to politically challenging proportions as creditors of planters and miners in the Americas, no less than had their predecessors in the ancient eastern Mediterranean, throughout the Islamic world, and in early modern Africa. Through the end of the seventeenth century New Christians and then Dutch encroached on subjects of the Iberian monarchies and also of France in precisely this sense, condemned as smuggling. In Brazil as well as in North America they eventually financed the indebted planters who expelled monarchs. Parallel to the peasant families indebted in the ancient Mediterranean, who had given up daughters to relieve threats of indebtedness to their families, American borrowers survived—some growing wealthy—by passing along the burden of covering the personal debt they had contracted to the slaves whom they had bought with it. They accordingly worked them hard, sometimes to death, and sold them off when even these efforts failed to produce commodities of values sufficient to cover what they owed.

Finance was thus as fateful or, in less rhetorical terms, as historically efficacious in the Euro-American Atlantic as it was in Africa, and slaves were critical among the collateral behind the debt that financed the speed with which the Atlantic economy grew. In Africa, the fast pace at which Europeans introduced debt overwhelmed the institutions of a domestic political economy of human relationships, and African borrowers resorted to selling captives to cover the indebtedness on which they had thrived. European financial resources similarly indebted the Americas. In the economic sectors engaged in the production of commodities there, the growth engines of the region, collateralized labor was a principal basis for borrowing. To the extent that Africans enslaved in the Americas funded the merchants who extended the credit they supported into Africa, thus stimulating the captures and sales of their successors, slaves themselves were utilized to sustain the historical processes of enslaving them. Years ago, Michael Craton, observing the steady extensions of slaving from the British Caribbean to the North American seaboard in the seventeenth century, remarked rhetorically that "slaving begat more slaving."[43] Craton's comment has historical substance: commercialized slaving was a core component of the fundamental processes of capital accumulation and market organization that financed further slaving in Africa and the Americas.

Slaving in the Americas Historicized: Political Problematics of Monarchy

Merchant slavers, accordingly, were threats to the formative monarchies in Europe in the sixteenth and seventeenth centuries. The early history of Atlantic slaving features ambivalent royal efforts, first, to contain the potential traders and planters operating in trans-oceanic areas beyond effective administrative reach from Europe, and then to buy into the business. Aspiring rulers in fifteenth- and sixteenth-century Iberia marginalized this sensitive strategic innovation by contracting overseas commerce to foreigners safely subject to monarchical authority, without competition from others within their territorial domains. Traders were economically useful, but politically they were tolerated, not embraced.[44] The principal commercial investors in Portuguese and Spanish legal domains in the sixteenth and seventeenth centuries were Italians and Germans and, later, Dutch-based Sephardic Jews who had been expelled from

Iberia, effectively in pursuit of dampening the local threat of commercial grown too strong for the comfort of kings primarily reliant on military resources. The confined territorial spaces of maritime Europe were becoming more and more constraining for the plunder on which military monarchies supported themselves as they expanded and consolidated their territorial domains.[45] In relation to the vast spaces and numerous populations of Asia, and with Ottomans blocking territorial conquests in that direction, or compared to the militarily uncontested European spaces that the Romans had plundered a millennium and a half earlier, the legacy of supporting political consolidation at home with military expansion abroad was reaching its geostrategic limit.

These constraints on available conquests tipped fifteenth-century Europe in favor of the merchant interests among the triad of Eurasian political history, militaristic strategies of slaving by conquest balanced by mercantile strategies of using slaving to consolidate the territories conquered, with priestly establishments endowed by and in turn supporting military rulers. By the macro-logic of slaving as a strategy of challenging from the margins, and only secondarily of defending the established authorities challenged, the landed military aristocracy and Catholic clerical interests in Spain and in Portugal were protecting themselves at home by displacing the dangerously dynamic potential of commercial development, initially via sugar, to the safely remote islands of the eastern Atlantic, and then on overseas to the Americas. The strategy was to exile commercialization, in the Atlantic pursued largely through slaving, as in Africa, seemingly safely beyond the maritime horizon.[46] Monarchs then attempted to limit the inevitable impact on the home front of expansive mercantile investment abroad through all the restrictions and monopolies and licenses familiar in the conventional narrative of imperial administration in the Iberian Atlantic.

But in this case out of sight was not beyond the range of the global historical dynamics of commerce that were gathering momentum beyond the visions of Christian military monarchs in Europe, no less personalistically and territorially minded than their contemporary counterparts in western Africa. For the consolidating monarchs in early sixteenth-century Madrid and Lisbon, the political problem of slaving was that of gaining control of distant American raiding grounds—not yet colonies in any integrated sense—with the clear or at least fantasized and thus strongly motivating economic potential to overwhelm their nominal masters in Europe.[47] For Spanish monarchs in Madrid, the first step (as is widely recognized[48] but still worth emphasizing here in terms of my accent on the political contexts of slaving[49]) was to limit the private, autonomous access of their military agents in the New World, the first generation of *conquistadores* in the 1520s and 1530s, to local residents to enslave and thus to exclude from direct access by the monarchy.

The early slaving among native populations was no less a contradiction of the direct and personal authority of monarchy in New Spain than enslaving by indebting had been two thousand years earlier in Palestine, or in the preceding two hundred years to consolidating monarchies in Scandinavia and England. Spaniards in the 1520s and 1530s had mounted massive military raiding for native captives all around the Caribbean and elsewhere, to replace local island populations already captured or sent into all-but-terminal decline by disease.[50] Similar captures and enslavement of the vastly larger populations of the mainland richly demonstrated the threat that rampaging mounted warriors posed to political control from Europe. The sprawling mainland estates claimed by Hernán Cortéz and other conquistadores, with the Native Americans living on them potentially under the exclusive control of their conquerors, threatened to embolden breakaway warrior-aristocrats rather than to create the loyal and dependent royal servants that monarchs in Spain intended. The New Laws of Charles II of Spain, decreed in 1542, whatever the theological and legal discourses of saving Indian hearts and minds for Christ in which they were debated, asserted the direct authority of the Crown, through appointed representatives and through missionaries and other allies in the Catholic Church, over the natives of the Americas, their bodies as well as their souls.[51] People excluded from the unitary authority of monarchy as slaves posed no lesser political threats in Madrid than in northern Europe, where slaving declined in direct proportion to the consolidation of monarchy.

The Spanish Crown, then, constrained foreign mercantile investment in its New World domains by consigning deliveries of Africans as slaves to foreign traders, under the famous *asiento* contracts.[52] Further, by allocating the Native American laborers, whom the Crown controlled, to the key productive agricultural and then mining sectors of the economy, monarchs in Spain restricted uses of the enslaved Africans delivered to positions much more politically benign, dispersed among the domestic retinues of its own appointees and allies in the cities or in familiar and controllable urban artisan employments. Except for lethal employment of Africans in production of alluvial gold in the Colombian Chocó, where no one else could be compelled or sacrificed and where few survived, slaves employed on significant scales in productive projects in Spanish domains were mostly safely confined to plantations of the Crown's ecclesiastical allies, principally Jesuits.[53] That is, in the sixteenth century, Spanish monarchs preserved Old World politics of household slaving by marginalizing the slavers, both late-medieval military conquerors and early modern merchants, not only from Iberia but also from the economic axes, commercial agricultural, pecuarial, and particularly mineral, of its possessions in the New World.

In succeeding with this strategy of defending monarchical interests in the Americas by quarantining slaving there, Spanish authorities evaded the next step, taken by others, in commercializing slaving in the Atlantic: the massive numbers of enslaved African males delivered to the sectors of the American economy developed as sources of agricultural commodities. However, monarchs in sixteenth-century Portugal, unlike their Spanish counterparts, depended on merchants, specifically on foreign ones, for the capital resources they could bring to American regions that proved (initially) lacking in precious metals and marginal to their principal interests in African gold and Asian spices.[54] Portuguese investors focused on Spanish silver, abundantly available by the 1560s, to deliver African captives to sell for pieces of eight in the Spanish mainland colonies in the Americas under the first asiento contracts in the 1590s.[55] The initial *asientistas* covered their investments by taking advantage of the late sixteenth-century[56] drought-induced distress in Angola to acquire refugees and captives widely available there at affordably (but very exceptionally) low cost, increasing the scale of the trade by a factor of ten from one decade to the next between the 1580s and 1590s.

Some of these captives helped to convert early struggling production of sugar in northeastern Brazil to the first large-scale production of an agricultural commodity in the New World. The access to Spanish silver that the Portuguese achieved through these asiento contracts allowed them to cover the high mortality costs of the initial transatlantic transport of of captives in these unprecedentedly large numbers, effectively financing deliveries of Africans to the Americas in multiples of previous numbers there or in Europe.[57] Distress in Africa covered the costs of the inevitable inefficiencies of the adaptations required to extend household slaving in the Spanish Americas to agricultural production in Brazil. Dutch-based commercial capital seized the opportunity of slave-laden vessels passing northeastern Brazil en route to the Spanish Indies, as well as lusophone connections through Sephardic merchants expelled from Portugal during the Iberian Union, to finance purchases by the Portuguese of some of the captives to extend to the Americas, for the first time on appreciable scales, earlier successes with sugar in the eastern Atlantic. As a result, monarchs in Lisbon ended up consigning their fortuitous territorial claims in the Americas to what became Brazil to a succession of commercial interests, backed substantially by foreigners. One of the persisting characteristics of Old World slaving had been the small-to-modest-scale of demand there for servants, mostly women, distributed among households. Larger concentrations of unassimilated male slaves in ancient Rome and in the Muslim world had been notable primarily for the challenges that the private strategies of slaving that produced them had turned out to pose for public authority.[58] Hasty abandonments of these dangerous experiments made them the exception that proved the rule of viable strategies of enslaving that dispersed women and children in domestic households.[59] In the New World, commercialization prevailed, initiated by financing on the backs of the people enslaved. And the other financial strategies that later were brought to bear on integrating a fast-growing Atlantic economy built incrementally, as always, on its start from slaving.

Answers to Isolation: Reconstituting Community in Slavery

The Africans, mostly men, who found themselves cutting cane in northeastern Brazil arrived there as isolated individuals. But eventually and relatively belatedly, ca. the 1620s, they found themselves entering aggregations of field laborers of substantial size. These allowed newcomers to convert the strategies of belonging craved by the enslaved from seeking places within their masters' households to finding associations among others enslaved in what can be termed communities only very crudely, in the sense of a secure environment of mutual moral commitment.[60] This prospect of even limited solidarity within slavery was radically new in the global history of slaving. Later, elsewhere in the Americas, it enabled the American-born descendants of other slaves to act publicly as slaves, in collaborative ways that their predecessors had found themselves able to approach only rarely. Community among the enslaved in the Old World had functioned primarily within, as support for its members;[61] in the New World it became a means to perform collectivity without, as a collective political presence.

To consider these incipient communities within the framework of the historical epistemology I am emphasizing, we must see them as strategies that their members adapted in incremental, processual ways, through time, to engage the changing social and cultural contexts that motivated and enabled them to act. In most times and places in the Americas, the communal character of such aggregates was barely incipient, since purchases, sales, escapes, and ubiquitous deaths made them anything but stable in terms of personnel. In this sense, these ad hoc groupings were extreme examples of the collective fragility that throughout world history had prompted bloody immolations of enemies to create or recover community. But their members were themselves slaves and seldom had the means to appropriate outsiders as victims.[62] The integrity and internal composition of an aggregate of male slaves in the Americas, unlike, say, a true community in Africa based on shared descent and hence in significant part on biological reproduction, suffered from the involuntary movements through it of its always temporary and contingent members. In the Americas, as fungible property slaves were essentially mobile, unwillingly and isolatingly so, both in entering enslavement by violent uprooting and forced transfer and then in leaving whatever groupings they could form through deaths and distributions of their masters' estates, of which they were themselves major components, or through sales.[63] This inherent, ongoing process of constant, complex, and contested movements through these aggregates, the varying rhythms of entering and leaving, was the historical focus of slaves' lives in the large numbers in which they were assembled in the Americas.

Over time, to take an example from among the clichés of slavery as an institution, the inability of the enslaved in the Americas to create communities of the integral sort that transcends the generations born into them explains why collective attempts at revolt were so infrequent, so partial when they did occur, and then so often betrayed from within. Revolt succeeded militarily in only a single instance—Saint-Domingue, in 1791–1804—and then only with evaporation of opposition, extensive European armed interventions, and only momentarily in any unified sense. In the commercialized American context, slaves' agency lay rather in their struggles to create community among themselves, prior to appropriating a resulting solidary institution against their masters. Most of them sought not to escape but to remain. Leaving through escape succeeded only through the ambiguous marginality of "maroon" communities established in the wilderness, and even these tended to stay in close touch with the slaves on plantations and sometimes even also with the masters.[64] Leaving slavery through individual manumission was no less ambivalent in the limited degree of separation sought, or established, by those freed into continuing, if negotiated, dependence on former masters. When emancipated, eventually, they withdrew from the market that had been the bane of their attempts to constitute community through family formation and sought legal recognition of their marriages to stabilize families.

Hence, we should expect (and the first hints of research along these lines are starting to appear)[65] that the vulnerability of the enslaved to repeated uprooting and to mortality figured prominently among their preoccupations. In seeking ways of limiting involuntary mobility, in creating techniques of social reconstitution under continual threat of destruction of the bonds they formed among themselves, and in staying in contact with the departed in their spiritual imaginations lay the primary strategies of people otherwise repeatedly and desperately isolated by their enslavement. The fundamental isolation of enslavement also nurtured the fierce individualism and creativity that later sustained its survivors in slavery and in freedom.

The Enslaved as Public Problems in the Americas

For masters in the Americas, by the early eighteenth century the aggrega-
tion of enslaved men in such massive numbers and the opportunities that the
men enslaved made of them posed entirely novel and largely unanticipated
problems. Analysts in Europe, political economists sensitive to the New
World realities more than theologians keyed on Old World ethics, acutely and
immediately recognized them as such. The profound demographic dominance
of the enslaved and their public prominence in the Americas, for me, help to
resolve Davis's classic problematization of why Europeans only then began
to extend their long-standing concern for the private morality of slaving into
the realm of its public political and economic viability, as commercialized on
these disquieting scales.[66] Racialization itself was not the causative change,
but a later aspect of the public categorization of persons generic to a commercializing world.

Spain had headed off the problem by protecting Native Americans and
limiting imports of Africans, and the Portuguese had enveloped the Africans
assembled to cultivate sugar in Brazil within a late-medieval ideology of
paternalistic, hence private control, secular and clerical. Before the late seventeenth century, nothing like the public, governmental problematic of massive
numbers of enslaved Africans had existed in new sugar-producing plantations
on the English and French islands in the Caribbean. They required public,
institutionalized responses, harbingers of the direct legal authority over individuals that is the other, and hardly less problematic, side of civic freedoms
in modern nation-states.

The problems of institutionalizing slavery in the Americas emerged on both
sides of the Atlantic, police and discipline for masters in the Americas and consolidation of monarchical authority in Europe. Locally, from the 1670s English
masters devised "slave codes" to support individual planters with an added
level of police discipline, first in the precocious sugar island of Barbados and
then extended to settlements in the Carolina Lowcountry and the Chesapeake
on the North American mainland. But the background political problematic
centered on the challenges that large, remote populations of slaves in prosperous private hands posed for the still formative model of monarchical absolutism
in Europe. Louis XIV in Paris (but not his counterparts in Lisbon, weak and
distracted as the recently restored autonomous Portuguese monarchy was in
the second half of the seventeenth century) tried to respond with codifications
of royal law that applied the ethical standards of the Old World slavery they
knew to the commercial and political realities that large gangs of enslaved
Africans in the New World were forcing them also to take into account.[67]

In the conventional logic of comparing types of slavery, abstractly contrasted as harsh or mild, the French *Code Noir* (1685) appears to be a self-
contradictory blend. This old saw of the literature on slavery as an institution contrasts cultural traditions, legal precedents in Roman law, and other
continuities across an Anglo-Iberian divide, extended to France through a
loose Protestant-Catholic analog. But as a moment in the historical process
of adapting Old World slaving toward New World slavery, the *Code Noir*
was routinely incremental. It threaded the woof of the new through the warp
of the older elements running through the moment, as legal authorities at the
French court tried to comprehend the radical novelty of large populations of
anonymous African males massed in segregated barracks on the basis of prior
European experience with small numbers of females of diverse backgrounds
dispersed among numerous households and living there close to their nominal
masters. The African men assembled in such potentially threatening numbers
in the Americas became, for the first time, not the concerns of personal ethics
but very immediate problems of public policy. Monarchies then stepped in,
promptly enough; social philosophers redefined slaving in the language of
political economy and eventually of liberal economics to take account of its
overwhelmingly commercial applications in the Americas; and populist dissenters and politicians took up the contradictions of a corresponding humanist
vision of people treated as property—not without accompanying overtones
of protest at the political power that personal property in other humans gave
to unrestrained, free masters—as causes under the banners of abolition.[68]

The bottom line was financial. A parallel sequence of historical processes
(rather than a time-transcending typology of sociological abstractions) ran
through the growing availability of capital in the early seventeenth century
that financed the transition in strategies of employment other than slaving. Against the broad background of indebtedness that financed the early
Atlantic economy, these began as low-investment, negotiable, short-term
personal entailments – the contracts of indenture characteristic of English Atlantic colonies in the early seventeenth century. By the nineteenth century, they
had moved toward use of the even shorter-term and individual worker-financed
informal contracts characterized as wages. Later ideological representation of
these later arrangements as free opposed them to permanent employer investments, as collateralizable property, in slaves.

On the other hand, viewing these strategies of labor mobilization historically and thus incrementally highlights them as ways of diverting scarce liquid
capital from labor to fund much large investments in labor-saving material
(not human) technology. Waged employment in mechanized industry was a
further step in a series of extensions from employer-financed apprenticeships,

indentures, and slavery to employee self-financed services, paid only after the effort and leaving the worker bearing the entire risk of the implicit contract. Advances of credit against wages to be earned are binding debts on the worker, although waged workers effectively finance the working capital of the employer. Freedom in economic terms did not bring the unmitigated opportunity that its celebration as a civic virtue is intended to suggest. In northeastern Brazil, recent research on *candomblé*—Afro-Brazilian communities long styled as religious and attributed romantically to origins in the Yoruba-speaking parts of modern Nigeria—is revealing how slaves freed as slavery declined there in the nineteenth century banded together in self-help associations by importing discourses of community (therapeutic cults of affliction) from Africa to heal the ills of isolation imposed by legal freedom in a society composed of clienteles, enslaved and freed.[69]

Wages and slavery, the two strategies of commercializing human relations, are usually contrasted as abstractions but in fact were regionally specific complements, mutually contextualized alternative strategies of a single, pan-Atlantic process of commercialization. Non-cash-waged slaving in the Americas financed the concentration of cash in Europe, paid in growing part in wages there in the context of increasingly commercialized economic growth at rates that strained the limits of the specie available to finance it—in Europe and the Americas as well as in Africa. As a result, continental Europe and England expanded their local uses of wages from a strategy largely confined to specialized temporary engagements in a larger context of other, longer-term arrangements not remunerated directly to a generalized strategy of ongoing employment by concentrating the specie not expended in acquiring and maintaining the African populations toiling in the Americas as slaves.[70]

Modern Atlantic slaving thereby applied an old strategy of building relationships, households in Europe and lineages in Africa, through slaving to new, commercialized ends of buying strangers. In the Americas, merchants could invest in production, using enslaved Africans as laborers, uninhibited by competing aristocratic or ecclesiastical claims to land and its residents. With capital backed by the unprecedented cornucopia of wealth in New World silver and eventually also Brazilian gold, they integrated the world of commercialized slaving centered on plantations, worked by highly fungible human collateral. By the eighteenth century, their prominence then led to institutionalization of slavery as a public status of exclusion from significant initiatives in this emergent public space. The enslaved might earn small amounts of cash, but they could not invest in the main game of cash-earning production.

These contradictions emerged most strongly in the wealthiest, or best-financed, regions, primarily British. The patron–client tone of Old World domestic slaving remained the ideology, though by the late 1700s its practice survived mostly in such economically less dynamic regions as northeastern Brazil and parts of the Spanish Americas. The regions under Spanish royal authority kept slavers there within bounds also by extending the paternalistic tone of monarchical protection to the royal courts that administered the king's justice, routinely intruding into the generally prevailing domestic slaving that survived there, accommodated—significantly, as an aspect of the historical context—by a legal framework that had applied the essentially household notion of slaving from Roman times to the no-less-domestic practices of thirteenth-century Iberia. The Catholic Church used its sacraments similarly. Slaving in the Americas had become a public problem on multiple levels, long before modern civic regimes racialized the American children of enslaved Africans to exclude them from formative national polities.

Contextualizing Abolition as Historical Process

These novelties of slavery in the New World, as a political problem (and not racism, in the relevant politicized sense of the term), bring us finally to abolition, the problem behind the problematization of slavery that has prompted this book. Abolition, both in the British sense of ending the Atlantic trade and in the American sense of emancipating the enslaved, redefined slavery as a political problem subject to public, not private, resolution. Within the confines of this chapter, I cannot gloss the intellectual and political details of a narrative already told elegantly by Davis and others. In fact, descending into details from the pan-Atlantic and *longue durée* of the historical processes I am attempting to define would risk distracting readers from my analytical approach, which is to highlight moments that illustrate historically significant changes in slaving as a strategy.[71] In that selective spirit, I'll move directly to North America, partly because the antebellum United States is so seductive a source of the contemporary politicized paradigm of slavery as an institution, even though its institutionalization there was the least representative instance of the processes of slaving in the global perspective that I want to establish here. The United States, against the background of Great Britain, is thus also most revealing of the misleadingly modern premises of attempting to understand slaving in world history in terms of slavery as the institution that it became there, uniquely.

The commercial strategies in the sixteenth- and early seventeenth-century Atlantic that I've emphasized in their incipient, most problematic and contested phases became dominant (and thus no longer problematical) at the end of the seventeenth century. The English defeated the Dutch for the leading position in what then became an era of intensely competitive and formatively rapid commercial growth in New World commodities produced by slaves. The American commodities were led by Caribbean sugar, with corresponding intensification in Atlantic slaving and in the sizes of the incipiently threatening quasi-communities of enslaved Africans in the Americas. The eighteenth century was also the most intense period of slaving in Africa, as I outlined in chapter 3. More than half of the people taken from Africa to the Americas crossed the Atlantic between the 1670s and about 1810.[72]

In the Caribbean and Brazil, the increasingly diverse backgrounds of the growing numbers of Africans introduced there and mortality among the enslaved turned the focus of agency of the enslaved from belonging in the more personal senses that had earlier characterized slaving to staff the households of the possessions of Spain and Portugal toward working out neo-ethnic identities among themselves.[73] Ethnicity is a particularly modern historical strategy, one to which people resort when thrown together without prior personal connections.[74] Africans did it, as the preceding chapter describes. Modern nation-states do it now. For the enslaved in the commercialized Atlantic, the corresponding circumstantial associations, seized on to create moral communities of belonging, derived from their origins as the commercial property they had become. Accordingly, African ethnicities in the Americas related more to the various ports along the African coast where they had entered the commercial world of the Atlantic, often building on broadly shared linguistic backgrounds in the regions from where they had come, than to the other communities in which they had previously lived.

Such New World ethnicities were entirely viable historical strategies, appropriated in the changing contexts through which the enslaved were moved. The slaves who invented them

1. for newcomers, negotiated places for themselves within the aggregates formed by their predecessors that they entered, or to establish networks on a colonywide basis to ease further transitions of being moved from owner to owner or plantation to plantation, as well as

2. provided an approximation of the community necessary to give decent burials to those departed through the ubiquitous deaths,

3. protected claims to favored treatment among the ethnic guilds thus created, particularly against newcomers from other parts of Africa, whom they thus forced to respond by organizing in parallel ethnic idioms, and

4. with regard to their masters, asserted a public character, allegedly inherited and consequently extending the African strategy of accommodating change by honoring antiquity, thus in theory independent of the demeaning and

demanding identities otherwise conferred entirely by their enslaved status in the Americas, however unreflective these performative American identities may have been of the socially pointless personal biographies that the people claiming them had lost

5. and in contexts with large numbers of manumitted or otherwise free persons of slave descent, creating neo-ethnic communities transcending the legal distinctions of slavery itself.

These ideological identities of the enslaved in the Atlantic as historical strategies paralleled the simultaneous creation of no-less-novel ethnicized communities of refugees and slaves in Africa.[75] The strategy also paralleled those of the slavers and of their European opponents in being formed significantly around the presence of Africans enslaved in socially and culturally viable aggregations, that is, in the historically catalytic contexts created by slaving. Neo-African ethnicities in the Americas, similarly imagined, were likewise useful. Once historicized in this way, they were modern and manipulated rather than inherited and inert, thus thoroughly historical strategies of clustering to manage change. They also tended to define places for the enslaved in public spaces other than the marginalized ones politicized by monarchical courts or, later, by constituted nations.[76]

All these historically specific ethnicizing strategies of the enslaved contrast with the identities that the enslaved in North America developed around family. As early as the middle of the eighteenth century, enslaved women and men in the Chesapeake began to reproduce families of their own.[77] Having families shifted their strategic focus from neo-ethnic (or ethnicized) competition among cohorts, mostly males, of new arrivals from Africa to formation of the effective control they exercised over reproducing communities of their own. These "generations of captivity"[78] did so in spite of recurring dispersals of their formative families among many small, often isolated residential units, accompanied by a near-total commercialization of their enslavement in proprietorial terms through sales. Simultaneous crushing exclusions from an emerging civic sphere turned them from pursuit of public recognition through performance of ethnicity to exploiting private patronage by owners radically empowered by the local and civic politics of a new republic. In the United States, unlike in Brazil or the colonies of Spain or even in the French Caribbean, slaves had no king's justice in which to seek refuge.

These historical and consequently varied strategies and processes of slaving and of living in enslavement generated no less diverse reactions throughout the Americas, according to the marginal positions of the slavers. From one end of the Americas to the other owners asserted their private proprietorial powers in degrees that approached the inverse of the influence over their slaves achieved through personal familiarity with them. Perhaps more significantly, property became the first proslavery line of defense in direct proportion to the marginality of the slavers in the larger political communities within which they relied on their property in humans to promote or secure their positions. Only where growing monarchical or, eventually, national political authority threatened to intrude on historically private patriarchal domains did they seriously defend their possession of human property.

To take Brazil as one example of manumissions and ultimately of emancipation as a nonevent: the lords (*senhores*) of the great houses (*casas grandes*) of the large agricultural estates and the town houses prominent in the memory of Brazilian slavery, assiduous in proclaiming their loyalty to the Portuguese Crown but also and accordingly careful in practice to evade its limited influence, exercised domestic intimacy of an intensity later sexualized and celebrated in the initial postslavery generation's memorialization of the era of its parents.[79] Sugar barons and their household retinues in Brazil shared loyalty to a distant king and after 1822 to an emperor in Rio de Janeiro; they felt little sense of themselves as members of a Brazilian and even less a Portuguese civic community, even well beyond the ending of slavery there in 1888. In the relative absence of monarchy or its nineteenth-century sequel, phrased as an empire to acknowledge local autonomies and in utter innocence of nationalism, they embodied the independence based on slaving that stronger monarchies in northern Europe had displaced to the Americas.

In composite/compound polities like Portuguese and independent imperial Brazil, allegiance was generally negotiated honorably between patrons and clients. Public abolitionist sentiments therefore emerged in Brazil in the nineteenth century only faintly and belatedly, when European immigrants of various backgrounds posed the novel problem of defining a civic identity in inclusive terms that could be modernized as national. Three centuries of only incidentally racialized patronage diminished the viability of modern politicized race as a way to assert a white national identity on the vast and variegated scale of Brazil. For the established barons of the great agricultural manors and town houses in the northeast, emancipation barely disturbed their ongoing relations of clientage radiating out through families of all shades, affines, freed former slaves, and clients of every public status. The slaves on the newer, more commercial coffee estates of central and southern Brazil simply decamped into rural peasantries.

For the absentee owners of huge early nineteenth-century plantations in the West Indies, emancipation was a matter of grasping the least of a set of looming economic evils. For them, personal relations with the enslaved workers on these rural "factories in the fields" were all but inconceivable, except for the most selected, mostly females, with their often-freed descendants. The issue of human property in this overwhelmingly commercialized context became principally a financial one. Since a way of life was not at stake, emancipation of human property was ultimately negotiable between the separate spheres of liberal politics, with its humanitarian enthusiasms in England and the resolutely fiscal and military concerns of conservative colonial strategists.

Parliament and metropolitan popular politics prevailed, with general emancipation coming in 1834–38. By the early nineteenth century, British slave traders and West Indian owners of slaves were both sufficiently marginal to the domestic politics of industrializing Britain to be sacrificed to emerging national interest. Formative working classes there could assert participatory roles in emerging politics of inclusiveness by championing the cause of even more benighted fellow workers in the canebrakes of the Caribbean. Established landed and industrializing interests could seize on their enthusiasms to play domestic working-class complaints of political exclusion and economic hardship off against stereotypes of modern enslavement in the Americas, safely remote from primary political concerns in Britain, as even more excluding and harsh. Thus the empowered interests in England conceded more in sentiment than in reality at home and ultimately also tolerated a limited and delayed sort of emancipation in a buyout in the islands. In doing so, with great public clamor, they contributed to the image of slavery as an institution of domination that now characterizes the literature in the field.

In France and the French Americas, the Paris (1789) and Haitian (1791) revolutions and subsequent continental wars all but ended slaving and rendered possession of slaves in the Antilles peripheral to more pressing concerns of converting republican revolutionary ideals to a French national civic identity. Abolitionism in France remained mostly an intellectual conceit, and emancipation itself in 1848 was a nonevent in political terms, marginalized by the domestic turmoil of that year throughout Europe. Culture, not politics, became the route opened to inclusion in the colonies through assimilation, including in Africa.

Finally, the United States, the paradigm of abolition that frames the historiography of slavery as an institution: all of the North American dynamics of slaving and slavery were unique. By the time the realities of erecting a new, effectively united Republic on a wobbly platform of thirteen (and soon more) differing colonial legacies forced rebellious former colonials to face themselves without a shared threatening enemy in London, well before imports of new slaves ended in 1807, most of those enslaved in the ideologically formative Chesapeake were Americans, not Africans. They were increasingly native-born

and English-speaking, their children eventually also Christian, and potentially disturbingly, as often unacknowledged members of the same extended
"*American* famil[ies] black and white."[80] To indulge in a "Charlottesville
moment," Mr. Jefferson and Ms. Hemings remain powerful symbols of this
transgression of all of the dichotomized ideological premises of slavery in the
United States: she was a woman enslaved, racially ambiguous, included in
the household of her owner in the most intimate ways, not disabled, perhaps
not even vulnerable. She was long obscured in the admiring historiography
of her nominal master. This obscurity derived from the implied and therefore
also powerfully denied—status of Hemings as a "founding mother" along with
Martha Washington, Abigail Adams, and Dolley Madison, if acknowledged
as consort of the nation's founding father.[81]

Simultaneously, and contradictorily, the characterization of these enslaved
Americans (if not also kin) as property became exaggerated by the 1820s
because of the profound commercialization of slavery in the industrializing
Chesapeake and in the cotton South and also because of the value of these
human beings as collateralizable property to gentlemen farmers seeking dignity and autonomy by mastering slaves but who were themselves increasingly
mastered in a commercial sense by creditors in Britain and later in northern
banks and eventually by the federal government. Jefferson is once again paradigmatic: his slaves, except for a few, perhaps his children, whom he freed,
were sold from his estate to pay off debts left from his otherwise rich and
creative (whether or not also procreative) life.[82]

Republican politics in the nascent United States further exaggerated the
contradictions of community within the broadly commercialized and individuating contexts of Atlantic slaving. Civic ideals of imagined inclusion in
North America were intense and volatile, amidst the challenges of forming
a functionally national identity among residents of unprecedentedly—and
also increasingly—diverse origins, recency of arrival, and unsettled relations
among themselves, except in terms of an invented shared whiteness. By the
1830s operative participatory politics generated intense public pressures
on both slavery and on perceptible, as socially ascribed, African ancestry.
The United States in the 1840s and 1850s thus entered one of those fragile
moments, which I have dated here from the dawn of humanity and history, of
uniting around exploitation of the vulnerability of the alien trapped within,[83]
if not also against enemieswithout.

The growing consciousness and sensitivity of civic inclusiveness identified
as anomalous and immoral anyone who would exclude native-born residents,
many of them kin, as slaves. Masters also held these people entirely beyond
the sphere of civic regulation on which the free found themselves anxiously

dependent. The ability of slavery to support personal power in the public realm from human bodies held as private property appeared imminently erosive of the integrity of a body politic increasingly understood in corporate terms as a nation. The United States Congress and the federal judiciary debated slavery in these terms for an entire generation. Slavery as thus institutionalized—that is, as politicized ideology—generated a broadly inclusive response through the familiar story of rising popular alarm at its place (rather less than the personal places of those enslaved)[84] as part of the process of consolidating a truly national politics, in the senses both of popular and participatory and of transregional, beyond the local communities in which people up to them had primarily lived their daily lives.

This fast-changing and urgent political context rendered legal and tactical compromises once tenable in less inclusive constitutional times no longer acceptable. The political debates accordingly took place precisely in terms of more and less strict constructions of an originary charter, the Constitution, more or less willing to acknowledge the emergent novelties of nationalism. These followed the familiar path of reinterpreting remembered pasts to fit present contexts, according to another originary logic that reached back to Roman times on both sides, slaveholders and republicans. The originary fallacy of selective memorialization of the past for purposes in the present is a very modern temptation, the opposite of restorative African tendencies to reconstrue the present to meet standards attributed to the past. Abolitionist tropes also portrayed slavery as a violation or inversion of the emerging commercial and national identities of the nation, with relatively incidental acknowledgment of the more complex realities of living in or with slavery.

Nineteenth-century Americans of ascribed African ancestry confronted in stark terms the problem of living under this highly ideologized slavery, rendered more and more perpetual by proprietorial concerns and by the growing sensitivity of their presence in a civic, participatory political culture. Anywhere else in the world they would have been acknowledged as the native-born sons and daughters of the land that they were.[85] Survivors of enslavement elsewhere have generally moved through some form of admission into other forms of dependency within private, domestic households. But such corporate dependency was not possible in a democratic nation of recognized, even participating, individual voters, strongly contrasted with and even defined by the ultimately nonparticipatory status of slavery. Hence, sales away to other owners, not manumission through self-purchase, became the principal, highly commercialized strategy of recognizing the personal value that the enslaved achieved by skills and ability, appropriating it in a financial sense.

As cotton boomed on the southwestern frontier, the families and communities of slaves in the Chesapeake and in the Carolina Lowcountry replaced Atlantic slaving as the principal sources of fungible collateral, as removable people.[86] Sales "down the river" from the U.S. seaboard removed recalcitrants who strained at restraint or guilt- and hostility-provoking unacknowledged potential heirs and severely challenged the communal strength the enslaved had built up through family strategies, by then for generations. The ephemeral single antebellum generation of the 1840s and 1850s from Georgia to Texas, individuals isolated by their removal, upon arriving on the highly commercial frontier plantations of the cotton South, had to find other ways to create communities of their own, other places to belong.

As a moment in a process influenced profoundly by Americans in slavery, the hypothetical question—had the national problem of slavery not intervened in the form of civil war—is what problems their children, growing up and living where they had been born, with families to defend and another generation's experience, would have created for their owners in the 1860s and 1870s. As it was, Union victory in the war released them to reconstitute the families dispersed in the preceding decade, as far as possible, aided by the Freedmen's Bureau. Then, betrayed by the failure of Reconstruction (for them, at least), they and their emancipated children lived in commercialized tenancy not dissimilar to the continuing personal dependency of other slaves manumitted elsewhere in the world. Commercialization had, by then, proceeded far enough that modern strategies of direct, individuated debt smoothly succeeded legal bondage as a means of control, though, in the impoverished postwar South, not sufficiently to fund wages. As increasingly populist, progressive politics of the modern United States prevailed, they had no significant places. The liberal reaction to these failures that followed from the 1930s to the 1950s framed the neo-abolitionist tone, with which we still live today, of condemning slavery as institutionalized, and then abolished, uniquely in the United States.

An Integrated Historical Dynamic

In the course of this sketch of slaving in the world's history, it has probably never been more apparent how much I have left unsaid about specific applications of treating slaving historically than here at the conclusion of the story, with the legal institutionalization and governmental abolition of slavery in the United States.[87] I hope that the preceding three chapters have sufficiently problematized slaving in its full, inherent, and dynamic historicity to raise new and interesting questions about a subject, at personal, societal, and global scales, that we have not known as well as we thought we did. Historicized, slavery in the United States appears "peculiar" not as a throwback to elite authoritarianism in an age of popular democracy or as an archaic form of labor in the age of capitalist progress, but as a run-of-the-mill historical adaptation of slaving to the commercialized modern Atlantic world, eventually unsustainably in the context of a uniquely civic political context, the modern nation-state.

African gold and then American silver, supplemented latterly by modern financial techniques of banking and insurance, were the primary means to this pervasive commercialization of the world, as well as of the slaving in it. Slaving in Africa's domestic political economy of people, which exported the metal precious in the Atlantic and imported textiles and other wares to invest in human relationships, was the indirect means by which marginal interests in all three of the continents involved, merchants with fewer cash resources in Europe, groups and individuals in Africa with fewer people, and indebted commodity producers in the Americas, gained places in the main Atlantic game of accumulating financial resources. Owners of the Africans delivered in the Americas financed the rapid growth of commodity production in significant part by collateralizing their human resources as personal property. The speed with which European financial capacity grew, accelerated through these complementing strategies of the marginal, in turn financed the European credit that overheated the African economy to the violence that generated still more captives, to be sold as slaves. In history, there are no single causes; there are always multiple engaged actors, with multiple motivations in multiple contexts, all complementing and competing at the same time.

However, mass commercialized enslavement of adult males in the Americas brought the political problematic of slaving, long-standing in Eurasia, to the fore in Africa and the Americas. In the composite polities of Africa and in Eurasian contexts with rival claims to local populations among military, ecclesiastical, and merchant interests, competitive slaving maintained a supple balance among the interests involved. In the fifteenth-century Mediterranean, the balance of slaving, mostly domestic and female, tilted in favor of growing merchant cities,[88] and the merchants in them extended their commercial capacity to supply slaves to collateralizing them to finance agricultural production on Atlantic islands, and on then to the American mainland. Slaves as property thus entered the public domain of commercial law. The large numbers of African men assembled in the Americas brought them, in differing ways, into the growing domains of monarchical law in Europe and also into the police regulations and other local legal spheres, not least wills and estates, in the colonies. In the indebted context of rapid economic growth in the Atlantic, property mattered as the principal form of security for private ambition funded by creditors in Europe.

Politically, the commercial Atlantic was no more reassuring. Its great distances and mobility individuated the Europeans active there, not unlike the repeated individuation of the enslaved, repeatedly isolated as financial assets by deaths and by sales. The Atlantic became an acutely, motivatingly anxious space for all, a space in which masters clustered in local participatory communities for the personal security that monarchies in distant Europe could not provide. Uneasy masters and vulnerable slaves, contextualized in the novel and fast-changing historicized circumstances of the Atlantic, shared more in their individuation than the modern politics and abstract polarities of the master–slave dyad have inclined students of the subject to notice.

In the intellectual context of growing enlightened humanism, the political exclusions of public slavery became an intolerable problem, as implemented politically in inclusive territorial, civic, and incipiently national states, particularly in North America. Citizens turned to their new, untested representative governments to terminate the institutionalized and legally formulated slavery that their predecessors had created by means that national governments could access. The economic failures of the resulting emancipations, at least from the point of view of the people freed, demonstrated the limits of the constructed legal aspect of the enslavement thus terminated.

Slavery as an institution, however symbolically valuable emancipation may have been to politicians in the process of building political nations out of the many communities living within the boundaries of the monarchical territories they had inherited, was only one aspect of deep-running historical processes of slaving. In a world in which the enabling historical process was that of consolidating commercialized modernity, former masters in the U.S. South turned to the familiar methods of sharecropping to try to recapitalize from the legislated loss of their collateralized human assets. In the British West Indies, government compensation paid off the planters, and the former slaves withdrew from the commercial economy. The seigneurial estates in northeastern Brazil had long been drifting toward a commercially marginal mixture of clienteles, which they sustained through emancipation (1888) and well into the republican era that succeeded the empire in 1889. Elsewhere in the Americas, the enslaved were too few and too little engaged in production to become significant problems in the very limited civic participatory politics of the independent Hispanic republics established in the 1820s. So long as Cuba remained Spanish, and subsequently under American tutelage, the civic nation-building politics of abolition would not emerge.

Modern commercialized slaving of males for production of commodities was also problematic when contextualized in its global legacy of recruitment of outsiders, mostly of females and children, for the domestic, private purposes

of insiders. The resulting presence of the enslaved posed only indirect challenges to the public interests and authorities who were dominant in formal
political terms, and so concerns about potential abuses of the enslaved had
formerly arisen largely in the realm of personal ethics, charging masters with
honorable and responsible patronage. But when slavery emerged in a non-
slaveholding world of radical individuation as a problem of overwhelmingly
public proportions, it became both institutionalized and problematic to the
degree that civic society and politicized racism in Europe and North America
replaced patronage as the structure of politics. Earlier adaptations of Eurasian
domestic slaving to the Americas in Hispanic colonies and in Brazil in the
sixteenth and seventeenth centuries had left legacies there of domestic households and personal and monarchical patronage that recognized its assimilative
or incorporative processes and accommodated the survivors of enslavement
and their children as clients and dependents of other sorts.

But in the United States, legal rights accorded the children of enslaved
women, an unacknowledged and therefore darkly looming proportion of
whom were sired by their masters, threatened the rights of legitimate heirs
defined as free and white. The enslaved became residents rather than uprooted
outsiders, reproducing communities rather than individuals imported and
thus isolated. They built private relational communities of their own rather
than seeking public protection and patronage from their masters. Community
shifted from internally heterogeneous households in Europe and Asia and lineages in Africa, united by public pressures external to them, to public, legal,
and eventually racialized categories that divided the communities in which
people lived. In the Americas, to the varying degrees that public politics institutionalized modern commercialized slavery they violated all the defining, and
elsewhere enabling, qualities of historical slaving: control became impersonal
rather than personal, thus dehumanizing the enslaved in an age of growing,
if still more abstract than implemented, humanism.

The problem of institutionalized slavery, rephrased as an anomalous modern outcome of long-term historical processes throughout the world, helps to
account for the highly politicized popular movements dedicated to abolition
and emancipation in parts of the eighteenth- and nineteenth-century northern Atlantic. These politically mobilizing causes, which Davis has helped
us understand in rich and erudite and sensitive intellectual specificity, were
constitutive components of localized processes of creating civic identities of
a virtuous intensity or an intense virtue, reassuring to subjects and citizens
otherwise drifting in the anonymity and isolation of modern individuation,
struggling to imagine new communities of a certainty as compelling as those of
the older worlds they had lost.[89] Abstractly constituted governments, the very

models of modernity,[90] demonstrated benign and protective recognition of the individuals within the territories for which they were responsible through the exercise of incipiently—or, in the case of the United States, intensely—national government authority, by force if necessary. Hence also, since today we live globally in terms of the national institutions, ideologies, and identities thus created, we continue to embrace the overwhelmingly familiar, highly politicized problematic of slavery as an abominable institution. It is the exclusionary ideological inverse of the inclusive standards of building modern nations, at least in the British, French, and U.S. models, that has obscured strategies of slaving elsewhere and earlier, and to the point of invisibility in an African past imagined as entirely ahistorical.

If this historicized phrasing only expands on elements of the familiar story of slavery as an institution, even nuances that are obvious when viewed from within the particular fields comprehended in this broad analysis, then I will have made my point about the insights yielded by the multiple perspectives that define world history: others' experiences reveal new wrinkles even, or particularly, in seemingly familiar faces, by contextualizing them in the dynamics of the incremental human historical strategies experienced only in particular ways throughout time and around the globe. It converts abstract typological contrasts of the modern mind into intuitively integrated processes motivated by the minds of others. The terms in which I have problematized slaving in the Americas as history are derived from dynamics of slaving evident on global scales, rather than from the modern perspectives on nationalized pasts that otherwise prevail throughout the discipline of history. The most familiar example, the historically very peculiar institution created in the antebellum United States, is also the most exceptional.

Hence, finally, my personal sense of urgency in presenting these ideas, both as a historian addicted to the ephemeralities of life and to appreciation of the infinite diversity of human ways of experiencing it, and also as an inhabitant of a modern world still torn by invocations of slavery—and of race—as institutions more permanent, hence unalterable, and thus more rigidly divisive than were actual historical practices of slaving in the past, including our own. The sufferings of the enslaved were not less than the civic disabilities implied by the model of the legalized institution but infinitely more diverse. People marginalized by historical change have always devised new strategies of slaving to challenge and in the end defeat monarchy and the nation-states that are its modern, militarized successors. By historicizing the diversity of slaving through all of the human past, we can accept the resulting diversity in the present not as immutably divisive but as an opportunity to embrace change and thus enrich all of our individual lives in the future.

APPENDIX

Schematic Historical Sequences of Slaving

Chapters 2–4

The following tables provide schematic references to the phases of the historical processes that underlie the epistemological structures of the discussions of slaving strategies in chapters 2 through 4. That is, the three columns in tables 2.1 through 4.2 represent three components of the logic of historical change elaborated in chapter 1. The column to the left frames the two columns to the right with calendar dates, most of them schematic referents to the generic contexts and strategies of slaving characterized in the latter two. The dating column is not so much a chronology or calendar of events as an ordering device to sequence the historical dynamics sketched to the right.

Historical dynamics are defined in chapter 1 as strategic initiatives of actors positioned in historical contexts, cultural, economic, and political. Novel contexts provoke or enable (or both) new initiatives, usually increments minimal in both scale and novelty, but cumulatively productive of the longer-term, large-scale changes that lie at the heart of history's epistemology. The resulting changes are dialectical in that each provokes further responses, accumulating in sequences of incremental initiatives. The tables sketch historical processes of slaving in these terms.

The middle column highlights the contextual changes that provoked and enabled the various strategies of slaving discussed in the chapters to which the tables refer. The resultant strategies – or strategic objectives – of slaving are sketched in the third, right-hand column. One may read these two columns together as a dialectical pair, alternating between them to follow each response (on the right) as leading to the altered context characterized on the following line of the column in the middle, which in turn provoked or enabled the further strategic response on the same line in the column to the right.

One thus reads most effectively across the columns in these tables at given points in time and then from the right-hand column's strategic response back through the (incidentally dated) column on the left to the novel context in the middle, then on to the strategic response on the right, and so on down through time. The set of schematically dated responses illustrates the principal moments in the processes of slaving as a strategy revealed by the historicization of the subject developed in this book.

Table 2.1, Political Contexts of the Past and Strategies of Slaving, presents slaving strategies as very broad categories, on a global scale. In keeping with my historical focus on strategies rather than on structures, I am dating and locating changes, not attempting to characterize periods as homogeneous or static. The periods in the left-hand column are multiplistic in terms of the strategies pursued, since historical contexts are always plural and dialectically contested. Nor are the strategies attributed to each unique to the periods to which they are assigned; rather, the periods are marked by the initiation *and success* of a *novel* strategy of slaving, in some part of the world, perhaps (and likely) in one marginal to the other historical strategies pursued there. Thus the dating offered is notional and framing for the historical columns to the right; it is not analytically substantive in itself. Strategies launched in earlier eras are understood to continue through succeeding ones, sometimes in regions where subsequent initiatives were elaborated and always in the remainder of the world.

Table 3.1, Epochs of the Past in Africa and Relevant/Formative Strategies of Slaving, treats the dating in the same schematic manner as table 2.1 but presents the historical dynamics in the middle and right-hand columns in terms of their specific realizations in Africa, the subject of chapter 3. The incremental steps in the historical processes thus elaborated are more refined and often constitute the precise increments and extensions that led to Africans' elaborations of their specific versions of the broad, generic epochs in table 2.1. Table 3.1 is thus an epistemological statement at a different level of historical logic than table 2.1; its detail offers a more dynamic depiction of the historical processes of slaving, with Africa as its focus.

Table 4 presents the comparable processual aspects of slaving in the Atlantic in terms of the sequence of new contexts it created in the Americas, over a rather shorter period of time but bridging the globally significant collapse of slaving as a sustainable strategy of effecting change to an ideologically structured target from the perspective of the unanticipated consequences of earlier slaving there. Accordingly, the table has two chronological sections. The earlier, table 4.1, Novelties in the Early Atlantic, traces contexts and the utility of the slaving that they produced from the fourteenth-century Mediterranean through the first (legal) strategies of institutionalization, initially commercial, then increasingly as aspects of consolidating monarchical authority in Europe. Owing to the sequence of different locations of significant initiatives in this pan-Atlantic process, the table introduces subdivisions by Atlantic regions, the islands in the eastern Atlantic, the Spanish Indies, Brazil, Barbados, and Martinique. The later, table 4.2, Novelties in the Modern Atlantic, shifts to the regional subdivisions relevant to the later period of dealing with the consequences of (and usually continuing) slaving in the emerging contexts of the modern nation-state as its standards of civic inclusion emerged in varying ways in England, the United States, France, and then, less sustainably, around the world, to the present resurgence of slaving in the global economy of weak, or weakening, nation-states and national cultures.

The last component of table 4, table 4.3, What Changed?, highlights the contrasts in the contexts of earlier eras, sketched in chapter 2 and elaborated for Africa in chapter 3, and the era of modernity, nation-states, abolition, and resurgent slaving—condemned not on grounds of constitutional theory but as universal human rights, and thus accountable to no significant legal authority in an era still dominated by the nation-state. It brings together in a list—with no logical or chronological structure—the analytical concepts and contrasts employed throughout the book to define the historicized alternatives to the modern concept of slavery as an institution. Insofar as it relates directly to a specific chapter in the book, it sketches specific elements of the historical logic elaborated in chapter 1.

Table 2.1 Political Contexts of the Past and Strategies of Slaving

Epoch (approximate date)*	Historical Challenge(s)	Strategies of slaving (responses)
"Reproducing" Communities (~20000–3000 BCE)	Creation of community ethos	Ritual immolation
Age of empires (~3000–1000 BCE) [and later, elsewhere in areas lacking horses]	Formation of military/ political institutions	Military seizure, temple, "state" slaving [Ritual immolation for political purposes, e.g. Aztecs]
Classical (a) (~1000 BCE–varying dates in first millennium CE)	Mercantile challenge (inclusive polities) (monotheistic religions)	(Military seizure, temple, state slaving) Household staffing
Classical (b) (~1000 BCE–varying dates in second millennium CE)	Preservation of ethos of community (era of ethnicity, kinship) (e.g. Africa)	Differential incorporation of hostages, "pawns," wives, slaves within ethos of collective integrity
Commercialization (~1000–1800 CE)	Mercantile challenge (and triumph)	Urban services, households Extension to production on Atlantic plantations
Modernization (~1750–1920)	Creating civic polities/ nations (early colonial rule) Wage economies eroding personal dependencies Emergence of modern categories of individuated anonymity	National integration and corresponding abolitionism, both at home and abroad
Modern (a) (1920–1950)	Consolidation of abstract categories of persons: class, race, gender, nation Era of nation-states	State totalitarianism (inc. colonial rule) Conscription of internal outcasts (gulags, concentration camps) in nationalist extremes International humanitarian campaigns against forms of forced/unfree labor

Table 2.1 (Continued)

Contemporary (b)	International human rights	Modern slaving—
(1950–present)	Weak governments in new nations	prostitution, other sexual labor, *Gastarbeiter*
	Extremes of wealth differentiation	"migrant child labor, other labor," undocumented aliens, commercialized
	Nongovernmental recruiting networks	forms of exploitation, mafia and warlord conscription
The Future?	[??]	[??]

* Dates are notional and Asia- and Euro-centric; some Amerindian and African epochs are later.

Table 3.1 Epochs of the Past in Africa and Relevant/Formative Strategies of Slaving

Epoch (approximate date)	Historical Challenge(s)	Strategies of slaving (responses)
~20000–5000 BCE	Formation of community	Ritual immolation (presumed)
~5000 BCE–~500 CE	Differentiation of communities (era of formative ethnicity), largely around environmental specializations	To incorporate strangers within communal ethos of reciprocity; internal differentiation; hostages—mostly women, children
~500–1500 CE (Era of atypical military regimes in Africa)	Supra-domestic political confederations; increasingly militarized in areas with horses Commercial networks supporting and being supported by military elites	To differentiate the polity or its claimant(s) from underlying domestic contexts in terms of personnel; countervailing intensification of domestic aggregation of outsiders
1500–1800 ("African slave trade" from European perspective, that is, intentionality and funding)	Commercial networks (extraction-based) and local trades developed by retaining captives	To extend and intensify commercialization and incorporation of outsiders on the Atlantic side of the continent Military regimes starting from defensive positions, first slaving through violence, then through commercial strategies (debt and foreclosure)
1800–1900	End of slave exporting, conversion from extraction to production by merchant and political interests Use of credit to create debtors and to foreclose by seizures of personnel.	To invest (people) in production of commodity exports of vegetable oils, beeswax, ivory, rubber Modern arms render military adventurers (warlords) less dependent on aggregating retinues—thus able to sell captives taken
1900–1940	Colonial regimes slowly finance wage labor and public (albeit authoritarian) regimes	End of public slaving; continuation of (hidden) domestic strategies of slaving to survive external pressures of modernity
1940–1970	Nationalist assertion of public political ideologies, i.e., civic equality, modern homogenization	Public embarrassment of private strategies of slaving; groups marginalized by national politics preserve slaves to survive
1970–present	Breakdown of national polities, cash economies, and civic/public politics	Warlords and others recruiting by violent neo-slaving strategies

Table 4.1 Novelties in the Early Atlantic

Background (approximate dates)	Historical challenge(s)	Strategies of slaving (responses)
European "domestic" Slavery (14th c.)	Mediterranean merchants constrained to trade in captive Slavs; superior urban Muslim markets for slaves	Sales to Islamic markets secondarily to Christian cities (merchants); women in urban households
1450s–1490s	Portuguese enter Atlantic, seeking African gold	Incidental Portuguese slaving, derived from slaving in Africa (cf. militarization in this era, area—table 3.1)
1490s–1530s	Merchants (foreign) move into production (sugar) on uninhabited islands— Madeira, São Tomé – under monarchical sponsorship	Shift to Africans for Iberian urban markets
		Extension to production of sugar, collateralization of labor, elaboration of proprietorial principle
	Managing slaves assembled	Manueline Code (Portugal 1516)
1520s–1560s		Elaboration of sugar production (with Italian capital) in São Tomé
Spanish colonies		
1490s–1510s	Staffing New World enterprises	Native American slaving
1520s–1530s	Monarchy constraining *conquistadores* in Americas	"New Laws" (1542)
	Legal protection of assets	Sugar lands, equipment, and labor entailed (1529?)
1580s–1590s	Silver mining	Specie supports early technical challenges (and costs) of Portuguese transatlantic transport of large numbers of Africans
1590s	Containing merchants	*Asiento* to externalize African slaving to foreign merchants Secondary deliveries of Africans to northeastern Brazil

(continued)

Table 4.1 (Continued)

Background (approximate dates)	Historical challenge(s)	Strategies of slaving (responses)
Brazil		
1610s–1630s	Technical advance in mechanical processing of cane; financing from Dutch	Growing numbers of Africans for agricultural production; male majorities
Barbados, Martinique		
(1650s)	Shift to large-scale, integrated plantations in West Indies	Europe: chartered companies (focused on American silver, African gold), debt financing of start-up costs (plantations, sugar) (1670s)
1670s–1690s	Jamaica acquired by English	
	Royal African Company	Barbados (and Virginia) slave codes (1670s–1680s)
	Male majorities (almost entirely new) of slaves	*Code Noir* (1684)

Table 4.2 Novelties in the (Early) Modern Atlantic

Background (approximate dates)	Historical challenge(s)	Strategies of slaving and abolition (responses)
Caribbean		
18th c.	Sustaining large-scale sugar plantations	Companies fail, private investors pick up the pieces
	Philosophical/economic/ethical/ disciplinary challenges	Political economy in Europe
		Police regulations in Americas
	Formulation of (European) ideologies of plantation model (England)	(Male) slaves forming pseudocommunities in Brazil, Caribbean; families in North America
	Abolitionism (Atlantic trade) emerges as expression of consolidation of liberal/civic nation-state in England (but not elsewhere in Europe)	
1790s	Haitian revolution	Confirms stereotypes of both "savage" Africans and liberal-inspired leaders
	French slavery problematized by republican (civic/national) ideology	
1810s–1820s	Slave violence, economic issues confirm doubts about British slavery	Leading to emancipation in British Caribbean colonies—1834/1838
1840s–1850s	Republican politics in France	Emancipation in French Caribbean colonies—1848
North America		
1770s–1790s	Elaboration of civic politics— forming a new nation	Exclusion of native-born slaves as blacks
	Native-born slaves come of age, slave families established	First rebellions (Gabriel, etc.)
		Cotton gin (1793)
		Imports end (1807)
1820s–1830s	Development of cotton production	Breaking up slave families
	Internal slave trade	Slave communities forming along racialized and religious lines
	Popular political culture	
1840s–1850s	"Old South"	Establishing new capitalized plantation systems
		Establishing new forms of slave community around Christianity
1860s	Civil War	National crisis
		Emancipation

Table 4.3 What Changed?

Old World	New World – Aspects of Modernity
Communal ethos	Commercial competition
Self = relational	Individualism
Wealth/power = people	Wealth monetized, then capitalized
Domestic economies	Capitalist economies
Slaving mostly female	Slaving predominantly male
Private/domestic authority	Public law
Real/collective estate	Personal property
Personal/negotiated politics	Civic politics
Composite polities	Morally unified polities (of growing direct involvement and intensity—monotheistic, then monarchies, then nations)
Slaves positioned	Slaves possessed
Slaves seek to belong	Some slaves seek (civic) freedom
Insignificant household debt	Commercial debt
Locally born majorities	Imported slave majorities
Slavers slave to acquire legitimacy	Slavers denied (national) legitimacy
Self-acquisition of slaves	Slaves acquired from foreigners
Slaves assimilated locally	Slaves concentrated in remote colonies
Slaving accelerates change (relative to alternatives)	Slaving retards change (relative to growth of financial assets)
Slavers' gains additive to established competitors; multiple domains of legitimacy	Slavers' gains at expense of existing establishment defined by origin, piety, honor, or other ranking

Notes

Chapter 1. The Problem of Slavery as History

1. In a broad sense, including the abstract modeling of all the modern social sciences in the phrases evoked here, sociology itself, political economy, economics, anthropology, and intellectual history or the history of ideas. All of these I contrast epistemologically with the historical approach I demonstrate here.

2. David Brion Davis, *The Problem of Slavery in Western Culture* (Ithaca: Cornell University Press, 1966; reprint New York: Oxford University Press, 1989). Davis's further, ongoing contributions receive appropriate mention in following notes.

3. For a recent comment on the distractions of this "originary fallacy," see Robin Blackburn, *The Making of New World Slavery: From the Baroque to the Modern* (London: Verso, 1997), 33, citing, in a slightly different sense, Marc Bloch, *The Historian's Craft*, trans. Peter Putnam, introd. Joseph R. Strayer (New York: Vintage, 1953; reprint Manchester: Manchester University Press, 1992), 24–29. Compare the originary tone of the centrality of ancient and medieval "precedents for the most striking traits of American slavery" in Davis, *Problem of Slavery*, 31; extended in *Challenging the Boundaries of Slavery* (Cambridge: Harvard University Press, 2003).

4. Moses I. Finley, *Ancient Slavery and Modern Ideology* (New York: Viking, 1980).

5. Although, historical processes working primarily indirectly, the short-term banishment of reform mobilized a nascent working class in Britain that in a succeeding generation brought the hawks of reform home to roost.

6. I am pleased to attribute this elegant aphorism to Jan Vansina, offered orally on the occasion of "Pre-colonial History in a Post-Colonial Age: Past and Present in African History," the forty-fifth anniversary conference, African Studies Program and Department of History, University of Wisconsin–Madison, March 11–13, 2005.

7. Bloch, *The Historian's Craft*.

173

8. See chapter 4 for details of this historiography.

9. Readers eager to anticipate the details may consult Curtis Keim, *Mistaking Africa: Curiosities and Inventions of the American Mind*, 2d ed. (Boulder: Westview, 2009).

10. The burden of chapter 4.

11. See, for example, Frederick Cooper, *Plantation Slavery on the East Coast of Africa* (New Haven: Yale University Press, 1977); numerous studies collected in Paul E. Lovejoy, *Slavery, Commerce and Production in the Sokoto Caliphate of West Africa* (Trenton, NJ: Africa World Press, 2005).

12. The quoted phrase refers to the title of a foundational work on slavery in the antebellum United States, an ironic invocation of a nineteenth-century euphemism for an institution of legal and political standings too contentious to characterize directly, with ironic force gained by indirection; Kenneth M. Stampp, *The Peculiar Institution: Slavery in the Ante-Bellum South* (New York: Alfred A. Knopf, 1956).

13. Joseph C. Miller (and various collaborators), "Slavery: Annual Bibliographical Supplement," *Slavery and Abolition* (1980–2004), third issue for each year, now ongoing by Thomas Thurston, under the auspices of the Gilder Lehrman Center for the Study of Slavery, Resistance, and Abolition (Yale University). Indexed print consolidations through the 1983 supplement appeared in Joseph C. Miller, *Slavery: A Worldwide Bibliography, 1900–1982* (White Plains, N.Y.: Kraus International, 1985), and all materials (10,351 entries) compiled since 1983 (through 1991) were corrected and consolidated in *Slavery and Slaving in World History: A Bibliography, 1900–1991* (Millwood, N.Y.: Kraus International, 1993). *Slavery and Slaving in World History* was republished (with further corrections) in 1998 by M. E. Sharpe, together with a second indexed volume consolidating the 3,897 entries compiled between 1992 and 1996. A web-based searchable database version of the bibliography, hosted by the Virginia Center for Digital History, was launched in April 2010: http://www2.vcdh.virginia.edu/bib.

14. For this vital insight into the embarrassment underlying the historiography of slavery, see Michael Salman, *The Embarrassment of Slavery: Controversies over Bondage and Nationalism in the American Colonial Philippines* (Berkeley: University of California Press, 2001). Salman considers the ongoing sensitivities of the issue that inhibited dispassionate consideration of the subject in the immediate postslavery era in the United States. It was not until after World War II that the modern historiography of slavery began—that is, treating it as a problem of the past rather than as current politics. The single notable exception was a very early sociological treatment, revealingly written by an heir to a national culture then (somewhat naively) unburdened by memories of its own history of slaving: H. J. Nieboer, *Slavery as an Industrial System: Ethnological Researches* (The Hague: M. Nijhoff, 1900; 2d rev. ed.: The Hague: Nijhoff, 1910). For recent memorialization of the slaving past of the modern Netherlands, see, for example, often led by its heirs in Suriname (descended from the Dutch colony), Gert Oostindie, ed., *Het verleden onder ogen: herdenking van de slavernij* (Amsterdam: Arena/Prins Claus Fonds, 1999), and translated (in the formerly British West Indies) as *Facing Up to the Past: Perspectives on the Commemoration of Slavery from Africa, the Americas and Europe* (Kingston: Ian Randle Publishers, 2001). I have explored aspects of the political vitality and volatility of abolition in the modern world in "Abolition as Discourse: Slavery as Civic Abomination" (unpublished paper, University of Nottingham, Institute for the Study of Slavery—"Discourses of Abolition," September 13–15, 2004; revised for Atlantic History Seminar, New York University, January 19, 2005), where I suggest that the modern civic/national governments asserted their popular legitimacy in significant part through the benevolence demonstrated in ending slavery. Less directly on this point, see Joseph C. Miller, "Introduction: Atlantic Ambiguities of British and American Abolition," special issue of the *William and Mary Quarterly* 66, 4 (2009), 675–703.

15. Historians have long agonized over the ideal of objectivity that we inherit from the late nineteenth-century positivists who defined the discipline and our seeming failings in attaining it. See, for example, Peter Novick, *That Noble Dream: The "Objectivity Question" and the American Historical Profession* (New York: Cambridge University Press, 1988). I will later attempt to define the realistic sense (awareness of the *perspectival* component of history's epistemology) in which historians can and must attain what I call detached contemplation, as distinct from politicized, or purely emotional, commitment. For a case for committed history, Allen Isaacman, "Legacies of Engagement: Scholarship Informed by Political Commitment," *African Studies Review* 46, 1 (2003), 1–41.

16. Davis, *Problem of Slavery*, 30.

17. *The Problem of Slavery in the Age of Revolution, 1770–1823* (Ithaca: Cornell University Press, 1975).

18. *Slavery and Human Progress* (New York: Oxford University Press, 1984). Moses I. Finley, "Was Greek Civilization Based on Slave Labour?" *Historia* 8, 2 (1959), 145–64, first proposed the ironic association of progress, at least as celebrated by nineteenth-century Progressives, with the moments in the past, particularly ancient Greece, that they identified as paradigmatic. In the United States, Thomas Jefferson, personal slaveholder and civic libertarian, has come to epitomize the apparent paradox yet again. See Jan Ellen Lewis and Peter S. Onuf, eds., *Sally Hemings and Thomas Jefferson* (Charlottesville: University Press of Virginia, 1999), and Annette Gordon-Reed, *The Hemingses of Monticello: An American Family* (New York: W. W. Norton, 2008).

19. Davis's latest and surely not last reflections: *Inhuman Bondage: The Rise and Fall of Slavery in the New World* (New York: Oxford University Press, 2006).

20. "True slavery persisted as a viable institution," Davis, *Problem of Slavery*, 31. Persistence forms the eventual theme of *Inhuman Bondage*.

21. My parenthetical accent in brackets is without implied need to apologize for a gendered phrasing from the early 1960s, however currently impolitic, historically inaccurate, and epistemologically unproductive. See Gwyn Campbell, Suzanne Miers, and Joseph C. Miller, eds., *Women and Slavery*, 2 vols. (Athens: Ohio University Press, 2007), and including Miller, "Introduction: Women as Slaves and Owners of Slaves: Experiences from Africa, the Indian Ocean World, and the Early Atlantic," 1:1–38, and "Displaced, Disoriented, Dispersed, and Domiciled: Slaving as a History of Women," 2:284–312.

22. As distinct from slavery's much clearer modern racialized legacies, and to a distinctive degree in the modern United States.

23. Oscar Handlin and Mary Handlin, "Origins of the Southern Labor System," *William and Mary Quarterly*, 3d ser., 7, 2 (1950), 199–222. See also Carl N. Degler, "Slavery and the Genesis of American Race Prejudice," *Comparative Studies in Society and History* 2, 1 (1959), 49–66, and other historians writing in the 1960s conveniently assembled in Donald L. Noel, ed., *The Origins of American Slavery and Racism* (Columbus: Merrill, 1972). The culminating point of this discussion was Winthrop D. Jordan, "Modern Tensions and the Origins of American Slavery," *Journal of Southern History* 28, 1 (1962), 18–30, and *White Over Black: American Attitudes Toward the Negro, 1550–1812* (Chapel Hill: University of North Carolina Press, 1968). For a recent summary, Rebecca Goetz, "Rethinking the 'Unthinking Decision': Old Questions and New Problems in the History of Slavery and Race in the Colonial South," *Journal of Southern History* 75, 3 (2009), 599–612.

24. E. Franklin Frazier, *The Negro Family in the United States* (Chicago: University of Chicago Press, 1939); Gunnar Myrdal, *An American Dilemma: The Negro Problem and Modern Democracy*, 2 vols. (New York: Harper and Brothers, [1944]).

25. Frank Tannenbaum, *Slave and Citizen: The Negro in the Americas* (New York: Knopf, 1947). A quarter century later, historians still shifted seamlessly between slavery and racism along the lines of this sort of comparison; see Carl N. Degler, "Slavery and the Genesis

of American Race Prejudice," *Comparative Studies in Society and History* 2, 1 (1959), 49–66; and id., *Neither Black nor White: Slavery and Race Relations in Brazil and the United States* (New York: Macmillan, 1971).

26. *Casa-grande e senzala* (Rio de Janeiro: Olympio, 1933), translated by Samuel Putnam as *The Masters and the Slaves: A Study in the Development of Brazilian Civilization* (New York: Knopf, 1946), and the immediate inspiration for Tannenbaum's solution to Myrdal's American dilemma.

27. One recalls the simultaneous deadly urge in Nazi Germany in pursuit of national homogeneity in racialized terms.

28. For a later, more sociologically phrased remix of the blending of race and slavery identified in Brazilian masters' tendency to manumit their slaves as a "mulatto escape hatch," see Degler, *Neither Black nor White*.

29. A conceptual muddle recognized by the foremost sociologist of slavery, Orlando Patterson, *Freedom in the Making of Western Culture* (New York: Basic Books, 1991).

30. The historical obscurantism is palpable in reasoning from abstractions of this sort. Since history is perspectival, a historian would immediately ask, "efficiency for *whom*?" The answer in this case, as defined by historians, is "from the perspective of the owner of the capital, who employs workers as cheaply as possible to bring maximal returns on minimal amounts invested in physical assets."

31. Harold D. Woodman, "The Profitability of Slavery: A Historical Perennial," *Journal of Southern History* 29, 3 (1963), 303–25; Hugh G. J. Aitken, ed., *Did Slavery Pay? Readings in the Economics of Black Slavery in the United States* (Boston: Houghton-Mifflin, 1971). Accordingly, a sophisticated economic analysis of slavery published in the early 1970s was received with barely concealed and sometimes unconcealed derision; Robert W. Fogel and Stanley L. Engerman, *Time on the Cross: The Economics of American Negro Slavery*, 2 vols. (Boston: Little, Brown, 1974). For examples of the scorn heaped on *Time on the Cross*, see Paul A. David, Herbert G. Gutman, Richard Sutch, Peter Temin, and Gavin Wright, *Reckoning with Slavery: A Critical Study in the Quantitative History of American Negro Slavery* (New York: Oxford University Press, 1976). Subsequently, Gavin Wright, *The Political Economy of the Cotton South, Households, Markets, and Wealth in the Nineteenth Century* (New York: Norton, 1978), and *Slavery and American Economic Development* (Baton Rouge: Louisiana State University Press, 2006).

32. A recent and intelligent version of this approach is Michael L. Bush, ed., *Serfdom and Slavery: Studies in Legal Bondage* (London: Longman, 1996); or Robert J. Steinfield and Stanley L. Engerman, "Labor—Free or Coerced? A Historical Reassessment of Differences and Similarities," in Tom Brass and Marcel van der Linden, eds., *Free and Unfree Labour: The Debate Continues* (Bern: Peter Lang, 1997), 107–26. The noncommercial spheres of the world's economies are visible through this lens only as a similarly undifferentiated and therefore analytically unproductive category of family labor. Gender and child labor have recently become tools used to pry open this particular conceptual black box.

33. I consider African alternatives in chapter 3; see chapter 4 for the historical dynamics behind the historiographical category discussed here.

34. This is the burden of chapter 4, against the background laid out here in general terms and illustrated contemporaneously in the following chapters on the Western tradition and on Africa.

35. Davis has confirmed, relatively recently, his sense that slavery in the New World essentially extended what had long been done in Europe. See "A Big Business (review essay: Thomas, *The Slave Trade*, and Blackburn, *Making of New World Slavery*)," *New York Review of Books* 45, 10 (1998), 50–53. See also the spirit of commitment in "Looking at Slavery from Broader Perspectives," *American Historical Review* 105, 2 (2000), 452–66, part of a symposium on "Crossing Slavery's Boundaries (AHR Forum)," with comments by

Stanley Engerman, Peter Kolchin, and Rebecca Scott; and elegantly again in *Challenging the Boundaries of Slavery*, and most recently in *Inhuman Bondage*.

36. And does so explicitly in the still-reigning sociology of slavery: Orlando Patterson, *Slavery and Social Death* (Cambridge: Harvard University Press, 1982).

37. Benedict R. Anderson, *Imagined Communities: Reflections on the Origin and Spread of Nationalism*, 2d new ed. (New York: Verso, 1991).

38. Patterson's first published monograph, *The Sociology of Slavery: An Analysis of the Origins, Development and Structure of Negro Slave Society in Jamaica* (London: MacGibbon and Kee, 1967), was explicitly in the tone of historical sociology.

39. Patterson draws this emphasis from the philosophical reflections of Georg Friedrich Hegel (1770–1831).

40. The most prominent objections were excited by Fogel and Engerman, *Time on the Cross*, and Philip D. Curtin, *The Atlantic Slave Trade: A Census* (Madison: University of Wisconsin Press, 1969). The critique of Curtin's counting has been deflected onto the massive database of slave voyages assembled by David Eltis and many collaborators, "Voyages: The Trans-Atlantic Slave Trade Database," http://slavevoyages.org/tast/index. faces. For a thoughtful reflection on the issues, see Stephanie Smallwood's review of *Rise of African Slavery in the Americas*, by David Eltis, and *The Trans-Atlantic Slave Trade: A Database*, ed. David Eltis, Stephen D. Behrendt, David Richardson, and Herbert S. Klein, *William and Mary Quarterly* 58, 1 (2001), 253–61.

41. Patterson does not refer to analogous psychoanalytic phrasings of the ambiguities and contradictions of this sort of relationship as a sadomasochistic pairing. This dynamic, including the master's ultimate dependence on the anything-but-totally-dominated slave, resonates for psychologists as a familiar pattern of dominators who attempt to displace internal pain by inflicting suffering on a particular other.

42. As John Edwin Mason terms freedom (in a different sense) in a fine study of the end of slavery at the Cape of Good Hope (southern Africa) in the 1820s and 1830s; see *Social Death and Resurrection* (Charlottesville: University Press of Virginia, 2003).

43. Generalized further as "weapons of the weak" by James C. Scott in *Weapons of the Weak: Everyday Forms of Peasant Resistance* (New Haven: Yale University Press, 1985).

44. If the concept of culture in Freyre's hands once saved Brazil from condemnation on racial grounds (see note 26 above), cultural nuances did not significantly deflect Patterson's focus on slavery's universality and corresponding sociological uniformity.

45. I will return in the final chapter of this book to the rarity of manumissions in North America.

46. And thus the background to Davis's resort to race in acknowledging potential novelty in slavery in the Americas.

47. Davis clearly held slavery constant as an institution in order to dramatize the change in attitudes in the eighteenth century and also because the lack of detailed evidence on the history of slavery in Europe or anywhere else at the time he wrote left him no real choice. Davis has not yet moved on to consider the utility of the cause of abolition to imperialists of the later nineteenth century; but see Joseph C. Miller, "The Abolition of the Slave Trade and Slavery: Historical Foundations," in Doudou Diène, ed., *From Chains to Bonds: The Slave Trade Revisited*, (New York: Berghahn, 2001), 159–93. Others have explored the intricate contradictions of the abolitionist rhetoric of the age of European imperialism, most recently and most comprehensively, Suzanne Miers, "Slavery and the Slave Trade as International Issues, 1890–1939," *Slavery and Abolition* 19, 2 (1998), 16–37, and *Slavery in the Twentieth Century: The Evolution of a Global Pattern* (Walnut Creek, Calif.: Altamira Press, 2003).

48. Which also does not distinguish slavery from innumerable other relationships of inequality, in social or civic terms, or overwhelming personal and psychological dominance, except as

publicly institutionalized. At base, it is the civic invisibility, the specifically "civic death," of the slave that underlies the logic of the field, as represented in this discussion by its two most insightful articulators, Davis and Patterson. Historiologically, however, civic identities did not acquire functional, or motivating (i.e., historical) significance—earlier ideological statements aside—until the 1830s and 1840s in Britain, the United States, and France. Elsewhere republican constitutions abolished monarchy but not the more personalistic, patron–client politics that kings had personified. For a version of this ambiguity, generated by framing the argument within the conventional typological (i.e., abstract, hence not historical) contrast between (rather than the ambiguous, incremental, contradictory process leading from) empire and (toward, rather than the reifying to) democracy, see Jeremy Adelman, "An Age of Imperial Revolutions," *American Historical Review* 113, 2 (2008), 319–40.

49. The logic of this dynamic reverses the vectors of energy denoted by the same word in Immanuel Wallerstein's *The Modern World System* (New York: Academic Press, 1974). For historians, margins are the growth points of the action, not the passive dependencies of Wallerstein's highly structural European core.

50. An epistemological aside, for readers tracking the nuances of describing human life historically, with regard to phrasing: singular nouns implicitly allude to abstracted ideas, while historians must write in the plural to accent the human multiplicity, variety, and particularity of the experiences alluded to. In this case, the literature on slavery generally would attempt to phrase my point in this sentence in the abstracting singular: "*A* historical *context* of change both motivated and enabled *a* specifiable *interest* in *it* to use slaving to appropriate *a change* already under way for *some purpose* of their own, depending on where in their particular historical *context* the slavers stood."

51. I appreciatively note the appropriately historicized plural nouns.

52. Consider the contrasting epistemology of history with the predominantly sociological tone of most of what passes for world history, not always sufficiently distinguished from avowedly sociological world systems analysis; e.g., Immanuel Wallerstein, *The Essential Wallerstein* (New York: New Press, 2000), or the profoundly economistic Andre Gunder Frank, *ReOrient: Global Economy in the Asian Age* (Berkeley: University of California Press, 1998). For a historical contemplation of the relationship between processes and particularities, see Joseph C. Miller, "A Theme in Variations: A Historical Schema of Slaving in the Atlantic and Indian Ocean Regions," in Gwyn Campbell, ed., "The Structure of Slavery in Indian Ocean Africa and Asia," special issue of *Slavery and Abolition* 24, 2 (2003), 169–94.

53. I make no claim as to history's necessity or sufficiency as a way of knowing, but only to its distinctiveness and value as such. Historians cannot think without drawing eclectically on the theorizing of our colleagues in the social and human sciences; the converse holds in the sense that social scientists draw selectively on historians' empirical research to demonstrate, or in the best-case scenario, test their models. However, the stronger the theory, the more inconvenient data become, except as statistical tendencies.

54. See chapter 3.

55. For a thoughtful contrast of similar events in the same locale, as experienced differently in differing temporal contexts, Jorge Cañizares-Esguerra, "Transformações ideológicas na atlântica América espanhola: as imagens as narrativas das rebeliões de 1624 e 1692 na Cidade do Mexico," in Júnia Furtado, ed., *Formas, sons, cores e movimento na modernidade atlântica: Europa, Américas e África* (São Paulo: Annablume, 2007), 173–84. Since motivation arises significantly from contexts conceptualized as external to the actor, an implicit further defining feature of historical epistemology is that it deals primarily with the collective (or social or cultural) reactions to human agency. Modern Western thought handles changes *internal* to the individual actor in the distinct modes of psychology or

religious experience and blends them with history in biographical or autobiographical self-examination of the self in relation to contexts, thus paradigmatically titled "So-and-So: Life and Times." The modern liberal emphasis on the individual as actor distinguishes the Western historical epistemology from collective agency of the sort inherent in Marxist political economy, as well as from most non-Western collective historical epistemologies. These modes of thought do not pose the classic modern apparent contradiction between the individual and society.

56. Edward Ayers, eminent historian of the nineteenth-century American South, formerly Dean of Arts and Sciences at the University of Virginia, now (2011) president of the University of Richmond.

57. Although often involved, like sadomasochistic impulses (see note 41 above), human greed is not a cause of slaving in a historical sense; rather, slaving enables abusive actions by placing vulnerable, isolated individuals at the unrestrained disposal of individual inclinations that society or culture or mores otherwise contain.

58. I find no inconsistency between the Hobbesian, or neo-Freudian, realism of this position and the determined idealism I also affirm. This morally ambiguous stance is, I argue, essential to historical epistemology and to effective engagement with the very real—in the sense of motivating—aspects of the human existence that historians must understand, whether or not they personally find them acceptable.

59. The historian's vision is sharper than that of the actors, if never quite attaining 20/20 clarity. Its lucidity derives not from knowing how things turned out; that retrospective would expose historians to the temptation of teleology. Rather, historians' explanatory insight arises from their ability to discern elements of contexts of which the historical actors were unaware, either because they were beyond their range of vision, or, more likely, because the actors systematically denied them. At the very least, they include novelties that actors are by definition incapable of appreciating coherently; they see and dismiss anomalies rather than recognizing incipient patterns in them. Ideology, which is retrospective, eventually makes sense of them, but usually only after what is recognized has begun to fade, when it is too late.

60. Merchants turn out to be the number twos most relevant to slaving, for the most part; younger sons and minor gentry were in similarly marginalized positions but without the access to external resources that merchants turned into slaving.

61. Patterson, *Slavery and Social Death*, 12. Patterson's italics, but my parenthetical glosses for implied emphasis relevant to the arguments of this paper.

62. Campbell, Miers, and Miller, eds., *Women and Slavery* (Athens: Ohio University Press, 2009), and Gwyn Campbell, Suzanne Miers, and Joseph C. Miller, eds., *Children in Slavery around the World*, 2 vols. (Athens: Ohio University Press, 2010-11).

63. Joseph C. Miller, "Retention, Re-Invention, and Remembering: Restoring Identities Through Enslavement in Africa and Under Slavery in Brazil," in José C. Curto and Paul E. Lovejoy, eds., *Enslaving Connections: Changing Cultures of Africa and Brazil during the Era of Slavery* (Amherst, N.Y.: Prometheus/Humanity Books, 2003), 81–121.

64. This definition is implicitly a commercial one since it does not stress the animalistic qualities attributed to the enslaved but the commercial value of livestock; it does not include pets, which often had places closer to the hearts of their masters than the same masters' slaves.

65. My bracketed extension of Davis' phrasing; see note 47 above.

66. I place the phrase in quotation marks to highlight the ironic vacuity of the negative characterization that two generations of scholarship have now begun to endow with the positive characterizations that these fields merit; for a version of the general argument, Joseph C. Miller, "Beyond Blacks, Bondage, and Blame: Why a Multi-Centric World History Needs Africa," *Historically Speaking* (Newsletter of The Historical Society) 5, 2 (2004), 7–12 ;

"Multi-Centrism in History—How and Why Perspectives Matter—Rejoinder," *Historically Speaking* (Newsletter of The Historical Society) 5, 2 (2004), 27–31.

Chapter 2. History as a Problem of Slaving

1. Eric Wolf, *Europe and the Peoples without History* (Berkeley: University of California Press, 1982).
2. Suzanne Miers is the leading authority on slavery in the twentieth century, including Anti-Slavery International, the League of Nations, and the colonial politics of slavery. Among her major works are *Britain and the Ending of the Slave Trade* (New York: Africana, 1975); with Richard Roberts, eds., *The End of Slavery in Africa* (Madison: University of Wisconsin Press, 1988); with Maria Jaschok, eds., *Women and Chinese Patriarchy: Submission, Servitude, and Escape* (Hong Kong: Hong Kong University Press, 1994); with Martin Klein, eds., "Slavery and Colonial Rule in Africa," *Slavery and Abolition* 19, 2 (1998), special issue; and *Slavery in the Twentieth Century: The Evolution of a Global Pattern* (Walnut Creek, Calif.: Altamira Press, 2003). Also see Amalia Ribi, "Humanitarian Imperialism. The Politics of Anti-Slavery Activism in the Interwar Years" (D.Phil. thesis, University of Oxford, 2008).
3. For an intricate study of slavery in Africa in these terms, Paul E. Lovejoy and Jan S. Hogendorn, *Slow Death for Slavery: The Course of Abolition in Northern Nigeria, 1897–1936* (New York: Cambridge University Press, 1993).
4. Three recent evocations of these politics are Apex A. Apeh and Chukwuma C. Opata, "Social Exclusion: An Aftermath of the Abolition of Slave Trade in Northern Igboland, Nigeria," *William and Mary Quarterly* 66, 4 (2009), 941–58; Sandra E. Greene, "Modern Trokosi and the 1807 Abolition in Ghana: Connecting Past and Present," *William and Mary Quarterly* 66, 4 (2009), 959–74; and Ella Keren, "The Transatlantic Slave Trade in Ghanaian Academic Historiography: History, Memory, and Power," *William and Mary Quarterly* 66, 4 (2009), 975–99.
5. Philip D. Morgan, *Slave Counterpoint: Black Culture in the Eighteenth-Century Chesapeake and Low Country* (Williamsburg: Omohundro Institute for Early American History and Culture, 1998); Walter Johnson, *Soul by Soul: Life Inside the Antebellum Slave Market* (Cambridge: Harvard University Press, 1999); Ira Berlin, *Generations of Captivity: A History of African-American Slaves* (Cambridge: Belknap Press, 2003). No similar syntheses yet exist for the Caribbean region, the Hispanic Americas, or Brazil. However, see Herbert S. Klein and Ben Vinson, *African Slavery in Latin America and the Caribbean*, 2d ed. (New York: Oxford University Press, 2007).
6. The recent controversies surrounding a very technical acknowledgment of the multiple backgrounds of classic Greek culture—including Egypt, construed by the publisher as African in a racialized sense—indicate the continuing extent of the sensitivities Finley highlighted in *Ancient Slavery and Modern Ideology*; see Martin Bernal, *Black Athena: The Afroasiatic Roots of Classical Civilization*, 3 vols. (New Brunswick: Rutgers University Press, 1987), and ensuring discussion in, for example, Mary R. Lefkowitz and Guy MacLean Rogers, eds., *Black Athena Revisited* (Chapel Hill: University of North Carolina Press, 1996); and David Chioni Moore, ed., *Black Athena Writes Back: Martin Bernal Responds to His Critics* (Durham: Duke University Press, 2001). These controversies continue.
7. For my characterization of African history generally in these sociological terms, see Joseph C. Miller, "History and Africa/Africa and History," *American Historical Review* 104, 1 (1999), 1–32; reprinted in Gad Heuman and James Walvin, eds., *The Slavery Reader* (London: Routledge, 2003), 707–38. An innovative attempt to extend the conventional framing of slavery as a legal institution to Africa was Paul E. Lovejoy, ed., *The Ideology*

of Slavery in Africa (Beverly Hills: Sage Publications, 1981); I discuss further details of the literature on Africa in the following chapter.

8. Or slavery had been emphasized primarily in terms derived from highly structural and abstract Marxist theorization of an ancient "slave mode of production," systematically overriding culture and meaning as well as sometimes straining evidence. For pioneering synthetic works, see James L. Watson, ed., *Asian and African Systems of Slavery* (Berkeley: University of California Press, 1980); Anthony Reid, ed., *Slavery, Bondage, and Dependency in Southeast Asia* (St. Lucia: University of Queensland Press, 1983); Martin L. Klein, ed., *Breaking the Chains: Slavery, Bondage, and Emancipation in Modern Africa and Asia* (Madison: University of Wisconsin Press, 1993). More recently, Gwyn Campbell, ed., "The Structure of Slavery in Indian Ocean Africa and Asia," and Edward A. Alpers, Gwyn Campbell, and Michael Salman, eds., "Slavery and Resistance in Africa and Asia," *Slavery and Abolition* 25, 2 (2004), both special issues.

9. Among recent notable examples, Claudio Saunt, *A New Order for Indians: Creeks and Seminoles in the Deep South, 1733–1816* (Cambridge: Cambridge University Press, 1999); James F. Brooks, *Captives and Cousins: Slavery, Kinship, and Community in the Southwest Borderlands* (Chapel Hill: University of North Carolina Press, 2002); Alan Gallay, *The Indian Slave Trade: The Rise of the English Empire in the American South, 1670–1717* (New Haven: Yale University Press, 2003).

10. In the European historiography of world slavery, the guilty heritage of colonial rule in the tropical world plays an obscuring role comparable to the American problem of the contemporary politics of race. For India, Indrani Chatterjee, *Gender, Slavery and Law in Colonial India* (New Delhi: Oxford University Press, 1999), and Indrani Chatterjee and Richard Maxwell Eaton, eds., *Slavery and South Asian History* (Bloomington: Indiana University Press, 2006). For comparisons of slavery with the debt bondage so often attributed to Asia, see Alain Testart, *L'esclave, la dette et le pouvoir: études de sociologie comparative* (Paris: Errance, 2001).

11. For the last, John O. Hunwick and Eve Troutt Powell, *The African Diaspora in the Mediterranean Muslim World* (Princeton: Markus Wiener, 2002); John Wright, "Morocco: The Last Great Slave Market?" *Journal of North African Studies* 7, 3 (2002), 53–66; Linda Colley, *Captives* (New York: Pantheon Books, 2002); Robert C. Davis, *Christian Slaves, Muslim Masters: White Slavery in the Mediterranean, the Barbary Coast, and Italy, 1500–1800* (New York: Palgrave/Macmillan, 2003); John L. Wright, *The Trans-Saharan Slave Trade* (London: Routledge, 2006).

12. For a reasonably wide ranging, up-to-date array of the known practices of slaving, see Paul Finkelman and Joseph C. Miller, eds., *Macmillan Encyclopedia of World Slavery*, 2 vols. (New York: Simon and Schuster, 1998), and (more briefly) Martin A. Klein, *Historical Dictionary of Slavery and Abolition* (Lanham, Md.: Scarecrow Press, 2002). Two other recent encyclopedias are designed on the same premise but achieve less coverage: Junius P. Rodriguez, ed., *The Historical Encyclopaedia of World Slavery*, 2 vols. (Santa Barbara: ABC-Clio, 1997), and Seymour Drescher and Stanley L. Engerman, eds., *A Historical Guide to World Slavery* (New York: Oxford University Press, 1998). One eagerly anticipates David Eltis, Stanley Engerman, Paul Cartledge, and Keith Bradley, eds., *Cambridge World History of World Slavery*, 4 vols. (New York: Cambridge University Press, 2011 and forthcoming).

13. A fuller narrative survey is in preparation, for the Cambridge University Press, based on the epistemological position developed here.

14. Archaeological and other evidence of much earlier (~100,000 bp) hominid collaboration, memory and sentiment, and purposive manufacture of complex tools and even machines (e.g., boats) may indicate an earlier phase of less creative communication (beyond signaling) that may have preceded the modern language families and the adaptability they

enabled. For a recent summary, Patrick Manning, "Homo sapiens Populates the Earth: A Provisional Synthesis, Privileging Linguistic Evidence," *Journal of World History* 17, 1 (2006), 115–58. However, for my purposes, the key distinction is between (earlier) occasional, even increasingly recurrent, strategizing in reaction to familiar challenges and fully historical creative initiatives eventually institutionalized through slaving. A historical inference from context that might explain such a global appearance would derive from climatic change so dramatic that only groups who developed, inter alia, new, presumably syntactical linguistic techniques of collaboration survived it, thus rendering obsolete all others' more rudimentary systems of communication. The sequence of key shifts—always incremental, since the law of Ockham's razor applies—would run from purely (and all but perpetually) instinctive animalistic behavior to individual awareness among hominids and eventually collective human imitation of advantageous accidents, to teaching and thus building reserves of advantageous reactions, which became the threshold of creative collective strategizing for advantage. This step-by-step sequence conceivably converts advantageous evolutionary physical capacity to historical strategizing and success. Awareness of individual heritages, arguably apparent much earlier in archaeological records of burials and other commemorative practices, was eventually extended to collective awareness of a future. Historical consciousness is thus social and derives from orientation toward a shared future rather than toward the past from which it draws its discourse; the past, also imagined as shared, is only fodder for a futuristic ethos.

15. And restoration, not progress, is the underlying ontology of many historical epistemologies in Africa and elsewhere. It is arguably more common among ourselves than the ideology of progress acknowledges.

16. As distinct from the culture heroes lionized in the memories of claimed heirs. Such semi-mythologized images are not historical but the products of the historical processes of creating them.

17. Without implying monothetic determinism of the sort that attempts to force an artificial choice between nature and nurture, both pervasively present in general, though one or the other may prevail momentarily in given circumstances, that is, historically. The false dichotomy prevails in numerous academic discourses about language, mind, reality, and so on—all singular, hence abstracted, rather than historicized and multiplistic.

18. "Who" in the sense of positionality, "why" in a motivated sense, and "how" again contextualized to assess historical actors' limitations in terms of ability to conceptualize.

19. Beyond personally sentimental, evidently much older among hominids, as an extension from primary maternal–infant bonding. The sequence suggested here would apply the notion of historical change as incremental to the emergence of human consciousness itself.

20. See the very suggestive opening remarks on the modern Tupinambá (Amazonia, in Brazil) in Patterson, *Freedom in the Making of Western Culture*, 13–15.

21. And resurrected in subsequent moments of crisis in collectivities in Africa; see following chapter. Also Orlando Patterson, *Rituals of Blood: Consequences of Slavery in Two American Centuries* (New York: Civitas, 1999). I am indebted to my former colleague Kris Lane at the College of William and Mary for reference to formal sociological consideration of these processes, in Walter Burkett, René Gerard, and Jonathan Z. Smith, *Violent Origins: Ritual Killing and Cultural Formation* (Stanford: Stanford University Press, 1987). The point is a mainstay of the broader sort of military history, e.g., Robert L. O'Connell, *Ride of the Second Horseman: The Birth and Death of War* (New York: Oxford University Press, 1995).

22. Consider this phrasing as a less teleological, less evaluative phrasing of the modern and Europe-centered idea that Davis considers as progress. As history, these are moments of clarification, or at least ideological definition, on which subsequent generations drew—always for the entirely different purposes of their own times and places. Africanists, who

must work with sources framed in terms of orally maintained traditions of ongoing continuity, have converted the static overtones of this phrase into the thoroughly dynamic and
creative and purposive processes that generate them by reference to "the (re-)invention of
tradition." A paradigm-shaping initial statement was that of Eric Hobsbawm and Terence
Ranger, eds., *The Invention of Tradition* (Cambridge: Cambridge University Press, 1983);
for a subsequent and elegant elaboration, see Jan Vansina, *Paths in the Rainforests: Toward
a History of Political Tradition in Equatorial Africa* (London: James Currey, 1990).

23. In chapter 3 I develop the contradictions internal to the communal ethos.

24. More detailed references to the key literature on these processes in Africa will follow in
the succeeding essay.

25. See chapter 3 for the definition of personal power in Africa, using slaves.

26. Or, in matrilineal contexts, uncles (and not females, except rarely).

27. And much of Patterson's *Slavery and Social Death* insightfully details this evidence in terms
of correlations with isolated elements of the circumstances that historians would integrate to
build the sort of thick (Geertzian) description that they appropriate as meaning-generating
context. Clifford Geertz, "Thick Description: Toward an Interpretive Theory of Culture,"
in *The Interpretation of Cultures: Selected Essays* (New York: Basic Books, 1973), 3–30.
In the context of this essay, Geertz thus historicized a rather abstracted ethnography (and
anthropology) by contextualizing its objects of study. However, such ethnography remains
less than historicized since it prioritizes context only as structural framing rather than
becoming fully *historical* by following the dynamics of change that such contextualized
(thereby motivated/meaningful) actions always generate in human (social) contexts.

28. Awareness of and thus motivation from what I am treating as context is overwhelming
in this communal ethos and contrasts strikingly with the tendency of our individualistic
ethos to encourage thinking that utterly disregards context (a.k.a. objectified reality
external to the observer and abstracted sociological modeling), often reaching narcissistic
proportions and sometimes, in degrees that endanger others, as megalomania. These are
mental diseases of civilization, to the (considerable) extent that we equate civilized with
individualism and its cognate, personal ambition.

29. Campbell, Miers, and Miller, eds., *Woman and Slavery*.

30. Miller, "Displaced, Disoriented, Dispersed, and Domiciled," and many studies on Africa
and on Native North Americans.

31. The dialectics presented here in historical terms parallel those phrased in neo-Marxist
terms by Claude Meillassoux in *The Anthropology of Slavery: The Womb of Iron and
Gold*, trans. Alide Dasnois, foreword by Paul E. Lovejoy (Chicago: University of Chicago
Press, 1991) (originally *Anthropologie de l'esclavage: le ventre de fer et d'argent* [Paris:
Presses Universitaires de France, 1986]). Fuller discussion follows in the third chapter in
this book.

32. In unilineal, kin-structured environments, numerous specific relationships of respect and
responsibility are complementary rather than competitive. Differentiation there according
to sex-based metaphors (not directly keyed to biology) is not equivalent to gender, which is
a prejudicially differentiating construct characteristic of modern civic societies; for further
discussion of this historicizing distinction from the theorized abstraction usually projected,
erroneously, into earlier, remote contexts, see Miller, "Introduction," in Campbell, Miers,
and Miller, eds., *Woman and Slavery*, vol. 1.

33. It is important, as a historian, not to enclose these designations within quotes, since the
status given vulnerable newcomers, at least once they had earned the places then accorded
them, was real to the people who granted it. Identities *were* relational and adaptable, not
immutable, isolated, abstracted, or individual. One may qualify such status with quotation marks only by invoking external (hence historically irrelevant) and abstract (again,
therefore irrelevant) and singular definitions of "wife" or "son."

34. For example, Theda Perdue, *Slavery and the Evolution of Cherokee Society, 1540–1866* (Knoxville: University of Tennessee Press, 1979), chaps. 1, 2.
35. For further discussion and references to relevant literature, see chapter 3.
36. Patterson, *Slavery and Social Death*, elaborating Moses I. Finley, "Slavery," *International Encyclopedia of the Social Sciences*, ed. David L. Sills (New York: Macmillan and Free Press, 1968), 14:307–13.
37. A further general point about history: success produces aggregates that are bulky, in which too many people in them are too invested to retain significant flexibility. They are therefore relatively stable and consequently vulnerable to changing contexts. Change originates at the margins, in the regions of instability. Whatever the specific limitations of the famous frontier thesis of American history, it was solidly based epistemologically, as history. For a productive discussion of open frontiers as the locales of change in Africa and a further comment on the ironies of tradition, see Igor Kopytoff, ed., *The African Frontier: The Reproduction of Traditional African Societies* (Bloomington: Indiana University Press, 1987).
38. A more nuanced sketch will appear in the monograph-length development of these strategies in preparation. For first-stage elaborations of more integrated versions of the general narrative, see my "Slavery," for the on-line edition of the *Encylopaedia Britannica* (as yet unpublished, to my knowledge). Elements of one eventual component appear in "The Historical Contexts of Slavery in Europe," in Per O. Hernaes and Tore Iversen, eds., *Slavery Across Time and Space: Studies in Slavery in Medieval Europe and Africa* (Trondheim: Dept. of History, Norwegian University of Science and Technology, 2002), 1–57. Other aspects of the general processes have emerged in the course of coediting the two volumes on *Women and Slavery*. See also "Slaving as Historical Process: Examples from the Ancient Mediterranean and the Modern Atlantic," in Enrico Dal Lago and Constantina Katsari, eds., *Slave Systems: Ancient and Modern* (Cambridge: Cambridge University Press, 2007), 70–102.
39. See chapter 1.
40. For provocative hypotheses regarding the composite structures of local communities underlying later militarized regimes, see Roderick J. McIntosh, "Clustered Cities and Alternative Courses to Authority in Prehistory," *Journal of East Asian Archaeology* 1, 1 (1999), 1–24, and, more elaborately theorized, id., *Ancient Middle Niger: Urbanism and the Self-Organizing Landscape* (New York: Cambridge University Press, 2005).
41. In implied contradistinction to chiefs in less militarized places like Africa, who maneuvered internally by coordinating the component interests of their chiefdoms through councils and other collaborative and participatory, i.e., integrative, devices.
42. But merely displacing the external resources that support local concentrations of wealth and power to the raw materials that became the focus of the strategies of modern imperial systems.
43. I will not pause here to take up Gerda Lerner's famous thesis in *The Creation of Patriarchy* (New York: Oxford University Press, 1986), in which she emphasized the capture of women by imperial adventurers of the sort sketched here; see also Gerda Lerner, "Women and Slavery," *Slavery and Abolition* 4, 3 (1983), 173–98. For discussion, see Miller, "Displaced, Disoriented, Dispersed, and Domiciled."
44. And that we usually attribute anachronistically to founders, without examining the strategies by which they acquired what their successors enjoyed. Seeing through this teleological fog is always complicated by calculated celebration in subsequent memorialization of the founders as regime-legitimating heroes.
45. New Kingdom, ca. 15th c. BCE.
46. The implication here is that many symbolic idioms other than race could express despicable alterity, but that the derisive and dismissive aspects of alterity were concentrated on those

rendered enslaveable by contingent historical circumstances. To rephrase this abstraction in terms of the familiar conundrum of modern Atlantic history touched on earlier (chapter 1), slaving preceded the derogation that in the Americas eventually become concentrated in a racial idiom. The incremental steps in this process in the modern Atlantic stretched out over two "long" (the seventeenth and eighteenth) centuries. Further footnoted aspects of the process of elaborating racial ideologies, ancillary to slaving itself, follow in chapter 4.

47. A thoughtful reflection on these intricacies in the instance of a recent counterpart is Sean Stilwell, *Paradoxes of Power: The Kano "Mamluk" and Male Royal Slavery in the Sokoto Caliphate, 1804–1903* (London: Heinemann, 2004).

48. "Innovative" and "cumulative" are other more historical analogs of what, in a teleological mode, is classed as progress.

49. The historical dynamic emphasized in Paul M. Kennedy, *The Rise and Fall of the Great Powers: Economic Change and Military Conflict from 1500 to 2000* (New York: Vintage Books, 1987), applies throughout the history of the militarized world.

50. For comments on unfree labor in the context of the historiography of modern slaving for commercial production, see chapter 4. I will integrate Asian regimes into this schema of slaving in *Slaving in World History* (New York: Cambridge University Press, in preparation). In terms of the alternative outcomes of competing military and merchant interests, the relevant distinction is between the cavalry-based inner Asian military regimes and the more mercantile regimes of the Indian Ocean rim and the southeastern Asian archipelago.

51. Which gave legal—that is, collective, or state—sanction to claims of individuals, not necessarily known to one another, as distinct from the prevailing communal ethos of consensus among familiars; the later distinction between personal property transferable at the will of an individual and the real wealth held in some degree of communal (later, state) trust derives from this transition from collective to private interest. Commercialized transactions represented only small parts of the lives of all but the most committed to cash and credit; writing here in a determinedly historical vein, I contextualize mercantile strategies as particular to a certain small segment of historical moments otherwise significantly conditioned by the communal ethos.

52. The implicit distinction here is between slaving as a strategy of recruiting outsiders, by purchase or by force, and other strategies of acquiring more limited rights over insiders through debt, including the practices in Africa termed pawning. Hostages were equivalent transfers of personnel across the boundary between insiders and outsiders.

53. In this case, given the form of the very limited evidence available, as defined by its public laws rather than by the communities in which the great majority of people in fact lived.

54. For development of this argument, see Miller, "Slaving as Historical Process."

55. Distinguished from emperors or theocracies in the ideological identification of the ruler with the welfare of people they claimed to rule, often in paternal metaphors extended from those of the communities of kinship on which they intruded. What distinguished kings from warrior-emperors was not the degree of power they exercised, but their paternalistic relation to the society they controlled by means of that power, as contrasted with the primary orientation of remote emperors toward the gods.

56. Davis, *Slavery and Human Progress*; also Patterson, *Freedom*, for another interpretation anchoring the invention of the ideal of civic freedom itself in the personal enslavement of the era, initially of women. The point, much debated, goes back to Moses Finley, "Was Greek Civilization Based on Slave Labour?" *Historia* 8, 2 (1959), 145–64.

57. As distinguished from sketching a history of slaving through a millennium of Roman history, which deserves another scholar and much greater detail.

58. I am aware of the agitated debate among specialists as to the prominence of slaves among the working populations of the rural estates of the Roman aristocracy. I assert their presence,

though not necessarily their dominance, on the basis of the general flows of resident rural Italians into the Roman legions and the city of Rome and on my reservations about the evidence cited essentially to prove their absence, that is, a negative. This alleged evidence consists primarily of the lack of archaeological remains of barrack-like housing resembling some modern, mostly Caribbean sugar plantations, i.e., the stereotyped modeling of slavery as an institution. I find much more plausible the village-like settlements of families that characterized nineteenth-century western Africa, per Meillassoux, *Anthropology of Slavery*, and various studies in Paul E. Lovejoy, *Slavery, Commerce and Production in the Sokoto Caliphate of West Africa* (Trenton: Africa World Press, 2005).

59. P. R. C. Weaver, *Familia Caesaris: A Social Study of the Emperor's Freedmen and Slaves* (New York: Cambridge University Press, 1972).

60. For a slightly more extensive application of this logic to Rome, see Miller, "Historical Contexts of Slavery in Europe"; also Miller, "Slaving as Historical Process."

61. Extending insights I owe to the late and lamented Thomas Wiedemann, "The Arming of Slaves in Classical and Islamic Societies" (unpublished paper, conference entitled "The Arming of Slaves from the Classical Era to the American Civil War," Gilder Lehrman Center, Yale University, November 16–18, 2000); unfortunately Professor Wiedemann did not live to review the paper for the eventual published proceedings of this occasion; Christopher Leslie Brown and Philip D. Morgan, eds., *Arming Slaves: From Classical Times to the Modern Age* (New Haven: Yale University Press, 2006).

62. A deliberated anticipation of similar issues of integrating abstract imagined political communities in the modern era, and a suggestion that military conscription has served often as an effective technique of political integration. Africanists know the efficacy of colonial conscription in the two twentieth-century world wars for the eventual course of nationalism in Africa in the 1950s.

63. As there is no recent synthesis of slaving in Rome, pending the appearance of Keith Bradley and Paul Cartledge, eds., *The Cambridge World History of Slavery*, vol. 1: *The Ancient Mediterranean World* (New York: Cambridge University Press, 2011), and the existing surveys hardly begin to historicize on the scale proposed here, I have no direct authority to cite for an interpretation deriving primarily from the epistemological considerations at the heart of this chapter. Further specifics will follow in *Slaving in World History*.

64. The schematic quality of this chapter allows no space to comment on such nuances as the distinction between sultanic figures and the early caliphs (and later claimants to the title), who attempted to combine the religious authority of the Prophet with the military power on which they, as successors capable of only a shadowy resemblance to the inimitably singular voice of the Prophet himself, enshrined in scripture, had to rely in practice.

65. The famous exception, the tens of thousands of eastern African Zanj assembled in the eighth and ninth centuries to drain the salt flats of the Persian Gulf, proved the rule: they revolted in numbers that required mobilization of much of the military forces of the central Islamic heartland and several decades to quell. On the Zanj, Alexandre Popovic, *La révolte des esclaves en Iraq au IIIe/IXe siècle* (Paris: Geuthner, 1976), translated by Leon King as *The Revolt of African Slaves in Iraq in the IIId–IXth Century* (Princeton: Markus Wiener, 1998).

66. For the domestic politics of gender, Miller, "Displaced, Disoriented, Dispersed, and Domiciled."

67. The massive research of Charles Verlinden remains classic, especially in this context, *L'esclavage dans l'Europe médiévale*. Vol. 2: *Italie—Colonies italiennes du Levant—Levant latin—Empire byzantin* (Ghent: Rijksuniversiteit te Gent, 1977).

68. Joseph C. Miller, "O Atlântico escravista: açúcar, escravos, e engenhos," *Afro-Ásia* (Centro de Estudos áfro-orientais, FFCH-UFBA—Bahia, Brazil) 19–20 (1997), 9–36 (translation of "Africa and the Atlantic in World History: Working Out the Lethal Combination of

Africans, Sugar, and Plantations in the Atlantic Basin" [unpublished, 1991–93]); earlier version also as "A dimensão histórica da África no Atlântico: açucar, escravos, e planta-ções," in *A dimensão atlântica da África* (II Reunião Internacional de História de África, Rio de Janeiro, October 30–November 1, 1996) (São Paulo: CEA-USP/SDG-Marinha/ CAPES, 1997), 21–40. The limited role of slavery in the marginal sugar industry of the later medieval Mediterranean features more fully also in Stuart B. Schwartz, ed., *Tropical Babylons: Sugar and the Making of the Atlantic World, 1450–1680* (Chapel Hill: University of North Carolina Press, 2004).

69. For recent perspectives on why slaving might have declined within western Europe, see David Eltis, *The Rise of African Slavery in the Americas: The English in Comparative Perspective* (New York: Cambridge University Press, 1999), and Blackburn, *Making of New World Slavery*. Both authors rightly focus on contingency but fall back on struc-turalist logic by citing absences of conditions that they thereby presumed normative or necessary according to theorized models. The novel emphasis in my approach is the his-torical contextualization of monarchy as politically incompatible with internal slaving; I will return in chapter 4 to the implications of Atlantic slaving, seemingly safely displaced across an entire ocean, for western European monarchies. My historical phrasing of these arguments works positively from contexts, in this instance the remote but significant attractions of Muslim commercial dynamism and the emergence of monarchical forms of military authority no more compatible with private retinues of slaves than the monarchies of the ancient Mediterranean. The religious ethic that both Blackburn and Eltis cite as minimizing opportunities to enslave within Christian Europe contradicts Davis's established emphasis on the compatibility of European urban household slaving with Christian ethics and surprisingly, in arguments with strong economic underpinnings, resorts to ethics as somehow causative. In my alternative historical calculus, Christianity was the monotheistic analog of the ideological and political inclusivity of secular monarchy. Both monarchy and monotheism were homologously singular and direct in the access they gave kings (or God) to individual subjects (or believers). They were thereby restrictive of the exclusion-ary access to personnel that slaving gave to competitors—merchants or militarists. Slavery remained politically acceptable only in transoceanic and thus legally ambiguous spaces; for the legal point, Lauren Benton, "Legal Spaces of Empire: Piracy and the Origins of Ocean Regionalism," *Comparative Studies in Society and History* 47, 4 (2005), 700–24, and extended in *A Search for Sovereignty: Law and Geography in European Empires 1400–1900* (Cambridge: Cambridge University Press, 2010).

70. Joseph C. Miller, "Retention, Re-Invention, and Remembering: Restoring Identities Through Enslavement in Africa and Under Slavery in Brazil," in José C. Curto and Paul E. Lovejoy, eds., *Enslaving Connections: Changing Cultures of Africa and Brazil during the Era of Slavery* (Amherst, N.Y.: Prometheus/Humanity Books, 2003), 81–121.

71. As one may read in the autobiographies of the survivors, including the famed Equiano: Vincent Carretta, ed., *Olaudah Equiano: The Interesting Narrative and Other Writings* (New York: Penguin Books, 1995), and Alexander X. Byrd, "Eboe, Country, Nation, and Gustavus Vassa's *Interesting Narrative*," *William and Mary Quarterly* 63, 1 (2006), 123–48. Also, particularly, Jerome S. Handler, "Life Histories of Enslaved Africans in Barbados," *Slavery and Abolition* 19 (1998), 129–41. Also E. Ann McDougall, "A Sense of Self: The Life of Fatma Barka (North/West Africa)," *Canadian Journal of African Studies/Revue Canadienne d'Études Africaines* 32, 2 (1998), 398–412, and Indrani Chatterjee, "Colouring Subalternity: Slaves, Concubines and Social Orphans under the East India Company," *Subaltern Studies* 10 (1999), 49–97, and id., "A Slave's Quest for Selfhood in Eighteenth-Century Hindustan," *Indian Economic and Social History Review* 37, 1 (2000), 53–86. Sandra E. Greene's biographies of people enslaved along the nineteenth-century Gold Coast (western Africa) elegantly emphasize precisely this

existential quality; *West African Narratives of Slavery: Texts from Late Nineteenth- and Early Twentieth-Century Ghana* (Bloomington: Indiana University Press, 2011). Recent literary studies of eighteenth-century captivity narratives promise an indirect route into arguably analogous experience.

72. As Carl N. Degler did, many years ago, with regard to the U.S. South, *Neither Black nor White: Slavery and Race Relations in Brazil and the United States* (New York: Macmillan, 1971).

73. Discussion of these alternatives follows, in the contexts of the epistemological issues that they raise, in succeeding chapters.

74. See note 6, chapter 1.

75. E.g., the role of durability played by so-called Roman laws of slavery in most synthetic work in this tradition; e.g. William D. Phillips, Jr., *Slavery from Roman Times to the Early Transatlantic Trade* (Minneapolis: University of Minnesota Press, 1985).

Chapter 3. Slavery and History as Problems in Africa

1. The phrase "same but different" yielded 210,000,000 hits on Google on May 21, 2010; "different but the same" yielded 204,000,000.

2. In fact, slaving has recently regrown in ways, for reasons, by means, and with consequences that vary well within the range of the political processes outlined in this book.

3. The principal exceptions, elaborated in chapter 4, were monarchies, with the ideology of a surrogate parent (rather than an absented godlike figure) enveloping the king or queen.

4. To incorporate the growing and insightfully deepening postmodern critique of progressive history, and its postcolonial/postnational emphasis on internationalism or globalization, with this useful phrasing developed by Frederick Cooper, as he asks (rhetorically) "What Is the Concept of Globalization Good For? An African Historian's Perspective," *African Affairs* 44, 1 (no. 100) (2001), 189–213. For how African historical processes fly under the radar of conventional history in Africa's more recent past, Steven Feierman, "Colonizers, Scholars, and the Creation of Invisible Histories," in Victoria E. Bonnell and Lynn Hunt, eds., *Beyond the Cultural Turn: New Directions in the Study of Society and Culture* (Berkeley: University of California Press, 1999), 182–216. This vague label ("networks") in fact refers faintly negatively to a vast array of specific strategies of political commitment that may be characterized more productively in positive, historically contextualized terms; for Africa, where abstractly dichotomous states and so-called stateless societies still distort efforts to understand political arrangements, the strongest, though still not fully articulate, statements are in Jan Vansina, *Paths in the Rainforests: Toward a History of Political Tradition in Central Africa* (Madison: University of Wisconsin Press, 1990), "Pathways of Political Development in Equatorial Africa and Neo-Evolutionary Theory," in Susan Keech McIntosh, ed., *Beyond Chiefdoms: Pathways to Complexity in Africa* (New York: Cambridge University Press, 1999), 166–72, and id., *How Societies Are Born: Governance in West Central Africa Before 1600* (Charlottesville: University of Virginia Press, 2004).

5. Not uniquely but representative of the fates of other similarly domestic communities around the world, as they attempted to assimilate commercial credit and then military weaponry. Other examples, all enduring sources of the slaves that, as historical strategies, commercialization and militarization require, include the Asian hill country surrounding its agrarian valleys, Slavic eastern Europe, island southeastern Asia, and most of the native Americas.

6. Africa's alleged isolation before the Atlantic slave trade has remained a trope of world history down to the present, even in, e.g., William R. McNeill's *Rise of the West* (Chicago: University of Chicago Press, 1963), in which progress in history arises from contacts among alien civilizations. For a recent attempt to consolidate a great many subsequent

demonstrations of the falsity of this impression, see Erik Gilbert and Jonathan T. Reynolds, *Africa in World History from Prehistory to the Present* (Upper Saddle River, N.J.: Pearson, 2004; 2d ed. 2008; 3d ed. 2011); an archaeological equivalent is Peter Mitchell, *African Connections: Archaeological Perspectives on Africa and the Wider World* (Lanham, Md.: AltaMira, 2005). Both attempt to integrate Africa into world history on the conventional terms of the militarized commercial world(s) surrounding them, relying mostly on such abstractions as universal religions and intercontinental trade. This essay, in contrast, attempts to assess these contacts historically, that is, as Africans experienced them and as they enabled initiatives usually characterized as foreign.

7. For non-Africanist readers: each of the principal phases in the modern historiography has reiterated the basic externalization of agency in early Africa, though in differing terms:

> First, trade and politics, roughly in the 1960s, in the nationalist era of political optimism in Africa, showed how eagerly Africans had welcomed long-distance trade with Europeans and how effectively they gained from it to construct strong and viable political systems (kingdoms). In this narrative, slaves barely appeared.
>
> Reaction followed in the 1970s, as an underdevelopment school turned the tables on international trade and African politics to show how unequal the exchange had in fact been and how collaborating African rulers had built their states, exploitively, on slaving. This approach showed how this demographic and economic drain pointed Africa toward the economic decline it began to suffer as these historians wrote.
>
> The 1980s differentiated the peasants, women, and other sorts of dependents—very prominently including slaves—victimized by the Bad Kings of the 1970s who had replaced the Good Kings of the 1960s. Since then, modern states in Africa have been reconsidered as fundamentally weak and exploitive, rather than nationalistically integrated and promising, from the wary perspectives of these peasants and others.
>
> The historiography of the 1990s moved toward sophisticated understandings of the devices—social, economic, cultural—by which modern regimes survive these processes of victimization in the past, with implications extended, though less commonly, to possible parallels in the past.

The obviously presentistic inspiration of this historiographical progression parallels that of the historical discipline as a whole and is no greater in Africa than anywhere else. In fact, Africa used contacts with Atlantic commerce to move from its equivalent of early modernity to modernity, just as Atlantic resources allowed Europeans, not to mention Americans, to transform themselves similarly. I have sketched some of these integrated parallels in "Beyond Blacks, Bondage, and Blame: Why a Multi-Centric World History Needs Africa," *Historically Speaking* (Newsletter of The Historical Society) 5, 2 (2004), 7–12 (lead essay in forum, with responses); also "Multi-Centrism in History—How and Why Perspectives Matter—Rejoinder," *Historically Speaking* (Newsletter of The Historical Society) 5, 2 (2004), 27–31 (rejoinder) (both reprinted in Donald Yerxa, ed., *Recent Trends in World History: The Place of Africa and the Atlantic World* [Columbia: University of South Carolina Press, 2007]); "History, World: Africa in," in John Middleton and Joseph C. Miller, eds., *New Encyclopedia of Africa* (5 vols.) (Farmington Hills, Mich.: Scribner's/ Macmillan, 2007), 2:568–75; and "The African Historical Dynamics of the Atlantic 'Age of Revolutions,'" in David Armitage and Sanjay Subrahmanyam, eds., *The Age of Revolutions in Global Context, c. 1760–1840* (Basingstoke: Palgrave Macmillan, 2010), 101–24 (nn. 246–50), as well as recent unpublished papers: "Does an Early-Modern Era Make Sense for Africa and Its Place in the World?—Answer: YES! And No" (Africa and the Early Modern: A Workshop, March 6–7, 2009, Johns Hopkins University), "Politics in Africa: Limits of the 'Law of Nations'" (Conference on "The Law of Nations in the Early Modern Atlantic World," Newberry Library—Chicago, Illinois, April 3, 2009),

"The 'Atlantic Slave Trade' as Byproduct of Historical Processes in Africa" (American Historical Association annual meeting, San Diego, 2010).

8. See Patrick Manning, *The African Diaspora: A History Through Culture* (New York: Columbia University Press, 2009).

9. As Henry Louis Gates, Jr., engaged precisely this issue in "Wonders of the African World: Into Africa" (PBS, aired October 25–29, 1999, and website <http://pbs.org/wonders/>), with subsequent discussion on H-AFRICA and other listserves, and summarized *West Africa Review* (on-line journal, <www.westafricareview.com/war/>); for the intellectual context of Gates's move, not always apparent in the television production, see his *Wonders of the African World* (New York: Knopf, 1999), esp. chap. 1.

10. For glimpses of these sensitivities, see Martin A. Klein, "Studying the History of Those Who Would Rather Forget: Oral History and the Experience of Slavery," *History in Africa* 16 (1989), 209–17. Also Apeh and Opata, "Social Exclusion"; Greene, "Modern Trokosi and the 1807 Abolition in Ghana"; Keren, "The Transatlantic Slave Trade in Ghanaian Academic Historiography."

11. Leading to a succession of studies: Frederick Cooper, *From Slaves to Squatters: Plantation Labor and Agriculture in Zanzibar and Coastal Kenya, 1890–1925* (New Haven: Yale University Press, 1980); Suzanne Miers and Richard L. Roberts, eds., *The End of Slavery in Africa* (Madison: University of Wisconsin Press, 1988); Paul E. Lovejoy and Jan S. Hogendorn, *Slow Death for Slavery: The Course of Abolition in Northern Nigeria, 1897–1936* (New York: Cambridge University Press, 1993); Suzanne Miers and Martin Klein, eds., *Slavery and Colonial Rule in Africa* (London: Frank Cass, 1999); Roger Botte, ed., "Esclavage moderne ou modernité de l'esclavage?" *Cahiers' d'études africaines*, nos. 179–80 (2005), special issue.

12. Carolyn A. Brown, "Epilogue: Memory as Resistance: Identity and the Contested History of Slavery in Southeastern Nigeria," in Sylviane A. Diouf, ed., *Fighting the Slave Trade: West African Strategies* (Athens: Ohio University Press, 2003), 219–28; also see note 39, chapter 2. Beyond Greene, *West African Narratives of Slavery*, several major international projects are currently and revealingly pursuing personal "memories of slaving" in Africa.

13. There is a considerable rhetorical challenge in presenting the aspects of African history that—collectively, generally—contrast with modern times without falling back into the racialized homogenization critiqued in the preceding section. Accordingly, I write generically about Africans' strategies as intending to differentiate themselves in myriad internally focused communities: the outcomes of a communal ethos. As a consequence, as introduced in the preceding chapter innumerable individuals attempted to transcend their boundaries, often, deliberately or not, through slaving. I beg the readers' indulgence in tolerating the degree of contrastive characterization needed to develop the broader argument of the book without extending these controlled rhetorical strategies to essentializing Africans, once again, as somehow different. My intent, and I hope also my delivery, are precisely the opposite. Also see n. 6. David Northrup, in particular, has called attention to this risk: "Imagining Africa in World History: Perspectives and Problems," in Jonathon T. Reynolds, ed., "Africa in World History" (special WHB focus issue), *World History Bulletin* 22, 1 (2006), 17–19.

14. The accent again falls on personal, as distinct from collectively held, or real, property held essentially in trust. As assets acquired from outside, that is, beyond the domain of property of concern to the collectivity, they could only be thus; the origins of captives in the personal seizures by warriors claiming valor and, even more, the individuating transactions of a commercial nature were quite consistent with this distinction.

15. The historical dynamics of modern individualism had eroded then-inherited senses of community among people of European descent, creating deeply felt needs to restore some equivalent sense of human security on the anonymous and abstract scale of modern

imagined nations and thus displacing the intense emotions of the process onto accessible and tangible neighbors. Parallel displacements of the anxieties of modernity into intimate contexts operate in families, in urban ghettos, and in evangelical churches in leafy suburbs. Chapter 4 will consider the ways in which slaves and their racially excluded descendants became the demonized enemies around whom intense political communities consolidated in the Americas, thus becoming heirs to the immolated enemies of the Tupinambá and others; a generation of lynchings was succeeded by another generation dedicated to national crusades to save and integrate them.

16. The Enlightenment impulse to normalize the world according to a universal, hence necessarily single, standard became the core of modern sensibilities. In terms of political theory, this impulse takes the form of civic equality, but it is also pervasive in the standardization implied by statistical reasoning and as achieved through mechanical production and mass, anonymous marketing. For moderns, difference is deviant and potentially divisive; for Africans, differentiation is enriching and complementary. Postmodern thought has fundamentally focused on the constraints of normative thinking on what is in fact normal human diversity and explored culture as a way of thinking about the fundamental particularity of history.

17. Though theoretically countable. Among many differing linguistics-based approaches to Africa's history one recent synthesis is Christopher Ehret, *The Civilizations of Africa: A History to 1800* (Charlottesville: University of Virginia Press, 2002).

18. As history, not complementary differences, since difference was not a given; people actively differentiated themselves and assembled communities to maximize personal diversity. For the latter point, Jane I. Guyer et al., essays on "Wealth in People: Wealth in Things," *Journal of African History* 36, 1 (1995), 83–90.

19. Wyatt MacGaffey, "Am I Myself? Identities in Zaire, Then and Now," *Transactions of the Royal Historical Society*, 6th ser., 8 (1998), 291–307; cf. John M. Cinnamon, "Mobility, Genealogical Memory, and Constructions of Social Space in Northern Gabon," in Allen M. Howard and Richard M. Shain, eds., *The Spatial Factor in African History: The Relationship of the Social, Material, and Perceptual* (Leiden: Brill, 2004), 177–219.

20. My principal statements on this historiography are in "History and Africa/Africa and History," *American Historical Review* 104, 1 (1999), 1–32, and "Life Begins at Fifty: African Studies Enters Its Second Half Century," *African Studies Review* 50, 2 (2007), 1–35.

21. See table 3.1.

22. Thus the importance, as an Africanist sees it, of the discovery of memory by historians working in the epistemology of the modern discipline. The difference is that modern historians must distinguish memory from history, while Africans leave that distinction to prying historians of Western persuasions. The historical processes in both cultural frameworks, as either side would understand them, are precisely the same.

23. Jan Vansina, "A Slow Revolution: Farming in Subequatorial Africa," *Azania* 29–30 (1994–95), 15–26; also Kairn Klieman, *"The Pygmies Were Our Compass": Bantu and Batwa in the History of West Central Africa, Early Times to c. 1900 C.E.* (Portsmouth: Heinemann, 2004).

24. One will sense here the strong implications for contemporary theorizing about globalization and its late and unlamented predecessor, modernization theory. Only historians of unproblematized progressive persuasions would expect emergent global awarenesses and dynamics to replace regional and local perspectives, coherence, vitality. Rather, local communities are dynamized as ways of proceeding incrementally, additively, through changes they see as parts of their own historical contexts. My own emphasis on historical processes as incremental adapts the African sensibility for what is there called the on-going reinvention of tradition.

25. In the language of development economics, this is also the shift from modernization theory to sustainable development and civic society rooted in the resources, knowledge, and initiative of local communities. Earlier Cold War–era conceptualizations of this essential withdrawal from global dynamics were presented as African socialism.

26. Often with all of the limitations of originary thinking as history that I emphasized in chapter 1.

27. Miller, "History and Africa/Africa and History"; for specifics, Ehret, *The Civilizations of Africa*, and, with differing method, Vansina, *Paths in the Rainforests* and *How Societies Are Born*.

28. I will not attempt to reference key methodological studies, other than to cite two recent compilations: Toyin Falola and Christian Jennings, eds., *Sources and Methods in African History: Spoken, Written, Unearthed* (Rochester: University of Rochester Press, 2003), and John Edward Philips, ed., *Writing African History* (Rochester: University of Rochester Press, 2005).

29. The breakthrough methodological work on oral traditions as historical sources was that of Jan Vansina, *Oral Tradition* (Chicago: Aldine, 1965) (English translation of *De la tradition orale* [Tervuren: Musée Royal de l'Afrique Centrale. Annales, 1961] Série in-8°, Sciences Humaines, 36]), fundamentally revised in *Oral Tradition as History* (Madison: University of Wisconsin Press, 1984). Vansina has not reflected theoretically on how his subsequent turn to linguistic evidence might reflect back on oral narratives.

30. A quest for rational coherence animated British structural-functional anthropology in the colonial decades; Wyatt MacGaffey, "African History, Anthropology, and the Rationality of Natives," *History in Africa* 5 (1978), 101–20.

31. A book that makes effective use of this principle of incoherent contemporaneity (or contemporaneous incoherence), resolved through historical linguistic methods in the Ehret tradition, is Klieman, "*The Pygmies Were Our Compass.*"

32. "African History, Anthropology, and the Rationality of Natives."

33. The two very different classics, both necessary to develop a full picture of the historiography of slavery in Africa, are Suzanne Miers and Igor Kopytoff, eds., *Slavery in Africa: Historical and Anthropological Perspectives* (Madison: University of Wisconsin Press, 1977), and Claude Meillassoux, *The Anthropology of Slavery: The Womb of Iron and Gold*, trans. Alide Dasnois, foreword by Paul E. Lovejoy (Chicago: University of Chicago Press, 1991). Less foundational but more comprehensive in mode is Paul E. Lovejoy, *Transformations in Slavery: A History of Slavery in Africa* (1983; new ed. New York: Cambridge University Press, 2000). Another integrated historical interpretation, based on demography, is found in Patrick Manning, *Slavery and African Life* (New York: Cambridge University Press, 1990). My own approach to history and slaving in Africa is in draft form as "Slavery" (for "Critical Themes in African History" pamphlet series, Boston University African Studies Center).

34. As opposed to material tokens of relationships. which were correspondingly ubiquitous. John Middleton, "Merchants: An Essay in Historical Ethnography," *Journal of the Royal Anthropological Institute* 9, 3 (2003), 509–26, shows the extent to which Africans converted the coins minted in towns along the Swahili coast, deeply embedded as they were in the commercial culture of the Indian Ocean, into distinctive and durable tokens of personal relationships, more characteristic of a communal ethos than of a mercantile economy. The famous "bell of kings" and copper crosses of central Africa are other examples of African tokens misrepresented as currencies in a commercial sense; they confirmed relationships among favored partners rather than establishing an individual proprietary right over the material itself; Jan Vansina, "The Bells of Kings," *Journal of African History* 10, 2 (1969), 187–97.

35. John Donne (1572–1631). It appears in *Devotions upon emergent occasions and seuerall steps in my sicknes—Meditation XVII*, 1624, though in a more abstractly humanistic sense.

36. People acquired collectively through the process known as pawning, i.e., as human collateral against credit extended between groups in ongoing relationships and integrated by the creditor to foreclose on a failed debtor, would not fall technically into the category of slave; as isolated outsiders they were held collectively rather than individually. But in the context of later commercialization they were often converted to disposable human assets. Discussion of commercialization follows.

37. This phrasing of the slave's position, like other aspects of my historicizing of slaving, states the slave's positive context, not the negative "kinless" usually used to describe this position. The positive statement also provides context for assessing the enslaved person's priorities and options, the enabling of her or him epistemologically as a historical actor.

38. David Schoenbrun, "Violence, Marginality, Scorn, and Honor: Language Evidence and the Genealogies of Slavery and Enslavement in the Great Lakes Region to the 18th Century," in Shane Doyle and Henri Médard, eds., *Slavery in the Great Lakes Region of Africa* (Oxford: James Currey Publishers, 2007), 38–75. Also id., "Violence and Vulnerability in Eastern Africa Before 1800: A Research Conspectus," *History Compass* 4, 5 (2006), 741–60.

39. In addition to the indelibility of slave ancestry stressed in Apeh and Opata, "Social Exclusion"; Greene, "Modern Trokosi and the 1807 Abolition in Ghana"; Keren, "The Transatlantic Slave Trade in Ghanaian Academic Historiography," see Joseph C. Miller, "Imbangala Lineage Slavery," in Miers and Kopytoff, eds., *Slavery in Africa*, 205–30.

40. Corresponding to the peak of the last glaciation of the higher latitudes, with corresponding lowered sea levels and dehydration of tropical climates around the world.

41. And thus the equivalents of the individuated post-traumatic stress disorder that has become a not uncommon experience of individuals in the second half of the twentieth century.

42. The infamous early seventeenth-century Jaga, or Imbangala; see Joseph C. Miller, *Kings and Kinsmen: Early Mbundu States in Angola* (Oxford: Clarendon Press, 1975), with restatements of the historical hypothesis in "The Paradoxes of Impoverishment in the Atlantic Zone," in David Birmingham and Phyllis Martin, eds., *History of Central Africa* (London: Longman, 1983), 1:118–51. For further specification, Vansina, *How Societies Are Born*.

43. The utility of slaving in political innovation corresponds to the efficacy of abolitionism in the creation of modern nation-states; see chapter 4.

44. Edna G. Bay, *Wives of the Leopard: Gender, Politics, and Culture in the Kingdom of Dahomey* (Charlottesville: University Press of Virginia, 1998), culminating an extensive historiography, though little of it emphasizing the historical dynamics of slaving I am attempting to bring out here.

45. Here the implicit reference is to the falsely cognate designation "tribe," which, as applied to Africa, inevitably invokes ancient and inherent conflict. For discussions of the concept and its limits in this sense, see Curtis Keim, *Mistaking Africa: Curiosities and Inventions of the American Mind* (Boulder: Westview, 1999), or "Talking about Tribe," http://www.africaaction.org.

46. Evidence of the initial achievements of these strategies appears in Africa's modern languages; we can also discern its traces by disaggregating recent practices observed ethnographically. A point of method: seen as an additive and often discordant accumulation of collective experiences from the entire past of the group observed, and not harmoniously and organically integrated in their modern contexts as the functionalist anthropology of the colonial era attempted to rationalize them. Instead, contemporary practices and ideologies may be separated and arrayed along a modern historical axis of linear time for epistemologically historical analysis, as opposed to the timeless simultaneity of the sociological approach.

47. No surprise there for modern capitalists, who reward individuals who appear to innovate, without accounting for the social costs they do not cover, while simultaneously reducing and often eliminating the personal exposure by insurance and other financial schemes that contractually deflect risks to society at large.

48. And forced thus to behave as such externally; in this precise historical sense, nations are the modern equivalents of what, when it is not recognized as politicized, is usually called ethnicity. For preliminary thoughts along these lines, Joseph C. Miller, "Introduction: Atlantic Ambiguities of British and American Abolition," special issue of the *William and Mary Quarterly* 66, 4 (2009), 675–703.

49. An African proverb expresses the flexible balance of conflict and collaboration in any relationship, in the language of the communal ethos: "We marry those whom we fight." The general historiography of slaving in Africa rests excessively on the premise of violence as its primary, even sole, method and on a teleological assumption that most or all of the resulting war captives ended up on the coast, sold as slaves to Europeans. Recent work has shifted to an acknowledgment that Africans kept more of the human products of slaving than they sold to Europeans as slaves, but it has retained the analogy of slavery to describe their fates in Africa. Strategies of deploying captives as hostages and thus redemption for the captured are becoming increasingly evident throughout the literature; they are featured, for example, in Paul Lovejoy, "Internal Markets or an Atlantic-Sahara Divide? How Women Fit into the Slave Trade of West Africa," in Gwyn Campbell, Suzanne Miers, and Joseph C. Miller, eds., *Women and Slavery*, 2 vols. (Athens: Ohio University Press, 2007), 1:259–79, and are evident in Kristin Mann, *Slavery and the Birth of an African City: Lagos, 1760–1900* (Bloomington: Indiana University Press, 2007). All of these examples represent recent distortions, in the context of hypercommercialization, of the older reconciliatory practices I am describing here. As such, and as I will go on to describe, they represent the incremental quality of change characteristic of history: familiar means put to new and distorting ends.

50. One notes that sex-based distinctions of gender produce the same hegemonic effect, so that ethnic identities are implicitly male and thus patriarchal. This accent extends the historicized restriction of gender to modern civic communities in Miller, "Introduction" (*Women and Slavery*, vol. 1), and "Displaced, Disoriented, Dispersed, and Domiciled," to the modern ethnicized equivalents in Africa. Tribes and nations are both prioritized political collectivities composed of people who are strangers to one another and possess no other means of collaborating under external pressures.

51. Recent literature on pastoralists generally in Africa has emphasized the ideological (and recently commercial tourist as well as national political) values of the appearance of ethnic purity and ahistorical stability; on this subordinate point, not involving slaving in a context of accessible ethnic complementarities, e.g., Thomas Spear and Richard Waller, eds., *Being Maasai: Ethnicity and Identity in East Africa* (London: J. Currey, 1993).

52. Margo Russell, "Slaves or Workers? Relations between Bushmen, Tswana, and Boers in the Kalahari," *Journal of Southern African Studies* 2, 2 (1976), 178–97; Thomas Tlou, "Servility and Political Control: Botlhanka among the BaTawana of Northwestern Botswana, ca. 1750–1906," in Miers and Kopytoff, eds., *Slavery in Africa*, 367–90; Suzanne Miers and Michael Crowder, "The Politics of Slavery in Bechuanaland: Power Struggles and the Plight of the Basarwa in the Bamangwato Reserve 1926–1940," in Miers and Roberts, eds., *The End of Slavery in Africa*, 172–200. The Dutch-descended Boer and, later, Afrikaner farmers in the region followed a closely parallel strategy.

53. For a recent statement in a large bibliography, Carolyn A. Brown, "Testing the Boundaries of Marginality: Twentieth-Century Slavery and Emancipation Struggles in Nkanu, Northern Igboland, 1920–29," *Journal of African History* 37, 1 (1996), 51–80.

54. This contrast between slavery as an unfortunate accident, happening to individuals, and an inherent destiny attributed to ethnicized peoples is well known from classical Greek formulations from the eighth to fifth centuries BCE; the same transition in the Americas changed people from Africa from infrequent and incidental and not always excluded newcomers in the sixteenth century (and in some areas into the seventeenth) to dangerous savages when structured deliveries of larger numbers followed in the Iberian colonies; the same conversion followed later in North America, at the end of the seventeenth century.

55. Not also without technological innovations (ferrous metallurgy, elaboration of agriculture, etc.) featured in progressive visions of history in Africa, though that fails to take fully into account the historical constraints of environmental contexts or of Africans' conceptualizing of change as restorative. A historical note: historicized, Africa was not the underpopulated continent that comparison in quantitative demographic terms makes it appear, and as it is accordingly described in a historiography still resting on abstract standards like this one.

56. A parallel analogy from chemistry would be the catalytic agent introduced, arbitrarily, into an otherwise chemically inert mixture of substances.

57. Commerce is particularly adaptable to slaving; other skills of males pursued widely through supracommunity mobility included smelting and hunting. The classic modeling of these arrangements is the "landlord–stranger" relationship defined by George E. Brooks, Jr., *Landlords and Strangers: Ecology, Society, and Trade in Western Africa, 1000–1630* (Boulder: Westview Press, 1994), and in other terms as "trading diaspora" in Philip D. Curtin, *Economic Change in Precolonial Africa: Senegambia in the Era of the Slave Trade* (Madison: University of Wisconsin Press, 1975), and id., *Cross-Cultural Trade in World History* (Cambridge: Cambridge University Press, 1984).

58. But not accounted for, left thus as exoticized curiosities in an ethnographic genre dependent on the prior production of curiosity-arousing exoticism for its essential explanatory epistemology of translation of cultures. Classical ethnography, as critical anthropology has been observing for years, renders intelligible to outsiders what is apparently unintelligible to them, thus necessarily in terms defined by the observer, not by the observed. The ethnographic subject remains merely described, not understood on her or his own terms, in ways that attribute intuitively intelligible but historically irrelevant motivation for the behavior observed.

59. Brooks, *Landlords and Strangers*. And greatly elaborated in Roderick J. McIntosh, *Ancient Middle Niger: Urbanism and the Self-Organizing Landscape* (New York: Cambridge University Press, 2005).

60. Vansina, *Paths in the Rainforests*, for a synthetic integration of the secret societies of the rivers.

61. This emphasis in Robert W. Harms, *River of Wealth, River of Sorrow: The Central Zaire Basin in the Era of the Slave and Ivory Trade, 1500–1891* (New Haven: Yale University Press, 1981).

62. After internal differentiation developed to the point of structuring distinctions between those in control of local resources and others within.

63. Contrast the distinct challenge of mounting political challenges to militarized imperial authority in early Asia; the parallel context of challenging militarized power in Africa came only later, and hence the parallel appropriation of slaving as a strategy of commercialization.

64. E.g., David Northrup, *Trade without Rulers: Pre-Colonial Economic Development in South-Eastern Nigeria* (Oxford: Clarendon Press, 1978).

65. Geographical considerations may have created a gender distinction between the northern African and southwestern Asian markets for women and a contrasting tendency in Muslim and Hindu India to favor African males. The former areas, universally Muslim (and later also integrated under Ottoman political authority), could not enslave locally and

so recruited male military slaves from their northern, central Asian fringes (Circassians, Slavs, etc.), leaving Africa a primary source for women. In caste-differentiated Hindu areas of India, families generated female slaves through a variety of local processes of indebtment and exchange. On the north, Muslim dynasties faced the Himalayas and central Asian steppes, leaving only Africa as a source of the males who turn up there as the military slaves.

66. Thus a crucial but little noticed redefinition of slaves from real to personal property in English law in American colonies at the end of the seventeenth century seems to have marked the development of commercial, public, institutionalized slaving from a legal background rooted in more collectivized interests in slave members of domestic households, thought of as preserved through the generations of the families holding them.

67. One of the classic debates of the early historiography of Africa pitted African against European initiative (with African agency celebrated for its responsiveness rather than its autonomous initiative) specifically in terms of political slaving. Compare Walter Rodney, "African Slavery and Other Forms of Social Oppression on the Upper Guinea Coast in the Context of the Atlantic Slave Trade," *Journal of African History* 7, 3 (1966), 431–44, with John D. Fage, "Slavery and the Slave Trade in the Context of West African History," *Journal of African History* 10, 3 (1969), 393–404. Rodney, a neo-Marxist, described political power in Africa as exploitive and attributed it to largely unspecified profits of selling people to Europeans; Fage, in nationalist-era celebration of African political initiative as unproblematically positive, emphasized the centrality of slaving to political centralization before the arrival of the Europeans. Neither significantly problematized political strategies in Africa as compositional.

68. Thus querying the celebratory and progressive overtones of the state- and empire-celebrating early historiography of Africa, starting with W. E. B. Du Bois and continuing through the trade-and-politics/nationalist phase of modern African historiography.

69. A basic political economy of predation, once admired in Africa in a neo-Marxist vein for its implicit relief of local peasantries from the costs of political overrule; see Catherine Coquery-Vidrovitch, "Recherches sur une mode de production africain," *La Pensée* 144 (1969), 61–78; translated as "Research on an African Mode of Production," in M. A. Klein and G. W. Johnson, eds., *Perspectives on the African Past* (Boston: Little Brown, 1972), 129–41. Also *Critique of Anthropology* 2, 4–5 (1975), 38–71, and other republications, e.g., David Seddon, ed., *Relations of Production: Marxist Approaches to Economic Anthropology* (London: Frank Cass, 1978), 261–88. As ideologies, tribute is personal and nominally voluntary, an expression of respect, integrated in a relationship; taxes are imposed, arbitrarily demanded by an entity external to those taxed. The mantra of rebellion in the English North American colonies and a subsequent core of political culture in the United States, no taxation without representation, expressed this transition from recognized and reciprocated contribution to a rhetoric of irresponsibly unreciprocated political slavery.

70. E.g., Walter Hawthorne, *Planting Rice and Harvesting Slaves: Transformations along the Guinea-Bissau Coast, 1400–1900* (Portsmouth, N.H.: Heinemann, 2003). What is now northern Ghana and so-called Mahi and Kabre in northern Togo and Bénin are others, among many. For Kabre, Charles Piot, *Remotely Global: Village Modernity in West Africa* (Chicago: University of Chicago Press, 1999). For Senegambia, Robert Martin Baum, *Shrines of the Slave Trade: Diola Religion and Society in Precolonial Senegambia* (New York: Oxford University Press, 1999).

71. For the best interpretation of that era along these lines, see Claude Meillassoux, "The Role of Slavery in the Economic and Social History of Sahelo-Sudanic Africa," in Joseph E. Inikori, ed., *Forced Migration: The Impact of the Export Slave Trade on African Societies* (London: Hutchinson, 1981), 74–99.

72. These are the African examples of the Islamic military states to which I alluded in chapter 2.

73. And not without tension with slaving by Muslim warrior regimes; John Hunwick, "Islamic Law and Polemics over Race and Slavery in North and West Africa (16th–19th Century)," in Shaun Elizabeth Marmon, ed., *Slavery in the Islamic Middle East* (Princeton: Markus Wiener, 1999), 43–68, and revised as "The Same but Different: Africans in Slavery in the Mediterranean Muslim World," in John O. Hunwick and Eve Troutt Powell, *The African Diaspora in the Mediterranean Muslim World* (Princeton: Markus Wiener, 2002), ix–xxiv.

74. Manning, *Slavery and African Life*, developed partially parallel distinctions to differentiate the actors in his demographic modeling of later Atlantic slaving for export.

75. The evidence now being recovered for pervasive memorialization of this intensely formative phase of modern Africa is found not in the consciously constructed, highly ideological oral narrative traditions but in community shrines and ritualized behavior; see, for example, Rosalind Shaw, *Ritual Memories of the Slave Trade: Ritual and the Historical Imagination in Sierra Leone* (Chicago: University of Chicago Press, 2002); Elizabeth Isichei, *Voices of the Poor in Africa* (Rochester: University of Rochester Press, 2002), chapters on slave-trade era.

76. And also to sustain complex European strategies of financing militarized monarchical consolidation in the Atlantic in the sixteenth and seventeenth centuries. These parallels are sketched in chapter 4 and will be developed in greater detail in my world history of slaving, for which these essays form an epistemological prelude.

77. Lovejoy, *Transformations in Slavery*, for an overview; the relevant dynamics appear in Lovejoy's work most clearly with regard to the nineteenth-century Sokoto caliphate in what is now northern Nigeria. See also Jan S. Hogendorn, "Slave Acquisition and Delivery in Precolonial Hausaland," in Raymond E. Dumett and Ben K. Swartz, eds., *West African Culture Dynamics: Archeological and Historical Perspectives* (The Hague: Mouton, 1980), 477–93. See also Miller, *Way of Death*, for western central Africa.

78. Jan Vansina, "Ambaca Society and the Slave Trade, c. 1760–1845," *Journal of African History* 46, 1 (2005), 1–27.

79. Joseph C. Miller, "Kings, Lists, and History in Kasanje," *History in Africa* 6 (1979), 51–96.

80. The least militarized and correspondingly most commercialized major slaving region was east of the lower Niger River, selling captives to Europeans through slaving ports along the channels of the Niger Delta and Cross River areas. Lovejoy and Richardson have emphasized the trust system of credit developed in this region by the most amply capitalized of the Europeans, the British; Paul E. Lovejoy and David Richardson, "Trust, Pawnship, and Atlantic History: The Institutional Foundations of the Old Calabar Slave Trade," *American Historical Review* 104, 2 (1999), 333–55; id., "The Business of Slaving: Pawnship in Western Africa, c. 1600–1810," *Journal of African History* 42, 1 (2001), 67–89; id., "'This Horrid Hole': Royal Authority, Commerce and Credit at Bonny, 1690–1840," *Journal of African History* 43, 3 (2004), 67–89; id., "African Agency and the Liverpool Slave Trade," in David Richardson, Suzanne Schwarz, and Anthony Tibbles, eds., *Liverpool and Transatlantic Slavery* (Liverpool: Liverpool University Press, 2007), 43–65. The literature on the canoe houses of the Niger Delta is classic; for recent treatments, Northrup, *Trade Without Rulers*, and Ralph A. Austen and Jonathan Derrick, *Middlemen of the Cameroons Rivers: The Duala and Their Hinterland, c. 1600–c. 1960* (New York: Cambridge University Press, 1999). Most recently and revealingly for the African strategies of organizing credit associations, Nicolas Argenti, *The Intestines of the State: Youth, Violence, and Belated Histories in the Cameroon Grassfields* (Chicago: University of Chicago Press, 2007). Since the composition of this essay, G. Ugo Nwokeji, *The Slave Trade and Culture in the Bight of Biafra: An African Society in the Atlantic World* (New York: Cambridge University Press, 2010).

81. In another context I will argue that Atlantic slaving accelerated that pace by enabling European commercial growth at rates beyond even those that the vast stores of specie imported from the Americas enabled. In this sense, slaving in Africa supported the slaving in the Atlantic that supported the European financial ability to stimulate more slaving in Africa. Only such a multiparty, self-dynamizing historical process could have produced a tragedy of proportions so far beyond the intentions of its initial participants.

82. Harms, *River of Wealth, River of Sorrow.*

83. Structures, including slavery as an institution, are naturalized ideologies. The social sciences developed out of the same logical premises that underlie structures/models and so are formal statements of the ideology. They are thus incapable of generating radical critiques of themselves.

84. Lovejoy and Hogendorn, *Slow Death for Slavery.*

85. A significant proportion of African slaving, though sufficiently distinct from commercial engagements with Saharan and Atlantic merchants that it cannot receive more than passing mention in the present context.

Chapter 4. Problematizing Slavery in the Americas as History

1. As the field of Atlantic history has begun to mature in the last ten years, scholars are becoming more aware of the limits of its origins in the respective national and imperial historiographies, and in particular the isolation of the southern Atlantic from its northern context, and vice versa. One example, from an African perspective, is Linda Heywood, ed., *Central Africans and Cultural Transformations in the American Diaspora* (New York: Cambridge University Press, 2002).

2. Beyond the epistemological limits of this selective strategy as history and the fact that it takes the legal language out of its wholly technical context and interprets it rhetorically and ethically as a direct characterization of the person enslaved, it assumes a coherent, universal body of quasi-codified European law; for the falsity of this assumption, see, for example, Lauren Benton, *Law and Colonial Cultures: Legal Regimes in World History, 1400–1900* (New York: Cambridge University Press, 2002), and much other recent work in the history of the law of nations and early modern European law. The same failing undermines the comprehensive and determinative (or, in historicized terms, motivating and enabling) uniformity given to Christianity in Eltis, *The Rise of African Slavery in the Americas.*

3. At the very early time of the definition of this principle, Roman laws expressed the challenges of consolidating a unified state claiming direct authority over its citizens out of a small urban republic of householders surrounded by family, client, and slave dependents, with only the last excluded from the human domain of the emergent polity. Such householders, heads of *familiae*, had responsibilities for the welfare of their dependents, expressed as honor and in other nonlegal ways balancing their domestic authority. The legal analogy to domesticated animals thus implied responsibility or custodianship as much as it implied arbitrary authority. A first step in historicizing applications of the analogy in the New World would trace its changes from an implied premise of personal responsibility in the cities of Spain's colonies to the impersonality of late seventeenth-century plantation labor and on to the civic freedoms and corresponding exemptions from social or public accountability that characterized the fully commercialized agricultural estates and other slave-worked enterprises of the eighteenth and nineteenth centuries.

4. This approach remains vital, particularly among economic historians working with the abstract assumptions of neoliberal economic theory; see Stanley L. Engerman, ed., *The Terms of Labor: Slavery, Serfdom and Free Labor* (Stanford: Stanford University Press, 1999). It also features, in this case appropriately enough, in intellectual histories of

abolitionism, e.g., Seymour Drescher, *The Mighty Experiment: Free Labor vs. Slavery in British Emancipation* (New York: Oxford University Press, 2002).

5. These legal rights to control residence themselves became commercialized to varying degrees in the eighteenth and nineteenth centuries, as landlords sought to realize cash to catch up with the intensifying exchange economies around them. Historically equivalent, contemporary New World strategies of cashing out on legal rights in dependents to buy into a commercial economy that was accelerating rapidly may be observed in the internal sell-offs of slaves from the seaboard United States and northeastern Brazil as newly integrated national economies shifted geographically southward and westward, or (like aristocratic households in imperial Rome) as urban slaveholders in Brazil as well as in Spanish colonies and their independent successor nation-states manumitted veteran slaves and their own progeny born of slave mothers in return for cash payments. The varying specifics of these strategies reflected varying degrees of monetized commercialization.

6. This was also the heart of the restrictions on residential mobility of African residents on white-owned farms in the Union of South Africa (c. 1910–60), to provide low-cost resident labor for a commercial agricultural sector feeding the country's burgeoning mining sectors, which otherwise would have allowed African farmers to support themselves.

7. In modern times, underfinanced modern nation-states have repeatedly fallen back on parallel strategies of intruding on local populations by deporting and interning, ranging from reservations to gulags and other concentration camps.

8. Roderick J. McIntosh, *Ancient Middle Niger: Urbanism and the Self-Organizing Landscape* (New York: Cambridge University Press, 2005).

9. The early strategies of *encomienda* and *repartimiento* in New Spain were adapted to increasing commercialization in the region, with peonage becoming the generic designation of later adaptations of these communal obligations to individuated debt.

10. See chapter 3.

11. See the opening quote from David Brion Davis (chapter 1, n. 16), which specifically invokes race as the distinguishing aspect of, not context for, slavery in the Americas.

12. For the same confusion in Muslim contexts, Bernard Lewis, *Race and Color in Islam* (New York: Harper and Row, 1971), with the blurring rendered explicit in the title of the revised version, *Race and Slavery in the Middle East: An Historical Enquiry* (New York: Oxford University Press, 1990), with some effort to track teleologically the formation of a defined process of racialization, thus evading the epistemological implications of the title's secondary claim to be historical.

13. Here one risks citing nearly the entire body of comparative scholarship originating in Frank Tannenbaum, *Slave and Citizen: The Negro in the Americas* (New York: Knopf, 1947); the most erudite elaboration of this tradition was Winthrop D. Jordan, *White Over Black: American Attitudes Toward the Negro, 1550–1812* (Chapel Hill: University of North Carolina Press, 1968), focused on race but taken by many appreciative readers as revelatory of slavery.

14. In addition to the original contributions, cited in chapter 1, Alden T. Vaughan, "The Origins Debate: Slavery and Racism in Seventeenth-Century Virginia," *Virginia Magazine of History and Biography* 97, 3 (1989), 311–54; reprinted in *Roots of American Racism: Essays on the Colonial Experience* (New York: Oxford University Press, 1995). Less racialized discussion is assembled in Edward Countryman, ed., *How Did American Slavery Begin?* (Boston: St. Martin's Press, 1999). Cf. chapter 1, n. 22.

15. The relationship between Europe and the Americas was fundamental to all of the American national historiographies in the early twentieth century, led by the high-volume production of history in the United States, as these former colonies faced transitions from external reaction (often presented as causality) to the internal integration that nationalist historians elsewhere in the world faced. The politics of displacing origins of the negative aspects of

this highly emotional and moralized process (e.g., slavery) to the Old World might be worth historiographical reflection, as distinct from earlier efforts to claim credit for more local aspects of the American experiences on the frontiers of the New World valued positively.

16. The transatlantic slave trade database allows an estimate of the numbers of the enslaved landed at ports serving plantation agricultural sectors in the range of 80 percent, and the great majority of the people sold there would have done time at hard field labor before some of them moved on to other sectors of these economies.

17. Stanley L. Engerman, "Europe, the Lesser Antilles, and Economic Expansion, 1600–1800," in Robert L. Paquette and Stanley L. Engerman, eds., *The Lesser Antilles in the Age of European Expansion* (Gainesville: University Press of Florida, 1996). I do not cite this passage because Engerman, a brilliant and eminent economist and historian, was alone but rather because he exemplifies the highly respected scholars who, in thinking about slavery in the Americas in institutional terms, drifted into this easy cliché to account for it in terms of structural continuities. See, for example, another able and distinguished contributor: "The answer to [Americans'] labor problems had already been suggested in the earlier experience of plantation management, in the Mediterranean and Atlantic islands," and the passage continues on to summarize the slow movement westward, though contradictorily "always on a small scale," of this strategy of integrating production on large scales; James Walvin, *Questioning Slavery* (London: Routledge, 1996), 3. Philip Curtin treated the story more historically, as the phrasing of the title of his book emphasized: *The Rise and Fall of the Plantation Complex*, 2d ed. (New York: Cambridge University Press, 1998), but within the framework of an institution-like complex.

18. With regard to sugar, I acknowledge, in particular, the history of sugar by John Galloway (oddly, a geographer rather than a historian, though one with laudably historical good sense): *The Sugar Cane Industry: An Historical Geography from its Origins to 1914* (Cambridge: Cambridge University Press, 1989); also see the earlier article by the same author, "The Mediterranean Sugar Industry," *Geographical Review* 67 (1977), 177–94. Other historians have acknowledged change but not exploited it analytically to explain the transition as one of incremental, dialectical historical process; e.g., William D. Phillips, Jr., "Sugar Production and Trade in the Mediterranean at the Time of the Crusades," in Vladimir P. Goss and Christine Verzár Bornstein, eds., *The Meeting of Two Worlds: Cultural Exchange during the Period of the Crusades* (Kalamazoo: Medieval Institute Publications, Western Michigan University, 1986), 393–406, which treats carefully the technical changes and the variety of forms of labor employed. A more historical treatment is found in Phillips, "Sugar in Iberia," in Stuart Schwartz, ed., *Tropical Babylons: Sugar and the Making of the Atlantic World, 1450–1680* (Chapel Hill: University of North Carolina Press, 2004), 27–41. This collection of essays as a whole marshals a systematic effort to contemplate these changes. My own statement appears as "Africa and the Atlantic in World History: Working Out the Lethal Combination of Africans, Sugar, and Plantations in the Atlantic Basin," unpublished but translated as "O Atlântico escravista: açúcar, escravos, e engenhos," *Afro-Ásia* (Centro de Estudos áfro-orientais, FFCH-UFBA—Bahia, Brazil), 19–20 (1997), 9–36 (and an earlier version as "A dimensão histórica da África no Atlântico: açúcar, escravos, e plantações," in *A dimensão atlântica da África* (II Reunião Internacional de História de África, Rio de Janeiro, October 30–November 1, 1996) (São Paulo: CEA-USP/SDG-Marinha/CAPES, 1997), 21–40.

19. William D. Phillips, Jr., *Slavery from Roman Times to the Early Transatlantic Trade* (Minneapolis: University of Minnesota Press, 1985).

20. I have made a first pass at considering Africans' passages from the Old World to the New in terms of the contexts through which they moved in "Retention, Re-Invention, and Remembering: Restoring Identities Through Enslavement in Africa and Under Slavery in Brazil," for José C. Curto and Paul E. Lovejoy, eds., *Enslaving Connections: Brazil and*

Western Africa during the Era of Slavery (Amherst, N.Y.: Prometheus/Humanity Books, 2003), 81–121; for a preliminary statement, see my "Central Africa During the Era of the Slave Trade, c. 1490s–1850s," in Linda M. Heywood, ed., *Central Africans and Cultural Transformations in the American Diaspora* (New York: Cambridge University Press, 2002), 21–69. I will not attempt here to cite the vast literature on "cultural survivals" dating back to Melville Herskovits and recentered by Sidney Mintz and Richard Price, *An Anthropological Approach to the Afro-American Past* (Philadelphia: Institute for the Study of Human Issues, 1976) (republished as *The Birth of African-American Culture: An Anthropological Perspective* [Boston: Beacon Press, 1992]). An exemplary historicizing approach is found in the works of Stephan Palmié, e.g., Palmié, ed., *Slave Cultures and the Cultures of Slavery* (Knoxville: University of Tennessee Press, 1995). For this reason I do not employ the word "creolization," an abstract cliché pervasive in the current literature, to describe the historical processes considered here. See following discussion on slaves' strategies, meant to replace this derivative of a thoroughly structural concept of culture. I therefore also do not invoke Ira Berlin's very popular concept of "Atlantic creoles" or rely on the continuities implicit in his related notion of a somehow determinative "charter generation." In addition to *Generations of Captivity*, also see *Many Thousands Gone: The First Two Centuries of Slavery in North America* (New York: Oxford University Press, 1998), and "From Creole to African: Atlantic Creoles and the Origins of African-American Society in Mainland North America," *William and Mary Quarterly* 53, 2 (1996), 251–88.

21. The renowned—and, in Africanist circles, ridiculed long before he endorsed the authenticity of the infamously fake Hitler diaries—Regius Professor of History at Oxford Hugh Trevor-Roper dismissed his critics with the remark that "the function of genius is not to give new answers, but to pose new questions which time and mediocrity can resolve." Eric Williams, *Capitalism and Slavery* (Chapel Hill: University of North Carolina Press, 1944). Reprinted with new intro. by Colin A. Palmer (Chapel Hill: University of North Carolina Press, 1994). Recent scholarship is rehabilitating Williams, after a period of obscurity in the intensely nationalist era of modern historiographies in Europe and the United States, and its accompanying neoliberal economistic isolation of the problem: William A. Darity, Jr., "Eric Williams and Slavery: A West Indian Viewpoint?" *Callaloo* 20, 4 (1997), 801–16; Heather Cateau and Selwyn H. H. Carrington, eds., *Capitalism and Slavery Fifty Years Later: Eric Eustace Williams—A Reassessment of the Man and His Work* (New York: Peter Lang, 1999).

22. Timothy H. Breen and Stephen Innes, *"Myne Owne Ground": Race and Freedom on Virginia's Eastern Shore, 1640–1676* (New York: Oxford University Press, 1980). The institutional paradigm of North American slavery that this book challenged remains paradoxically stable, in spite of three decades of consistent refutations of it. The book has been reissued in a "25th anniversary edition" (New York: Oxford University Press, 2005). Recently, John Coombs, *The Rise of Virginia Slavery, 1630–1730* (Charlottesville: University of Virginia Press, forthcoming).

23. Michael A. Gomez, *Exchanging Our Country Marks: The Transformation of African Identities in the Colonial and Antebellum South* (Chapel Hill: University of North Carolina, 1998).

24. Berlin, *Generations of Captivity*, has broken through the otherwise prevailing stasis, but still significantly within the framework of the master–slave dyad. I hope to suggest ways to integrate the changes he accents into a national narrative and to set that in turn into its hemispheric and global contexts.

25. The overwhelming power of presentism is seldom more evident than in the historiography of slavery in North America, which exhibits an almost unvarying tone of eternal rediscovery that slaves there were not as passive or dependent as American racism would incline us to think, or that an institution denigrated as pointlessly profitless in fact made a great deal of

202 Notes to Pages 134–138

money for some investors, or that slavery was a major feature of the history of the nation, or that slaves suffered in ways that some know all too well but that fail to impress others, and so on, and on. The stability of this structure of the debate, in spite of the consistent evidence to the contrary, among Americans of all backgrounds, might qualify it clinically as a national obsession.

26. At a preliminary level, Miller, "Resistance and Accommodation: Strategies of Survival in Slave Societies" (paper presented to conference "Meanings of Resistance in the Various Contexts of Enslavement," University of Nottingham, Institute for the Study of Slavery, September 8–10, 2003); also panel (organized by Jason Sharples) discussion entitled "Resisting 'Rebellion': Slaves' Collective Violence in Their Own Terms in Eighteenth-Century North America and the Caribbean" (Organization of American Historians annual meeting, Washington, D.C., April 7–11, 2010). Some readers will be anticipating the customary accent in the literature on slavery on the slaves as agents of their own liberation, as emancipated in the nineteenth century. The historical logic of positioning the sheer presence of the enslaved, in their massive numbers and public visibility, renders their implicit challenge to their own enslavement more profound than the infrequent and seldom efficacious instances of violence derived from falsely presumed domination. However, as with all historical action, the outcomes also were uncontrollable, unintended, and ironic.

27. The central argument of Miller, "Retention, Re-Invention, and Remembering." Since then see also James H. Sweet, *Recreating Africa: Culture, Kinship, and Religion in the African-Portuguese World, 1441–1770* (Chapel Hill: University of North Carolina Press, 2003); Paul E. Lovejoy and David V. Trotman, eds., *Trans-Atlantic Dimensions of Ethnicity in the African Diaspora* (London: Continuum, 2003). And Gwendolyn Midlo Hall, *Slavery and African Ethnicities in the Americas: Restoring the Links* (Chapel Hill: University of North Carolina Press, 2005).

28. Robin Blackburn, *The Overthrow of Colonial Slavery, 1776–1848* (London: Verso, 1988).

29. Or foreseen—other than, perhaps, by Jefferson; Thomas Jefferson, *Notes on the State of Virginia* (Query XIV, Laws, and Query XVIII: Manners) (published 1781–82); http://etext.lib.virginia.edu.

30. Davis's wording: "involving economic functions and interpersonal relationships ... for which we lack satisfactory data," *Problem of Slavery*, 30.

31. Supplemented by shipments of specie to Asia by merchants not significantly involved in slaving for the textiles and marine shells, or cowries, that slavers needed to do business in Africa. The only shipments of gold to Africa were by Brazilians, who sold it to English, Dutch, and French merchants along the Gold and Slave Coasts for northern European products they required to buy slaves. Spanish Maria Theresa silver thalers (dollars) became significant only in the 1840s as part of the complex negotiations of the illegal trade of that era and in the Indian Ocean trade built on earlier shipments of Spanish silver to Asia.

32. This paragraph generalizes, in the context of this book, arguments I have made in more specific ways in "A Marginal Institution on the Margin of the Atlantic System: The Portuguese Southern Atlantic Slave Trade in the Eighteenth Century," in Barbara Solow, ed., *Slavery and the Rise of the Atlantic System* (New York: Cambridge University Press, 1991), 120–50 (reprinted in Patrick Manning, ed., *Slave Trades, 1500–1800: Globalization of Forced Labor* [Brookfield, Vt.: Variorum, 1996], 214–44), and "Slavery and the Financing of the Atlantic World" (plenary address, conference entitled "Debt and Slavery: The History of a Process of Enslavement," Indian Ocean World Centre—McGill University, Montréal, May 7–9, 2009).

33. The failure to consider medieval western European history and particularly the struggle over rural laboring forces in relation to debt bondage rather than only in relation to slavery once again demonstrates the dominance of slavery in the consciousness of modern historiography. Debt bondage has received relatively cursory and very theorized attention in

relation to slavery (Evsey D. Domar, "The Causes of Slavery or Serfdom: A Hypothesis," *Journal of Economic History* 30, 1 [1970], 18–32); it developed primarily in eastern Europe and in western and southern Russia in circumstances on the margins of the growing commercial sectors of western Europe; Michael L. Bush, ed., *Serfdom and Slavery: Studies in Legal Bondage* (London: Longman, 1996). In Europe (e.g. Renaissance northern Italy), it was easier to evacuate lands than indebt their occupants; land enclosures in England reflected the same tendencies. Both supported conversions of land from peasant agriculture to grazing sheep for wool for early textile manufactories. The further contexts would be primarily in Asia. See Joseph C. Miller, "A Theme in Variations: A Historical Schema of Slaving in the Atlantic and Indian Ocean Regions," in Gwyn Campbell, ed., "The Structure of Slavery in Indian Ocean Africa and Asia," in special issue of *Slavery and Abolition* 24, 2 (2003), 169–94. However, in the American context peonage became an important successor strategy to slaving. In general, Alain Testart, *L'esclave, la dette et le pouvoir: études de sociologie comparative* (Paris: Errance, 2001).

34. They also faced other competition in the form of emerging waged labor and monarchical protections that excluded slaves from much of the protoindustrial sectors in central and northern Europe.

35. The Cape Verde Islands, too dry even for irrigated sugar, were left to marginal Iberian New Christian (i.e., Jewish) merchant investors. See, e.g., Tobias Green, "Amsterdam and the African Atlantic: The Role of Sephardim from Amsterdam in Senegal in the 17th Century," in Hilary Pomeroy, Christopher J. Pountain, and Elena Romero, eds., *Proceedings of the Fourteenth British Conference on Judaeo-Spanish Studies* (London: Queen Mary and Westfield College, 2008), 85–94. The small size of these islands, as historical contexts, provided hothouse conditions that elevated capacities, in this case financial, of a scale insignificant in larger contexts to efficacy of paradigmatic proportions. For parallel reasoning in terms of law, see Benton, *Search for Sovereignty*.

36. An important accent on enslaved labor as collateral in Barbara Solow and collaborators, "Capitalism and Slavery in the Exceedingly Long Run," *Journal of Interdisciplinary History* 17, 4 (1987), 711–37; Solow and Stanley L. Engerman, eds., *British Capitalism and Caribbean Slavery: The Legacy of Eric Williams* (New York: Cambridge University Press, 1987).

37. I will return to these famed *Siete Partidas* in their more direct application to the mainland Americas. Here the methodological point is, again, the limits of alleged continuities of law or culture in attempting to explain historical processes contextualized in changing times.

38. The same process as eroding Africa's communal ethos and wealth in people or in mutually responsible human relationships with commercial credit and aggressive, acquisitive individuation.

39. One may extend the economics of the argument cited in note 33 to emphasize the high leverage of converting labor from illiquid farmers resident on entailed and ecclesiastical estates to enslaved and therefore fungible additions to the local pool at a moment when commercial interests in Europe were struggling to create liquidity (e.g., banks in northern Italy) to expand local commerce to engage the wealthy Muslim economy. Thus, a further key moment in the legal definition of modern slavery was the elimination of residual public interest in slaves in the English Americas in the 1670s through redefinition of their property status as personal rather than real.

40. Miller, "Abolition as Discourse: Slavery as Civic Abomination." Also "The African Historical Dynamics of the Atlantic 'Age of Revolutions,'" in David Armitage and Sanjay Subrahmanyam, eds., *The Age of Revolutions in Global Context, c. 1760–1840* (Basingstoke: Palgrave Macmillan, 2010), 101–24 (nn. 246–50). Generally, Jeremy Adalman, "An Age of Imperial Revolutions," *American Historical Review* 113, 2 (2008), 319–40, and

id., *Sovereignty and Revolution in the Iberian Atlantic* (Princeton: Princeton University Press, 2006).

41. Thus creating an impersonal entity of the sort realized in the ultracommercialized context of Dutch cities as anonymous societies or, still later, as modern legal corporate bodies.

42. At least in their subsequent representation, if not also originally in practice.

43. Michael M. Craton, *Sinews of Empire: A Short History of British Slavery* (Garden City N.Y.: Anchor Press, 1974).

44. Compare the parallel exclusion of resident merchants from the domestic sphere in Africa under terms usually translated into English as landlord–stranger relationships; see discussion in chapter 3. Like Holmes in Victorian England, I take my clue from baroque Iberia, where the dog of modernity didn't bark. In terms of historical processes, baroque monarchical splendor represented a diversion of the gains from emergent commercialism into triumph in the last great crusade of late medieval Europe, a victory within the local context of Catholic Europe at a moment when the significant historical initiatives had, since the late fifteenth century, shifted to the powerfully external riches of the Atlantic and beyond.

45. The relevant comparisons lie not in the immediate, very different contexts in Europe but at similar points in parallel historical processes; in this case, the process involved the recurrent contest between incipient military regimes and the merchants on whom they depended, but who simultaneously threatened political consolidation on monarchical terms. Earlier instances had occurred, as I mentioned in chapter 2, in and around the eastern Mediterranean basin late in the second half of the first millennium BCE, and much of the history of slaving in the Muslim world revolved around the same struggle.

46. And the parallel in Africa took the form of its ethical exclusion of committed merchants from the communal ethos as witches, with many of the accused physically eliminated as slaves, some of them sold to Europeans. See chapter 3.

47. As all eventually did; the historical formulation of this process is not the teleological/originary search for anticipations of independence but the effectiveness of European monarchies in devising legal and eventually military techniques to manage such novelties in the North Atlantic for more than two centuries and even longer in the Iberian domains. For a sense of the ambiguities of the earlier phases of extending a European presence overseas, see Benton, *Search for Sovereignty*.

48. But primarily as an ahistorical/teleological/originary anticipation of abolition or of humanism, and then always acknowledging the paradox thus created of its apparently racist toleration of, even encouragement of, slaving for Africans; see, e.g., Blackburn, *The Making of New World Slavery*, 150–56.

49. And also illustrating the potential of world-historical perspectives to lend additional significance to familiar elements of local or regional narratives.

50. Though not as completely as traditional scholarship has emphasized.

51. The distinctions between slavery and the other forms of negatively characterized unfree labor—*repartimiento, encomienda, mita,* and so on—that succeeded slaving in Spanish America are vital in terms of the creation of monarchical and eventually national modern forms of political authority by intruding on relationships that had been well on their ways to autonomous local fiefdoms.

52. But significantly *not* contemporary Portuguese monarchs more dependent on foreign traders, increasingly English after 1680.

53. Where, in the end, their slaves helped to make even the order intolerably independent competitors of monarchical absolutism, leading to their expulsion from Portuguese territories in 1758; see Dauril Alden, *The Making of an Enterprise: The Society of Jesus in Portugal, Its Empire, and Beyond, 1540–1750* (Stanford: Stanford University Press, 1996); and in Spain's domains ten years later; Bertrand M. Roehner, "Jesuits and the State: A Comparative Study of Their Expulsions (1590–1990)," *Religion* 27, 2 (1997), 165–82.

54. Other than the gold of Elmina, in western Africa, modern Ghana.
55. António Mendes de Almeida, *La traite portugaise en Méditerranée et dans l'Atlantique, XVe–XVIIe siècles* (Paris: Editions Chandeigne, forthcoming); Linda A. Newson and Susie Minchin, *From Capture to Sale: The Portuguese Slave Trade to Spanish South America in the Early Seventeenth Century* (Leiden: Brill, 2007).
56. The circumstances provoking the Imbangala strategies of consolidating bandit gangs through immolatory slaving are sketched in chapter 3.
57. Again, as elsewhere, the epistemology of history reasons from the fullest relevant—here global—contextualizations: Brazilian sugar was a substantially new creation, catalyzing elements originating in Spanish law, African climate, the dispersal of the Sephardic community, and silver mining in Peru and Mexico as well as often-cited developments in Muslim nautical sciences, Ottoman closure of the eastern Mediterranean to Christian merchants, and invention of the three-roller mill for grinding sugar in China.
58. The reference here is to the famous revolts in late second-century BCE Sicily and southern Italy and to the Zanj revolt in late ninth-century CE southern Iraq. Note, in both cases, the strategic placement of significant numbers of enslaved men in locations remote from the centers of political authority in Rome and in Baghdad.
59. And conversely—as well as perversely—also made them instances of the heroic slave rebellion iconic in the modernist historiography of institutionalized slavery as domination. Other regimes supplemented local agricultural productivity with imports of slaves in sudanic western Africa, Tunisia, Morocco, and parts of Asia, usually to support new military regimes, but they settled the slaves as reproducing communities of peasants in composite, not unitary monarchical, polities.
60. As distinct from the notion of the slave community as a stable or at least consolidated entity, as developed and criticized in U.S. historiography; for the original notion, John W. Blassingame, *The Slave Community: Plantation Life in the Antebellum South*, rev. ed. (New York: Oxford University Press, 1979); initial criticism in Al-Tony Gilmore, ed., *Revisiting Blassingame's* The Slave Community: *The Scholars Respond* (Westport, Conn.: Greenwood Press, 1978). The parallel strategy in Spanish colonial urban environments produced the *castas*, urban populations usually viewed through ahistorical lenses of modern racial identities; in fact, mixed in ancestry as members of the castas may have been, their characterization described ancestry in the late medieval manner of categorizing people, not the categories keyed on color that modern historians have glossed onto them. Their principal affiliations were clientage (*compadrazgo*, etc.) to the patriarchal households of the cities, and these affiliations diminished the significance of civic distinctions (of import primarily in relation to a remote monarchy in Spain, and in any case alterable on the initiative of the enslaved) of slave and subject (*sic:* not free, a standing under modern civic law not even imaginable or desirable in seventeenth-century contexts of personalistic patron-client protections).
61. Ehud R. Toledano, *As If Silent and Absent: Bonds of Enslavement in the Islamic Middle East* (New Haven: Yale University Press, 2007).
62. But see Kathryn Joy McKnight, "Confronted Rituals: Spanish Colonial and Angolan 'Maroon' Executions in Cartagena de Indias (1634)," in Kathryn Joy McKnight and John Cinnamon, eds., "Enslavement and Colonialism in the Atlantic World," special issue of *Journal of Colonialism and Colonial History* 5, 3 (2004)—http://muse.jhu.edu/journals.
63. Escape and manumission were more voluntaristic ways of leaving; no one entered voluntarily. For an imaginative contemplation of death, see Vincent Brown, "Spiritual Terror and Sacred Authority in Jamaican Slave Society," *Slavery and Abolition* 24, 1 (2003), 24–53; id., *The Reaper's Garden: Death and Power in the World of Atlantic Slavery* (Cambridge: Harvard University Press, 2008).

64. Here is the distinction between the frequency of "marronage" throughout the parts of the Americas highly dependent on imports and its infrequency among the American-born slaves in North America: where communities were only nascent, greater prospects for the stability of belonging lay in flight into the forests, but where reproduction created families and stability within slavery, however limited, the enslaved opted for the community at hand rather than assuming the risks of starting over yet again.

65. Notably Philip Troutman, "Slave Trade and Sentiment in Antebellum Virginia" (Ph.D. diss., University of Virginia, 2000); also Calvin Schermerhorn, "Money Over Mastery: Slavery in the Antebellum Upper South (Baltimore: Johns Hopkins, University Press, 2011), and id., "Left Behind but Getting Ahead: Antebellum Slavery's Orphans in the Chesapeake, 1820–60," in Campbell, Miers, and Miller, eds., *Children in Slavery*, 1:204–24. Also the essential insights of Walter Johnson, *Soul by Soul: Life Inside the Antebellum Slave Market* (Cambridge: Harvard University Press, 1999).

66. I would place the discontents of the religious dissenters of the sixteenth and seventeenth centuries in Europe primarily in another process of local popular reactions to the growing power of secular monarchical authority and ethical alarms at the apparent risks of a commercial world; see Philip Gould, *Barbarous Traffic: Commerce and Anti-Slavery in the Eighteenth-Century Atlantic World* (Cambridge: Harvard University Press, 2003).

67. Not the Iberian *Siete Partidas* (1275?), but in the Atlantic era the Manoeline ordinances (1514) of Portugal's then-waxing monarchy, the French *Code Noir* (1685), and eventually the Spanish *Código Negro* (1784, 1789). In a broader sense, the royally chartered companies of the late seventeenth century and then the mercantilist regulation of private traders increasingly through the eighteenth century.

68. As Seymour Drescher is elaborating, in his ongoing imaginative revelation of unsuspected nuances in the process; most recently, *Abolition: A History of Slavery and Antislavery* (New York: Cambridge University Press, 2009).

69. João José Reis, "Candomblé in Nineteenth-Century Bahia: Priests, Followers, Clients," in Kristin Mann and Edna Bay, eds., *Rethinking the African Diaspora: The Making of a Black Atlantic World in the Bight of Benin and Brazil* (London: Frank Cass, 2001); Luis Nicolau Parés, *A formação do Candomblé: história e ritual da nação jeje na Bahia* (Campinas: Editora Unicamp, 2006), and id., "Memories of Slavery in Religious Ritual: A Comparison between the Benin Vodun Cults and Bahian Candomblé," in Andrew Apter and Lauren Derby, eds., *Activating the Past: Historical Memory in the Black Atlantic World* (Cambridge Scholar Publishing, 2010), 71–98; also L. E. Castillo and L. N. Parés, "Marcelina da Silva: A Nineteenth-Century Candomblé Priestess in Bahia," *Slavery and Abolition* 31, 1 (2010), 1–27.

70. The counterpart in Africa was the uses there of commercial resources from the Atlantic to preserve the ideology of domestic community. Africans commercialized pawnship by substituting imported goods on personal credit for collective liens against future females of communities of kin. For pawnship, though not developed systematically in these terms, which emphasize it as the equivalent of debt bondage in a political economy where "people are wealth," see Paul E. Lovejoy and David Richardson, "Trust, Pawnship, and Atlantic History: The Institutional Foundations of the Old Calabar Slave Trade," *American Historical Review* 104, 2 (1999), 333–55; id., "The Business of Slaving: Pawnship in Western Africa, c. 1600–1810," *Journal of African History* 42, 1 (2001), 67–89; Paul E. Lovejoy and Toyin Falola, eds., *Pawnship, Slavery and Colonialism in Africa*, exp. ed. (New Brunswick: Africa World Press, 2003). In general, Alain Testart, "The Pawning of Humans: Comparative Sociology of an Institution—La mise en gage des personnes: sociologie comparative d'une institution," *European Journal of Sociology/Archives Européennes de Sociologie* 38, 1 (1997), 38–67.

71. See appendix.

72. Details on line at http://www.slavevoyages.org; current reflections based on this massive database in David Eltis and David Richardson, eds., *Extending the Frontiers: Essays on the New Transatlantic Slave Trade Database* (New Haven: Yale University Press, 2008).
73. The neo-African *cabildos* and *naciones* in Hispanic America were later, parallel responses of the masses of Africans (many of them young boys) taken to Cuba in the nineteenth century in numbers that recreated the opportunities seized in neo-ethnic terms earlier in the British and French areas. Africans in Brazil appropriated Catholic lay brotherhoods and, later, Afro-Brazilian successor institutions like *candomblé* to similar ends of creating communities of their own. All of these private preserves were distinct from the public persona, phrased in deceptively parallel neo-African terms, in the literature. Examples include Mina and Bantu in Brazil, Eboe or Coromanee in Jamaica, Bambara or Angole among the French. These were masters' characterizations, largely for commercial purposes of valuation (in effect, brand-naming) and accordingly derived from the ports where people of many African backgrounds were homogenized into recognizable identities for purposes of marketing them. To the extent that Africans created ethnic identities of their own for similarly strategic purposes, ethnicization as a historical strategy may describe both, but as history, the creators must be accounted for: the ethnic identities in the Atlantic were imposed, not initiated, except as the slaves so characterized employed their assigned identities in the Americas for purposes of their own.
74. As a flood of scholarship on Africa is demonstrating in greater and greater detail. Among post-Enlightenment Europeans, individual mobility eventuated in the ethnicized, imagined community of the modern nation.
75. The literature on ethnicity in Africa has turned strongly in this direction; with regard to identities constructed out of the slaving process, the most thoroughly explored, so far, is Yoruba; Robin Law, "Ethnicity and the Slave Trade: 'Lucumi' and 'Nago' as Ethnonyms in West Africa," *History in Africa* 24 (1997), 205–19; J. Lorand Matory, "The English Professors of Brazil: On the Diasporic Roots of the Yorùbá Nation," *Comparative Studies in Society and History* 41, 1 (1999), 72–103. Also see David Northrup, "Igbo and Myth Igbo: Culture and Ethnicity in the Atlantic World, 1600–1850," *Slavery and Abolition* 21, 3 (2000), 1–20. The cultural traits that form the focus of most studies of Africanisms in the New World take little account of such initiative; one must approach them as symbols, not as inert survivals but as products of enslaved people adapting and applying them to the circumstances in which they found themselves, and not necessarily Africans, but perhaps even more urgently Americans seeking symbols distinguishingly their own. "Looking African," in terms of American stereotypes of Africa, would have been as important in public contexts as actual derivation from African antecedents. The case of Equiano stands in point; for references to doubts about the location of his birth, "Olaudah Equiano, The South Carolinian? A Forum [Vincent Carretta, Paul E. Lovejoy, Trevor Burnard, Jon Sensbach]," *Historically Speaking* 7, 3 (2006), 2–16. Without taking on the long genealogy of the debate on continuities from Africa, originating in the work of Melville and Frances Heskovits in the 1930s, one cites recent accents in Gomez, *Exchanging Our Country Marks*; Douglas B. Chambers, "'My Own Nation': Igbo Exiles in the Diaspora," *Slavery and Abolition* 18, 1 (1997), 72–97, and developed in id., "The Significance of Igbo in the Bight of Biafra Slave-Trade: A Rejoinder to Northrup's 'Myth Igbo'" [see above], *Slavery and Abolition* 23, 1 (2002), 101–20. An ambitious pan-Atlantic summary is Hall, *Slavery and African Ethnicities in the Americas*. The issue has resurfaced rather intensely in the debate over "black rice" occasioned by Judith Carney's systematic attempt to document the origins of South Carolina riziculture in western Africa. Judith A. Carney, *Black Rice: The African Origins of Rice Cultivation in the Americas* (Cambridge: Harvard University Press, 2001), followed by David Eltis, Philip Morgan, and David Richardson, "Agency and Diaspora in Atlantic History: Reassessing the African Contribution to Rice Cultivation

in the Americas," *American Historical Review* 112, 5 (2007), 1329–58, and id., "AHR Exchange: The Question of 'Black Rice,'" *American Historical Review* 115, 1 (2010), 123–71.

76. In an earlier note I asserted my intention of avoiding the ahistorical concept of creolization, which focuses on abstracted cultures rather than on historical human strategies. These comments on neo-African strategies of belonging in the Americas can, I am confident, resolve the ambiguities in this widespread aspect of the historiography of Africans and African Americans in the New World.

77. In a different context, the very evocative work of Jennifer Morgan, *Laboring Women: Reproduction and Gender in New World Slavery* (Philadelphia: University of Pennsylvania Press, 2004). Reproducing slave populations are no longer thought to be unique to North America, but the other examples cluster in similar contexts of limited or decreasing imports; the recent demographic evidence is summarized (and highlighted to make this point) in Herbert S. Klein, *The Atlantic Slave Trade* (New York: Cambridge University Press, 2010).

78. Berlin, *Generations of Captivity.*

79. Or, perhaps, sexualized in order to celebrate it in a later age, and not only in a North American environment that blurred distinctions between paternalism and paternity. In Brazil see the "soap opera" serialization of Júnia Ferreira Furtado, *Chica da Silva e o contratador de diamantes: o outro lado do mito* (São Paulo: Companhia das Letras, 2003), translated as *Chica da Silva: A Brazilian Slave of the Eighteenth Century* (New York: Cambridge University Press, 2009); also Furtado, "Chica da Silva: o avesso do mito," in Maria Beatriz Nizza da Silva, ed., *Sexualidade, família e religião na colonização do Brasil* (Lisbon: Livros Horizonte, 2001), 77–89.

80. Playing on the titles of Henry Wiencek, *The Hairstons: An American Family in Black and White* (New York: St. Martin's Press, 1999), and Edward Ball, *Slaves in the Family* (New York: Hill and Wang, 1998).

81. Jan Ellen Lewis and Peter S. Onuf,, eds., *Sally Hemings and Thomas Jefferson* (Charlottesville: University Press of Virginia, 1999); Annette Gordon-Reed, *The Hemingses of Monticello: An American Family* (New York: Norton, 2008).

82. Lucia Stanton, *Free Some Day: The African-American Families of Monticello* (Charlottesville: Thomas Jefferson Foundation, 2000).

83. Cf. chapter 2, on the formation of communities, chapter 3 on later political applications of this strategy in Africa, and Patterson, *Rituals of Blood.*

84. Again underscoring the vital importance of separating public racism from slavery.

85. With the possible exception of the similarly commercial French and English plantations in the Caribbean. However, even there the continuing relevance of a broader imperial context and the relative absence of the owners allowed acknowledgment of a local standing as colored and freedman. In the national political spheres in Europe, these island natives were safely remote and administratively contained as colonial subjects, posing no political challenge comparable to freedmen in the United States, where they were anathema and subject to further exclusion through deportation out of state or, in the extreme case, back to Africa. Here lay formulation of the close association of Africa with black, hence of race with place.

86. New work is emphasizing, appropriately, the financial aspects of slaving. The best work, so far, is Bonnie M. Martin, "The Power of Human Collateral: Mortgaging Slaves in the Colonial and Antebellum South" (Legal History Colloquium, New York University School of Law, October 22, 2008), and other papers.

87. The selectivity principle is inherent in, and in fact analytically vital to, history's epistemology. The relevant distinction between the kind of selectivity I condemn in originary forms and the selectivity I employ in focusing on processes of slaving is the differing principles of

selection employed. Originary logic is ahistorical because it applies presentistic standards to past times. Historical selectivity generates the behavior selected for analysis from the much more inclusive contexts of the times under study. It interprets behaviors as human strategies motivated by meanings/significances in the past; that is, in terms of who (in a contextualized sense) was acting, what (again in terms of that context) they were trying to accomplish, and how they were proceeding to do so (the focus of the analysis, in this case slaving as defined consistently and, as always, relative to context).

88. I have not taken up the story of slaving strategies in Asia from the fifteenth century to the present day in this book. As I intend to develop this history in another context, it will emphasize the continuing balance among territorial military rulers' uses of enslaved palace guards, particularly by new dynasties, peasants indebted to merchants and obligated to warlords and seeking refuge on ecclesiastical estates in non-Muslim regions, and growing urban markets for women and children as domestics as European commercial investment stimulated commodity production there. Europeans, very marginal figures in the region, slaved in order to maintain their toeholds, in varying ways, in these regional processes. Growing populations and collapsing commercial economies in the nineteenth century created widespread foreclosures on indebted peasants, and the people conceded were sent under contracts of indenture into the European world then in the throes of abolishing slavery. There, though worked like the enslaved Africans who had preceded them, the residential stability they and their descendants were able to sustain and their ability to accumulate commercial assets allowed them to survive and sometimes thrive even under the discriminatory regulations of twentieth-century colonial rule.

89. Classically, Peter Laslett, *The World We Have Lost* (New York: Scribners, 1965); Anderson, *Imagined Communities.*

90. Suggesting that the national processes of abolition in continental Europe and its American colonies were political processes distinct from those in Britain and the United States. Elsewhere in the world, the local politics of abolition, mostly of Atlantic trading rather than emancipation of the enslaved, were different yet again. Recent literature on abolition has moved revealingly in this historicized direction.

Index